Conflict
IN THE
Quorum

Conflict
IN THE
Quorum

Orson Pratt, Brigham Young,
Joseph Smith

GARY JAMES BERGERA

SIGNATURE BOOKS • SALT LAKE CITY
A SMITH-PETTIT FOUNDATION BOOK

Cover design by Ron Stucki

Conflict in the Quorum: Orson Pratt, Brigham Young, Joseph Smith
was printed on acid-free paper and was composed, printed, and
bound in the United States of America.

2013 2012 2011 2010 2009 2008   6 5 4 3 2

Library of Congress Cataloging-in-Publication Data
Bergera, Gary James.
Conflict in the Quorum : Orson Pratt, Brigham Young,
    Joseph Smith / by Gary James Bergera.
        p. cm.
"A Smith-Pettit Foundation book".
Includes bibliographical references and index.
ISBN 1-56085-164-3 (hardback)
        1. Pratt, Orson, 1811-1881. 2. Smith, Joseph, 1805-1844.
3. Young, Brigham, 1801-1877. 4. Church controversies—
Church of Jesus Christ of Latter-day Saints--History—19th
century. 5. Church of Jesus Christ of Latter-day Saints—
History—19th century. I. Title.

BX8695.P69 B47 2002
289.3'09'034—dc21
                                        2002036664

For my parents

CONTENTS

This is a study in interpersonal conflict and group dynamics. It is a story that illustrates issues of freedom and obedience and the fragile fabric they share.

Among the many beliefs embraced by members of the Church of Jesus Christ of Latter-day Saints (LDS or Mormon), few are as pervasive as the perception that harmony prevails within the First Presidency and Quorum of Twelve Apostles, the tightly knit core of the church's governing hierarchy. (There are other general authorities or officers, but all are subservient to the First Presidency and Twelve.) As former LDS church president and official Church Historian Joseph Fielding Smith once explained: "There is no division among the authorities, and there need be no divisions among the people, but unity, peace, brotherly love, kindness and fellowship one to another" (qtd. in Bruce R. McConkie, comp., *Doctrines of Salvation* [Salt Lake City: Bookcraft, 1954-56], 2:245-46). While such assurances stand as the rule, human nature and Mormonism's turbulent history suggest that within the highest councils, differences of opinion can and do erupt into debates among men who hold similar convictions yet possess vastly different temperaments.

An examination of the controversies arising between nineteenth-century LDS leaders Orson Pratt and Joseph Smith, and later between Pratt and Brigham Young, illustrates the degree to which such disharmony can affect church doctrine, policy, and organization. Aside from the personal views and experiences of these men, all of whom were deeply spiritual and strong-willed individuals, their influence and interplay in their quorums are what is significant. Their actions affected the entire structure of the ecclesiastical hierarchy and the rest of the church as well.

I focus on Pratt because he was the common denominator in these disputes. Given his eventual demotion in his quorum, he is the one who was most directly impacted by the controversies. However, it should not be inferred that the overriding characteristic of the church, during this period or later, was conflict. Nor do I mean to question the faith or inspiration of any of these men. My interest is in exploring expressions of faith when one leader clashed with an equally sincere and devoted colleague.

Neither the conflict nor the men themselves were "right" or "wrong," "good" or "bad." Their actions resulted in consequences that were favorable or unfavorable depending on the criteria one employs or judgments that are made. I have tried to consider each person's perspective in terms of how he interpreted his circumstances. If a reader suspects that I favor one man over another, another reader may see evidence that I side with a different individual. I have tried to set aside my own preconceptions and biases as much as possible and let their own words, and the context in which they were spoken, form the core of this study.

A note about the sources used. Much, but not all, of the research was undertaken in the historical archives of the LDS church beginning in the late 1970s. Policies regarding access to the papers of general church officers were different then. In some cases, I have had to rely on notes and photocopies without being able to examine the originals a second time. Nevertheless, I have tried to present these documents as faithfully as possible, including peculiarities of spelling and punctuation. I regret that interested readers will not be able to verify independently all of my references and transcriptions.

For their assistance, encouragement, and especially example, I thank Thomas G. Alexander, Lavina Fielding Anderson, Leonard J.

Arrington, Lisa Orme Bickmore, Martha Sonntag Bradley, Newell G. Bringhurst, David John Buerger, Eugene E. Campbell, Todd Compton, Everett Cooley, Scott H. Faulring, Steven Heath, Michael Homer, Scott G. Kenney, Stanley B. Kimball, Boyd Kirkland, Brigham D. Madsen, H. Michael Marquardt, D. Michael Quinn, Allen D. Roberts, John Sillito, George D. Smith, Susan Staker, Richard Van Wagoner, Dan Vogel, and David J. Whittaker. I also appreciate the support of Ron Priddis, Connie Disney, Jani Fleet, Greg Jones, Keiko Jones, and Tom Kimball. I have benefitted immensely from their perspectives and involvement.

Come martyrdom, come burnings at the stake, come
any calamity and affliction of the body, that may be de-
vised by wicked and ungodly men—let me choose that,
and have eternal life beyond the grave; but let me not
deny the work of God.

—ORSON PRATT

[Orson Pratt is] strangely Constituted. He [has] acquired a good deal of knowledge upon many things but
in other things He [is] one of the most ignorant men [I]
ever saw in [my] life. He [is] full of integrity & would lie
down & have his head Cut off for me or his religi[o]n if
necessary but he will never see his Error untill he goes
into the spirit world. [T]hen he will say Brother Brigham
how foolish I was.

—BRIGHAM YOUNG

O[rson] P[ratt] ... [has] caused trouble by telling stories to people who would betray me and [who] must believe these stories because his [Pratt's] wife told him so! I
will live to trample on their ashes with the soles of my
feet.

—JOSEPH SMITH

"Out of the Church"

*S*now had fallen intermittently throughout the week, but by the 10th of April 1875, the blue sky held only high clouds. For the tenth time since Tuesday, members of the Rocky Mountain-based Church of Jesus Christ of Latter-day Saints filled the Tabernacle in Salt Lake City to capacity for the 45th semi-annual general conference.[1]

During the two o'clock afternoon session, George Q. Cannon, the increasingly influential forty-eight-year-old assistant to aging church president Brigham Young, read the names of twenty-six church officers from president through the First Council of the Seventy. These men, Mormonism's elite, were endorsed "by the uplifted hand of over ten thousand Saints."[2]

Members had performed the same task six months earlier except that there had been no surprises at that meeting. Apostles Or-

---

1. For the weather and crowds, see Historian's Office Journal, 10 and 11 Apr. 1875, Church Archives, Family and Church History Department, Church of Jesus Christ of Latter-day Saints, Salt Lake City, Utah (hereafter cited as LDS church archives).

2. "Annual General Conference," *Deseret Semi-Weekly News,* 13 Apr. 1875, [2].

son Hyde and Orson Pratt had been sustained as the senior members of the Quorum of Twelve Apostles, next in line to assume the church presidency. Now the same men were reduced to third and fourth in rank behind Elders John Taylor and Wilford Woodruff.[3] Equally intriguing was that Taylor, who replaced Hyde as senior apostle, was not sustained as president of the Twelve, a position Hyde had held for the past twenty-seven years. Perhaps this was to soften the sting of the demotion. (Although Taylor would act as *de facto* president of the Twelve, a new quorum head would not be publicly announced until after the death of Brigham Young two years later.) No explanation was offered before or after the voting. Pratt addressed the conference the next day without alluding to it, and there is no record that a majority of attendees exhibited much surprise or curiosity.[4] Only the anti-Mormon *Salt Lake Tribune* commented, remarking sarcastically: "Orson Hyde, who has been President of the Twelve Apostles for nearly thirty years, has been degraded by his dread master to third man in the apostolic ranks; John Taylor is promoted to the primacy. As Brigham confers his favors upon men who have committed the most crimes for the Church, the irreverent outsider is left to the conclusion that the

---

3. George A. Smith would have been placed before Hyde and Pratt as well had he retained his position in the quorum and not become Young's first counselor.

4. Hyde's recent biographer believes the apostle was actually pleased by the change in seniority: "At age seventy his mind and spirit remained lively, but physical energy waned" (Myrtle Stevens Hyde, *Orson Hyde: The Olive Branch of Israel* [Salt Lake City: Agreka Books, 2000], 473, see also 456-57, 480). Hyde's immediate family felt differently. Six weeks after the realignment, Young complained publicly about Hyde's oldest son, who "has come pussying around me, and saying that his father had been misrepresented." The president said that Hyde "was not fit to be apostle ... [and] had not the spirit" (qtd. in ibid., 474). The next day Apostle Hyde said publicly, "I don't want to refer to chastisement yesterday, but God bless my family who took so much interest in me at Salt Lake as to go to the president about action concerning the Twelve Apostles at conference" (qtd. in Brigham Young Jr., Journal, 23 June 1875, LDS church archives; cf. Hyde, *Orson Hyde*, 474-75).

malignant John Taylor has earned his elevation by his greater infamy."[5]

Hyde's and Pratt's reassignment brought real consequences. Both men outlived Brigham Young and, under the emerging protocol of apostolic succession, Hyde would have replaced Young as president of the church in 1877. He would have been followed by Pratt the next year when Hyde died. Instead, Taylor, and then Woodruff, bore the burden of the president's mantle.

The issue was not explained publicly at the time but was broached privately. Shortly before conference, the Twelve were reminded that Hyde and Pratt had been "out of the Church" for several months some thirty-five years earlier and had presumably returned to positions behind Taylor and Woodruff, both of whom now "stood ahead of [these men] in the Quorum."[6] Following Young's death, George Q. Cannon would refer publicly to the demotion,[7] but an authoritative public explanation would not come for an additional four years until both Hyde and Pratt had died.

On 7 October 1881, four days after Pratt's passing, John Taylor, who would turn seventy-three the next month and had been presiding over the church for four years, delivered a sermon to the church's priesthood holders on "Succession in the Priesthood." Relying on Brigham Young's retrospective autobiography and the forty-year-old memories of several eyewitnesses, including himself, Taylor explained that because Hyde and Pratt had been "cut off" or "dropped" from the quorum in 1839 and 1842 respectively and later reordained, their seniority was based on the date of their reordination, not on the date of their initial appointment.[8]

The next year Cannon, now Taylor's counselor, agreed that

---

5. "City Jottings," *Salt Lake Tribune*, 13 Apr. 1875, [4]. By "crimes," the writer probably meant polygamy.

6. Scott G. Kenney, ed., *Wilford Woodruff's Journal*, 9 vols. (Midvale, UT: Signature Books, 1983-85), 7:224.

7. *Journal of Discourses*, 19:234-35.

8. John Taylor, *Succession in the Priesthood* (Salt Lake City: n.p., 1881), 18-20.

both Hyde and Pratt had "lost their standing" for some time, thus forfeiting their right to seniority.[9] Almost all subsequent commentators embraced Taylor's and Cannon's explanation without considering the circumstances—including the doctrinal issues and interpersonal dynamics—that preceded the realignment. By 1969, the 23rd edition of Joseph Fielding Smith's *Essentials in Church History,* which in its first printing fifty years earlier had reported only that Pratt had been "handled for his fellowship," now spelled out that he had been "excommunicated," "rebaptized," "[re]ordained," and realigned as a consequence of his excommunication.[10] Because of Smith's standing as an apostle, Church Historian, and later church president, his history—while not the first to narrate a version of Pratt's and Hyde's changes in status—became the standard, authoritative explanation for the incident.[11]

Under closer scrutiny, the events leading to, surrounding, and following Pratt's 1842 "excommunication" and 1843 "reinstatement" are more complex than this explanation allows.[12] All avail-

9. *Journal of Discourses,* 23:364; see also 24:275-76.

10. Joseph Fielding Smith, *Essentials in Church History* (Salt Lake City: Deseret Book, 1969), 575.

11. Almost all LDS histories either report Pratt's "excommunication" as a *fait accompli* or avoid reference to it altogether. The most recent "official" treatment of the episode reports that he was excommunicated in August 1842, then "reinstated in the Quorum of the Twelve Apostles in January 1843," without noting that his excommunication was declared illegal and that he was reinstated to his former position and standing (see David J. Whittaker, "Pratt, Orson," in *Encyclopedia of Mormonism,* 4 vols., ed. Daniel H. Ludlow [New York: Macmillan Publishing Company, 1992], 3:1114-15). I know of only two books published since 1970 that remain tentative on the topic: Leonard J. Arrington, *Brigham Young: American Moses* (New York: Alfred A. Knopf, 1985), 376, and Richard S. Van Wagoner, *Mormon Polygamy: A History* (Salt Lake City: Signature Books, 1986; 2nd ed., 1989), 30. The earliest discussion of the problems surrounding Pratt's excommunication was Mark J. Taylor's privately circulated "Orson Pratt: Conflict and Restoration," written in 1973 for a history class at Brigham Young University, copy in my possession. An anonymous chronology, "Orson Pratt and Brigham Young," no date but prior to 1973, has also circulated privately, copy in my possession.

12. A brief summary of Orson Hyde's case may be helpful. In mid-October

able evidence suggests that no binding action was taken against Pratt, that his "excommunication" was not legal but was intended, not to deprive him permanently of his position, but to quell his objection to Joseph Smith and plural marriage. When Pratt stopped resisting his prophet and the new doctrine, his standing as a full member of his quorum was reaffirmed. Young's restructuring of the quorum thirty-three years later had other issues as its cause and

---

1838, he voluntarily withdrew from the church because of Mormon violence in Missouri (for context, see Stephen C. LeSueur, *The 1838 Mormon War in Missouri* [Columbia: University of Missouri Press, 1987]). At the time, Hyde wrote unequivocally: "I have left the Church called Latter Day Saints for conscience sake, fully believing that God is not with them, and is not the mover of their schemes and projects" (attached to Thomas B. Marsh and Orson Hyde to Brother [Lewis] and Sister [Ann] Abbot, ca. 25 Oct. 1838, Joseph Smith Papers, LDS church archives [Ann was Marsh's sister]; see also Hyde to Brigham Young, 30 Mar. 1839, in Brigham Young, Diary, LDS church archives). Together with Apostle Marsh, Hyde signed an affidavit denouncing the Saints' actions. Missouri state officials used this document, with others, to charge church leaders with treason. (One of Hyde's biographers credits his actions to poor health; see Hyde, *Orson Hyde,* 100-10.)

The following January 1839, the First Presidency instructed Apostles Brigham Young and Heber C. Kimball to fill the double vacancy in their quorum occasioned by Marsh's and Hyde's removal (see Sidney Rigdon, Joseph Smith, and Hyrum Smith to Kimball and Young, 16 Jan. 1839, Joseph Smith Papers). Two months later, the church excommunicated a number of "apostates" including Marsh *(Times and Seasons* 1 [Nov. 1839]: 15), but Hyde, who had already contacted officials about returning, was not among them. When Joseph Smith wanted to excommunicate Hyde in early May 1839, others intervened, and the prophet suspended him pending a satisfactory explanation of his actions. Hyde "made his confession and was restored to the Priesthood ... in full fellowship by a full vote of the Council" (qtd. in Scott H. Faulring, ed., *An American Prophet's Record: The Diaries and Journals of Joseph Smith* [Salt Lake City: Signature Books in association with Smith Research Associates, 1987], 237; Kenney, *Wilford Woodruff's Journal,* 1:340-41; see also Minutes, 5 Oct. 1839, Joseph Smith Papers). The man who was tentatively chosen to replace Hyde died in late January without being ordained to office. Hyde was never excommunicated, as some have incorrectly suggested (see Howard H. Barron, *Orson Hyde* [Bountiful, UT: Horizon Publishers, 1977], 105-107; Wilburn D. Talbot, *The Acts of the Modern Apostles* [Salt Lake City: Randall Book, 1985], 46, 53). Rather, he left the main body of Saints, then re-

cannot be explained satisfactorily by appealing only to Pratt's difficulties in 1842.[13]

Like other controversial events in the past, attempts to understand Pratt's *ex post facto* realignment, as well as his roller-coaster relationship with Presidents Smith and Young, are hindered by conflicting reports of what happened, a tendency to interpret mid-nineteenth-century terms and actions in light of later definitions and practices, and the lack of, or inaccessibility to, relevant documents. Using available sources, the ensuing discussion details the sometimes contentious relationship between Pratt, Smith, and Young, not only in 1842 but throughout their careers, culminating in Pratt's eventual demotion in apostolic seniority.

---

turned before formal action was taken against him. Unlike Pratt, Hyde believed that he had temporarily left Mormonism.

13. Two years after John Taylor's *Succession in the Priesthood* was published, "The Book of the Law of the Lord," a special history kept by Joseph Smith and his scribes in Nauvoo, Illinois, was revived at Taylor's request. Elder Franklin D. Richards wrote to Taylor: "Here would seem to be the proper place for a complete and accurate statement of the reasons why you were, at that time, President of the Twelve Apostles instead of Elders Orson Hyde and Orson Pratt, both of whom were then alive; and the former had been sustained and published as the President of the Twelve for a number of years" (Richards to Taylor, 26 Dec. 1883, LDS church archives; see allusion to investigation by Richards and Wilford Woodruff in early 1883 in Kenney, *Wilford Woodruff's Journal,* 8:225). The original manuscript of "The Book of the Law of the Lord" is controlled by the First Presidency of the LDS church.

ONE.

"My Sorrows Are Greater Than I Can Bear!"

According to John Taylor's 1881 recital, Orson Pratt's demotion began thirty-three years earlier in 1842 after Joseph Smith introduced "the Celestial Order of Marriage" to his closest associates.[1] Born on 19 September 1811 in Henderson, New York, to Jared and Charity Pratt, Orson converted to Mormonism through his older brother Parley in late summer 1830 just four months following the organization of the Church of Christ, as it was then called. By the end of that year, the young, intellectually gifted convert, anxious to learn the Lord's will, felt instructed by revelation to "lift up your voice as with the sound of a trump, both long and loud, and cry repentance unto a crooked and perverse generation, preparing the way of the Lord for his second coming." "You are my son," Pratt had

---

1. Taylor, *Succession in the Priesthood*, 18. The best introduction to plural marriage is Van Wagoner's *Mormon Polygamy: A History*.

Pratt and Smith had two earlier altercations worth noting. The first in early 1836 centered on the pronunciation of a Hebrew word (see Joseph Smith, *History*

7

been told; "And blessed are you because you have believed" (Doctrine and Covenants 34:6, 3-4). Before the end of the decade, Orson—now twenty-eight and among the first group of twelve apostles called to spread Mormonism's good news—was sent with other colleagues on a proselyting mission to England and Scotland.[2]

During Pratt's sixteen-month absence from church headquarters, Joseph Smith began taking plural wives as part of the "restoration of all things." His first recorded plural marriage ("sealing")

---

of the Church of Jesus Christ of Latter-day Saints, Period I, ed. B. H. Roberts, 7 vols. [Salt Lake City: Deseret Book Co., published for the church, 1974], 2:356; Breck England, *The Life and Thought of Orson Pratt* [Salt Lake City: University of Utah Press, 1985], 44). "A mans faults," Pratt later complained, "if they [a]r[e] written[,] ought to have carried out their whole meaning—or else it is despicable in my eyes. [T]hat thing that Warren Parrish [Joseph Smith's scribe] wrote[—]'O Pratt manifested a rebellious Sp[irit]'—it was all ab[ou]t the pronounciation of a Hebrew word[, which] was decided in my favor. [F]uture generat[io]ns wo[ul]d think I [h]ad done some great fault" ("Minutes of Councils, Meetings, & Journey on a mission to the Saints on the Pottawatomie Sands," 5 Dec. 1847, LDS church archives). Parrish actually recorded: "Attended the Hebrew School [and] divided them into classes. Had some debate with Elder Orson Pratt. He manifested a stub[b]ourn spirit, which I [Joseph Smith] was much grieved at" (Faulring, *American Prophet's Record,* 97).

In the second instance, Pratt apparently cosigned a letter addressed to the church's bishop in Kirtland, Ohio, in mid-1837 during the so-called Anti-Banking Society scandal. It charged Joseph Smith with "lying & misrepresentation—also for extortion—and for speaking disrespectfully against his brethren behind their backs" (qtd. in Elden J. Watson, comp., *The Orson Pratt Journals* [Salt Lake City: editor, 1975], 531; England, *Life and Thought,* 50-51; Taylor, *Succession in the Priesthood,* 13). Shortly afterwards, Pratt reported that his accusation was based on hearsay and that he had no personal knowledge of any wrongdoing by Smith (see Mary Fielding to Mercy Fielding Thompson, 8 July 1837, LDS church archives). Neither Smith nor any other known source made further reference to either the Hebrew class or the letter.

2. See James B. Allen and Malcolm R. Thorp, "The Mission of the Twelve to England, 1840-41: Mormon Apostles and the Working Class," *BYU Studies* 15 (Summer 1975): 499-526; and especially James B. Allen, Ronald K. Esplin, and David J. Whittaker, *Men with a Mission, 1837-1841: The Quorum of the Twelve Apostles in the British Isles* (Salt Lake City: Deseret Book Co., 1992). One of Orson's converts, Marian Ross, would become his plural wife in 1847.

occurred in early April 1841 to twenty-six-year-old Louisa Beaman.[3] By the end of August 1842, Smith had married at least twelve other women ranging in age from seventeen to fifty-three; he was also still married to his first wife, Emma Hale. Eight of his plural wives (nearly two-thirds) had living husbands. A few of the husbands were non-believers or estranged from their spouses, but a majority, according to historian Todd Compton, were faithful Latter-day Saints.[4]

In taking additional wives, Smith maintained that he followed, under penalty of spiritual death, a divine commandment to strengthen the family and to exercise his prerogative as one of the Lord's chosen. Compton terms this a "theology of degreed exaltation by quantity of family."[5] As Smith advised his personal secretary in February 1843: "It is your privilege to have all the wives you want."[6] "[T]he Lord had given him the keys of this sealing ordinance," Smith's cousin later remembered, and "he felt as liberal to others as

---

3. See Andrew F. Ehat, "Joseph Smith's Introduction of Temple Ordinances and the 1844 Mormon Succession Question," M.A. thesis, Brigham Young University, 1982, 102; George D. Smith, "Nauvoo Roots of Mormon Polygamy, 1841-46: A Preliminary Demographic Report," *Dialogue: A Journal of Mormon Thought* 27 (Spring 1994): [60] (hereafter *Dialogue*); and Todd Compton, *In Sacred Loneliness: The Plural Wives of Joseph Smith* (Salt Lake City: Signature Books, 1997), 59.

4. Compton, *Sacred Loneliness*, 4-7; see also Danel W. Bachman, "A Study of the Mormon Practice of Plural Marriage before the Death of Joseph Smith," M.A. thesis, Purdue University, 1975, 333-36. These already married women and the dates of their sealings to Joseph Smith are (married names in parentheses): Zina Diantha Huntington (Jacobs), 27 Oct. 1841; Prescinda Lathrop Huntington (Buell), 11 Dec. 1841; Sylvia Sessions (Lyon), 8 Feb. 1842; Mary Elizabeth Rollins (Lightner), late Feb. 1842; Patty Bartlett (Sessions), 9 Mar. 1842; Marinda Nancy Johnson (Hyde), Apr. 1842; Elizabeth Davis (Goldsmith Brackenbury Durfee), before June 1842; and Sarah Kingsley (Howe Cleveland), before 29 June 1842 (see Compton, *Sacred Loneliness*, 4-7).

5. Compton, *Sacred Loneliness*, 455.

6. Qtd. in "William Clayton's Testimony," 16 Feb. 1874, rpt. in George D. Smith, ed., *An Intimate Chronicle: The Journals of William Clayton* (Salt Lake City: Signature Books in association with Smith Research Associates, 1995), 557. Later

he did to himself. He [Joseph] remarked that he had given Brigham
Young three wives, Heber C. Kimball two, John Taylor three,
Orson Hyde two, and many a number of others, and said to me
'You should not be behind your privileges.'"[7] Despite the associated hardships, Smith was convinced that his actions blessed forever
not only the plural wives, their parents, and families, but—
through the sealing ordinances of eternal marriage and adop-
tion—united their husbands and families in an ever-expanding web
of familial and social inter-relationships.[8] Indeed, the Lord himself,
speaking through Smith, promised one of the church's leaders in
late July 1842 who had agreed to "consecrate" his seventeen-
year-old daughter to the prophet: "[T]he thing that my servant Joseph Smith has made known unto you and your Family and which
you have agreed upon is right in mine eyes and shall be rewarded
upon your heads with honor and immortality and eternal life to all
your house both old & young."[9] "If you will take this step," a
young bride reported Smith telling her, "it will insure your eternal
salvation & exaltation and that of your father's household & all of
your kindred."[10] "I know that I shall be saved in the Kingdom of
God," another plural wife recorded of her sealing. "I have the oath

---

sealing records occasionally refer to the prophet's early plural wives as his "eternal
possessions."

7. George A. Smith to Joseph Smith III, 9 Oct. 1869, in Journal History of
the Church of Jesus Christ of Latter-day Saints, daily entries, multi-volume, unpublished scrapbook, LDS church archives.

8. See, e.g., Rex Eugene Cooper, *Promises Made to the Fathers: Mormon Covenant Organization* (Salt Lake City: University of Utah Press, 1990), 138-47.

9. Qtd. in "A Revelation to N[ewel] K. Whitney," 27 July 1842, rpt. in *The
Essential Joseph Smith* (Salt Lake City: Signature Books, 1995), 165. "A main mo-
tive of some plural marriages seems to have been to extend this saving power
through the sealed woman to members of her family" (Cooper, *Promises Made to
the Fathers,* 140).

10. Helen Mar Kimball, qtd. in Richard S. Van Wagoner, *Sidney Rigdon: A Portrait of Religious Excess* (Salt Lake City: Signature Books, 1994), 293. "The promise
was so great," Kimball admitted, "that I willingly gave myself to purchase so glorious a reward." See also Donna Hill, *Joseph Smith: The First Mormon* (Garden City,
NY: Doubleday, 1977), 355.

of God upon it and God cannot lie. All that he [Joseph] gives me I shall take with me for I have that authority and that power conferred upon me."[11]

Failure to obey the Lord's commands through his prophet could spell damnation for a woman and her family. "[P]repare thy heart to receive and obey the instructions which I am about to give unto you," the Lord proclaimed in the revelation on plural marriage; "for all those who have this law revealed unto them must obey the same. For behold, I reveal unto you a new and an everlasting covenant; and if ye abide not that covenant, then are ye damned; for no one can reject this covenant and be permitted to enter into my glory" (Doctrine and Covenants 132:3-4). "Believing that one's eternal exaltation depended on Joseph Smith," observes LDS historian Kathryn M. Daynes, "ensured loyalty to him, especially when his power extended not only to his plural wives but also to their families. Mormons' concern with their salvation was strong and immediate because of their millenarian belief that the end of the world and the second coming of Christ would happen, not imminently but in the not-far-distant future."[12]

As a result, Smith judged that all contracts which were not sanctioned, or sealed, by the power of his restored priesthood authority—in the case of married women, their civil marriages—were ultimately invalid.[13] "He that is called of God is not only a minister of the Law given by God," he explained, "but is also anointed to make

---

11. Qtd. in "Remarks by Sister Mary E. Lightner, Who Was Sealed to Joseph Smith in 1842. [An Address Delivered at] B.Y.U., April 14, 1905," 3, LDS church archives.

12. Kathryn M. Daynes, *More Wives Than One: Transformation of the Mormon Marriage System, 1840-1910* (Urbana: University of Illinois Press, 2001), 26.

13. See Bachman, "A Study of the Mormon Practice of Plural Marriage," 124-36; and Compton, *Sacred Loneliness,* 17-18. Mormons continued to contract civil marriages. Joseph himself personally performed at least twelve such marriages in Nauvoo; his older brother Hyrum performed twenty-six. See Lyndon W. Cook, comp., *Nauvoo Deaths and Marriages, 1839-1845* (Orem, UT: Grandin Book Co., 1994), 89-114.

Law according to their Authority."[14] "No marriage is valid in the morn of the resurrection," his brother Hyrum echoed, "unless the marriage covenant be sealed on earth by one having the keys and power from the Almighty God to seal on earth as it shall be bound in heaven."[15] "All covenants, oaths, vows, performances, connections, associations, or expectations," the Lord said,

> that are not made and entered into and sealed by the Holy Spirit of promise, of him who is anointed, ... are of no efficacy, virtue, or force in and after the resurrection from the dead. ... Therefore, if a man marry him a wife in the world, and he marry her not by me nor by my word, and he covenant with her so long as he is in the world and she with him, their covenant and marriage are not of force when they are dead, and when they are out of the world; therefore, they are not bound by any law when they are out of the world. (Doctrine and Covenants 132:7, 15)

"[T]he Prophet felt," LDS educator Danel W. Bachman concluded,

> that only those who had his approval could properly exercise the religious ordinance [of marriage], and that he could void marriages that were not valid in eternity. Indeed, there is evidence that Smith and others willfully "annulled" civil marriages at Nauvoo. They likened this activity to their practice of rebaptizing converts. That is, on some occasions they honored marriages by non-priesthood authority no more than the baptisms by non-Mormon ministers.[16]

---

14. Qtd. in Bachman, "A Study of the Mormon Practice of Plural Marriage," 125-26.

15. Hyrum Smith, discourse, 8 Apr. 1844, Miscellaneous Minutes Collection, LDS church archives. The previous year, Hyrum explained to John and Julia Pack that "all former covenants and contracts in marriage would be null and void after death, and that it was his [Pack's] privilege to have his wife sealed to him for time and for all eternity" (John Pack, affidavit, 22 July 1869, in Joseph F. Smith Affidavit Book, 1:56-57, LDS church archives).

16. Bachman, "A Study of the Mormon Practice of Plural Marriage," 127. D.

"[C]ontracts and the like, not entered into during mortality by the proper authorization of God and his servants," Bachman wrote, "are of no lasting significance in the resurrection."[17] "Smith eliminated civil marriage as a viable alternative for faithful Saints," Mormon historian M. Guy Bishop has added; "[his] usurpation of civil authority to perform weddings was an audacious move."[18] "[P]riesthood law transcended human convention," concurs LDS researcher Rex E. Cooper.[19]

Although some writers have postulated that these "celestial marriages" were to be consummated only in the hereafter, Smith, according to Bachman, Compton, and other scholars, was sexually intimate with "a number"—though not all—of his wives, including those already married.[20] Perhaps more importantly, especially within the context of the church's "culture of secrecy,"[21] rumors did not allow for such distinctions. For those who embraced the new

---

Michael Quinn terms this a doctrine of "theocratic ethics"; see his *The Mormon Hierarchy: Origins of Power* (Salt Lake City: Signature Books in association with Smith Research Associates, 1994), 88.

17. Danel W. Bachman, "Polygamy 1830-52," in *The First Annual Church Educational System Religious Educators Symposium* (Provo, UT: Brigham Young University, 1977), 36.

18. M. Guy Bishop, "Eternal Marriage in Early Mormon Marital Belief," *The Historian* 52 (Autumn 1990): 83, 84.

19. Cooper, *Promises Made to the Fathers,* 85.

20. Ibid., 136-42; and Compton, *Sacred Loneliness,* 12-15. In fact, Cooper suggests that one of the purposes of plural marriage was to "legitimize sexual relations" (see Cooper, *Promises Made to the Fathers,* 142). Daynes cautions: "Some historians have assumed that because some plural marraiges involved sexuality, probably most, if not all, did so, a conclusion that goes beyond documentary evidence. That is particularly the case in the Nauvoo period" (Daynes, *More Wives Than One,* 29).

21. The phrase is Susan Staker's; see her "'The Lord Said, Thy Wife Is a Very Fair Woman to Look upon': The Book of Abraham, Secrets, and Lying for the Lord," in Bryan Waterman, ed., *The Prophet Puzzle: Interpretive Essays on Joseph Smith* (Salt Lake City: Signature Books, 1999), 300. "Early Mormonism was steeped in secrecy," agrees Bachman ("A Study of the Mormon Practice of Plural Marriage," 192).

doctrine, the promise of future exaltation offset the passing condemnation of fellow church members and the ridicule of unbeliev-
ers. "To nineteenth-century leaders," observes Compton, "the
principle was not just an optional revelation—they viewed it as the
most important revelation in Joseph Smith's life, which is what he
undoubtedly taught them. If they accepted him as an infallible
prophet, and if they wanted full exaltation, they had no recourse
but to marry many plural wives."[22] "Essential ... to understanding
why Latter-day Saints did not immediately and vociferously reject
such proposals so repugnant to their ingrained traditions," Daynes
adds, "is their central belief that God revealed his will to humans
and that Joseph Smith as his prophet was the conduit through
whom such revelations were received."[23]

Upon his return to Nauvoo in mid-July 1841, Orson Pratt, at
the time not quite thirty, sold religious pamphlets he had printed
abroad and conducted classes in elementary mathematics at the
boomtown's fledgling university. By November, he was elected to
the city council. In both church and civic circles, he encountered
the loquacious newcomer to Mormonism, John C. Bennett, who
had arrived late the previous summer. The thirty-six-year-old
Bennett had quickly become chancellor of the university, mayor of
the city, and, most importantly, acting assistant president and intimate confidant to Joseph Smith. Talented and opportunistic, Bennett had used his keen political and oratorical skills to ingratiate
himself to Smith and, presumably, to other church members. While
residing in the prophet's home for nearly ten months,[24] he helped
supervise the draining of the swamp lands adjoining the city and
successfully steered the far-reaching Nauvoo city charter, which he
largely wrote, through the Illinois state legislature. Seduced for a

---

22. Compton, *Sacred Loneliness*, 456.

23. Daynes, *More Wives Than One*, 27.

24. Andrew F. Smith, *The Saintly Scoundrel: The Life and Times of Dr. John Cook Bennett* (Urbana: University of Illinois Press, 1997), 56.

time by Bennett's charisma, Smith and others overlooked his many shortcomings.[25] "Clearly," wrote future LDS Church Historian Leonard J. Arrington, "the [Mormon] kingdom was in need of a man with Bennett's talents, and could profit from his ambitions. This is apparently what Joseph Smith saw in him, and the Prophet was at least persuaded that Bennett was sincere in hitching his career to the rising star of Mormonism."[26]

Pratt left no contemporary account of his initial impression of Bennett, but his biographer feels that the two must have become friendly.[27] Nor did Pratt reveal the extent of his own knowledge, if any, of "the new and everlasting covenant" of marriage before mid-1842.[28] Joseph Smith taught the new revelation to many of Pratt's colleagues in the Quorum of the Twelve Apostles following their return from England. Elders Brigham Young and Heber C.

---

25. Smith, *Saintly Scoundrel,* is the best biography of Bennett. Venerable LDS historian B. H. Roberts wrote: "It must be confessed that both President Joseph Smith and the people of Nauvoo erred greatly in their treatment of John C. Bennett, by being too indulgent and long-suffering with him." Roberts identified the following as among Smith's "limitations": "a too great tenacity in friendship for men he had once taken into his confidence after they had been proven unworthy of that friendship, and by which taint of their sins, in hypercritical minds, attached somewhat to him" (B. H. Roberts, *A Comprehensive History of the Church of Jesus Christ of Latter-day Saints. Century I,* 6 vols. [Provo, UT: Brigham Young University Press, for the church, 1965], 2:146, 358).

26. Leonard J. Arrington, "Centrifugal Tendencies in Mormon History," in *To the Glory of God,* ed. Truman G. Madsen and Charles D. Tate (Salt Lake City: Deseret Book, 1972), 168. Arrington's is the most generous treatment of Bennett to date.

27. England, *Life and Thought,* 75.

28. In 1878 Pratt reported that Smith had "made known ... as early as 1831, that plural marriage was a correct principle ... but that the time had not come to teach or practice it in the Church but that the time would come" (qtd. in "Report of Elders Orson Pratt and Joseph F. Smith," *Millennial Star,* 16 Dec. 1878, 788; also "Orson Pratt's Testimony" in the *Historical Record* 6 [May 1887]: 230). Pratt's biographer thinks he "must have been aware of the possibility that the plural marriage covenant might someday be required of the Saints" (England, *Life and Thought,* 76). If so, his behavior in 1842 suggests that he was unprepared for its practice in his own household.

Kimball both took additional wives before August 1842.[29] Bennett was aware of Smith's teachings, sometimes called "spiritual wifery," because after his disaffection from the church, Bennett published specific details that, despite sensational embellishments, only an informed insider could have known.[30] Meanwhile, rumors of polygamy had begun to surface in nervous meetings of Nauvoo's stake high council and Relief Society. In fact, several members of the all-female Relief Society had married Smith without the knowledge of the society's president, the prophet's first wife, Emma.[31]

Pratt's standing as an apostle should have placed him in the inner circle of polygamists,[32] but it seems clear that, for at least the first nine months following his return home, he was unaware, or refused to acknowledge, that plural marriage had been restored among some of the Saints in fulfillment of the "fullness of times." When he did learn of it and its place in the church, it was not from Smith or from his brethren in the Twelve but from his wife of nearly six years, Sarah Marinda Bates.

---

29. See Smith, "Nauvoo Roots of Mormon Polygamy," 49-50, 67-68; also England, *Life and Thought,* 76-77; Ehat, "Joseph Smith's Introduction of Temple Ordinances," 102; Arrington, *Brigham Young,* 420; Stanley B. Kimball, *Heber C. Kimball: Mormon Patriarch and Pioneer* (Urbana: University of Illinois Press, 1981), 311.

30. "When he was relieved of his offices and left Nauvoo," wrote Leonard Arrington, "Bennett took with him an intimate knowledge of some of the confidential conversations and hopes and designs of the Church and its leaders" (Arrington, "Centrifugal Tendencies," 169). England, *Life and Thought,* 77, agrees that Bennett was "fully aware" of Smith's new doctrine. Bennett's anti-Mormon writings first appeared in the *Sangamo Journal* but are most accessible in his *History of the Saints; Or an Exposé of Joe Smith and Mormonism* (Boston: Leland and Whiting, 1842; rpt. 2000 by University of Illinois Press, Urbana), esp. p. 256. See also Smith, *Saintly Scoundrel,* 100-103.

31. See Nauvoo High Council Minute Book, 20, 24, 25, 27, 28 May, 10 June 1842, copy in my possession, original in LDS church archives; and Staker, "'The Lord Said, Thy Wife Is a Very Fair Woman,'" 298-304; Linda King Newell and Valeen Tippets Avery, *Mormon Enigma: Emma Hale Smith,* 2nd ed. (Urbana: University of Illinois Press, 1994), 106-18; and Van Wagoner, *Mormon Polygamy,* 47-59.

32. England, *Life and Thought,* 76-77.

According to Sarah's third-person 1884 recollection,[33] Smith, accompanied by Bennett, invited her to become his plural wife in the fall of 1840 when Orson was in Great Britain. Only twenty-three years old, Sarah was alone in Nauvoo and "dependent for means of support as well as companionship." Smith "appeared much interested in her affairs and brought Dr. John C. Bennett once or twice with him when he called." Initially, the prophet's "calls were made upon her in her home where she was living with another family," that of Stephen and Zeruiah Goddard. After Sarah moved that November to "a little house by herself," Smith's "attentions became more frequent." One time he told her that his own wife, Emma, "had become jealous of her." Sarah soon assured Emma "of the folly of such an idea" and stressed that she was "thoroughly bound up in her husband ... and had no thought for any one else."

A short time later, Smith again called and told Sarah "he knew she must be lonely now that her husband was away, and that it was not at all necessary that it should be so. She needed the company of some man," he continued, "and he would stay with her when she wished it; that there was no sin in it as long as she kept it to herself; that the sin was wholly in making it known herself to her husband or any one else."[34] She indignantly rejected him, saying "she loved her husband most devotedly." Reportedly fearing exposure, Smith threatened that "if she told of it [his proposal,] he had it in his power to ruin her character."

---

33. Anon., "Workings of Mormonism Related by Mrs. Orson Pratt, Salt Lake City, 1884," LDS church archives. Although reflecting Sarah's beliefs and accurate in many of its details, this document is retrospective, and by 1884, Sarah was a critic of the church. The last three paragraphs of the chronology are confused and the author misidentifies Sarah twice as "Mrs. Orson Hyde."

34. "Happiness is the object and design of our existence," Smith wrote to another prospective plural wife who rebuffed him. "That which is wrong under one circumstance, may be and often is, right under another. ... Whatever God requires is right, no matter what it is, although we may not see the reason thereof till long after the events transpire" (Smith to Nancy Rigdon, ca. 11 Apr. 1842, rpt. in *Essential Joseph Smith*, 158-59).

Deeply troubled by this "insult" from "one who was almost as a god to her," but ignoring Joseph's warning, Sarah confided in an older friend "in whose virtue and faithfulness as a wife ... she had implicit confidence," fully expecting "to receive her [friend's] hearty sympathy." Much to her surprise, her "old and tried friend" said, "You must think nothing of that; why I myself have been his [Smith's] mistress for the past four years."[35] Sarah "saw for herself, with her eyes now opened, that there were houses whose back doors [Smith] entered on the sly, guarded as he was by Bennett." Bennett himself "would tell [Sarah] to watch Smith's entrance[s] and exit[s] here and there," and other women "would admit to her their intercourse with [Smith] and offer her opportunities of convincing herself that what they said was true."[36]

Orson returned home in mid-July 1841. About a year later in April 1842, according to Bennett's exposé published a few weeks later on 15 July, Smith renewed his invitation to Sarah and attempted to kiss her.[37] While Sarah had kept silent about his earlier advances, now infuriated, she complained to Orson who immediately confronted Smith. The prophet denied the story, saying that the real culprit was Bennett. Bennett hotly rejected the charge. By this time, Bennett had become both an embarrassment to church leaders and an easy target because of his messy attempts to arrange

---

35. If true, this would date the beginning of Smith's relationship with Lucinda Pendleton (Morgan Harris) to 1837 or 1838, three or four years before Smith's known marriage to Louisa Beaman. See Compton, *Sacred Loneliness,* 47-48, 650.

36. Two years after this reminiscence was recorded, non-Mormon journalist Wilhelm Ritter von Wymetal quoted Sarah as saying that Bennett "knew that Joseph had his plans set on me [Sarah]; Joseph made no secret of them before Bennett, and went so far in his impudence as to make propositions to me in the presence of Bennett, his bosom friend." Bennett, being "of a sarcastic turn of mind[,] used to come and tell me about Joseph to tease and irritate me" (W. Wyl, pseud., *Mormon Portraits* [Salt Lake City: Tribune Printing and Publishing Co., 1886], 61).

37. Bennett, *History of the Saints,* 231.

sexual liaisons for himself and others without Smith's imprimatur.[38] Faced with having to choose between his wife's charges and Smith's denials, Pratt, who by now must have heard rumors of the prophet's plural marriages, sided with Sarah.

Unfortunately, Smith did not leave an account of his dealings with Sarah Pratt since presumably his perspective would have been different. But while Sarah's account is not without problems, its main point seems accurate: Orson first learned about polygamy from his wife because of her anger over Smith's advances. Since returning from England, Orson had undoubtedly learned that the prophet had propositioned other apostles' wives. Joseph had approached Heber C. Kimball and John Taylor directly, asking that they give him their wives. When they reluctantly responded in the affirmative, he proclaimed that he had merely tested their loyalty.[39] In a third case involving Orson and Marinda Hyde, Joseph married Marinda in April 1842 while her husband was in Europe and Palestine on a church mission.[40]

The traditional explanation for this aspect of Nauvoo polygamy emphasizes that Smith wanted to evaluate his associates' devotion. A counselor in the First Presidency, Jedediah M. Grant explained two years after plural marriage was publicly announced:

---

38. Smith required that a ceremony be performed with his permission prior to sexual contact. Bennett believed that worthy individuals could engage in sexual activity if they kept their conduct secret. "If Bennett had not moved [al]together so fast[,] all would have been well now, as I look at things with them," observed ex-Mormon Oliver Olney, writing from Nauvoo in the early 1840s (qtd. in Lawrence Foster, *Religion and Sexuality: Three American Communal Experiments of the Nineteenth Century* [New York: Oxford University Press, 1981], 316).

39. Van Wagoner, *Mormon Polygamy*, 37.

40. See ibid., 224; Van Wagoner, *Sidney Rigdon*, 294; Hyde, *Orson Hyde*, 161; and Compton's more conservatively phrased discussion, *Sacred Loneliness*, 4-5, 235-44. "[L]et my handmaid Nancy Marinda Hyde hearken to the counsel of my servant Joseph in all things whatsoever he shall teach unto her," Smith's *History of the Church* (4:467) quotes a revelation of 2 December 1841, "and it shall be a blessing upon her and upon her children after her, unto her justification."

When the family organization was revealed from heaven—the patriarchal order of God, and Joseph began, on the right and on the left to add to his family, what a quaking there was in Israel. Says one brother to another, "Joseph says all covenants are done away, and none are binding but the new covenants; now suppose Joseph should come and say he wanted your wife, what would you say to that?" "I would tell him to go to hell." This was the spirit of many in the early days of this Church. ... Did the Prophet Joseph want every man's wife he asked for? He did not but in that thing was the grand thread of the Priesthood developed. The grand object in view was to try the people of God, to see what was in them.[41]

If Grant is correct, Pratt was not the only one who was angry or perhaps believed his wife over the prophet. Pratt would certainly be inclined to see this as an assault on his wife's virtue if he knew of other *sub rosa* proposals, especially in cases where Smith had consummated the marriage.[42]

A few weeks later, on 15 June 1842, the first public indication of Orson's growing difficulties with Joseph appeared. The church's *Times and Seasons* announced Bennett's expulsion from the church, but Pratt's name was conspicuously absent from the list of those endorsing the action.[43] Bennett claimed that Pratt refused to sign be-

41. *Journal of Discourses,* 2:13-14.

42. Rachel Ridgway Ivins, Sarah M. Kimball, Jane Law, and Nancy Rigdon all rebuffed Smith's overtures. Kimball and Law had living husbands. See Ronald W. Walker, "Rachel R. Grant: The Continuing Legacy of the Feminine Ideal," *Dialogue* 15 (Autumn 1982): 109; Van Wagoner, *Mormon Polygamy,* 30-32, 40-41, 63-66. What Rachel Ivins is alleged to have replied to Joseph Smith is quoted in Smith, "Nauvoo Roots of Mormon Polygamy," 24: "[I would] sooner go to hell as a virtuous woman than to heaven as a whore."

43. "Notice" of 11 May, *Times and Seasons,* 15 June 1842, 830; see also William Clayton on Bennett's excommunication in Smith, *Intimate Chronicle,* 533; and Joseph's longer, 23 June, denunciation, "To the Church of Jesus Christ of Latter Day Saints, and To All the Honorable Part of Community," *Times and Seasons,* 1 July 1842, 839-42. Three of the signatories were out of town at the time: Apostles Lyman Wight, William Smith, and John E. Page. Bennett said the authorities ante-

cause "he knew nothing against me."[44] The absence was deliberate: Pratt's name appeared with the other apostles' on a flyer the previous month, and two months later it would be included with the others on a general notice. Most significantly, if Pratt believed Smith's charge that Bennett had made advances toward Sarah, he most likely would have sustained the action against Bennett.

From this point on, the apostle was in open, if anguished, conflict with the prophet—a "sullen rebel" his biographer calls him.[45] Church leaders launched a program of damage control. During this period, Pratt stopped associating socially with other members of the Twelve, refused to join his brethren in embracing Freemasonry, and held back on becoming a member of the Quorum of the Anointed or Holy Order (the earliest initiates into what would become the Mormon temple endowment ceremony).[46] In the meantime, a deeply embittered Bennett left Nauvoo, highly offended by Smith's treatment of him, and began publishing a lurid account of his years in Nauvoo in the nearby *Sangamo Journal*.[47] Never before had Smith and his church been subject to such a scabrous attack. In the 15 July 1842 issue, Bennett gave his account of the prophet's proposals to Sarah Pratt. "Sister Pratt," he quoted Smith as having said, "the Lord has given you to me as one of my *spiritual wives*. I have the blessings of Jacob granted me, as God granted holy men of old, and as I have long looked upon you with favor, and an earnest desire of connubial bliss, I hope you will not repulse or deny me." "I

dated the notice to make it appear he had not first withdrawn of his own accord (Bennett, *History of the Saints,* 41). Smith was informed of Bennett's marital status in late 1840 and again about ten months later (Smith, "To the Church," 839-40).

44. Bennett, *History of the Saints,* 41. Bennett's biographer agrees that Pratt refused; see Smith, *Saintly Scoundrel,* 100.

45. England, *Life and Thought,* 78.

46. See Heber C. Kimball to Parley P. Pratt, 17 June 1842; Brigham Young to Parley P. Pratt, 17 July 1842, LDS church archives.

47. Smith, *History of the Church,* 5:35-40; Kenney, *Wilford Woodruff's Journal,* 2:179; for a full account, see Smith, *Saintly Scoundrel,* 98-128.

care not for the blessings of Jacob," Sarah countered, "I have one good husband, and that is enough for me." "Sister Pratt," Smith allegedly replied, "I hope you will not expose me; for if I suffer, all must suffer; so do not expose me. Will you promise me that you will not do it?" "If you will never insult me again," Sarah promised, "I will not expose you, unless strong circumstances should require it."[48]

Furious over Bennett's disclosures, Smith responded by assaulting not only Bennett but also Sarah and Orson Pratt. He went so far as to publicly brand Sarah a "—— [whore?] from her mother's breast."[49] "The man who promises to keep a secret and does not keep it," he later elaborated to the city council in reference to the "spiritual wife system," "he is a liar and not to be trusted. ... When a man becomes a traitor to his friends or country who is [are] innocent, [and becomes] treacherous to innocent blood[, I] do consider it right to cut off his influence so that he could not injure the innocent ..."[50] This definition of "lying"—breaking a confidence, in other words—may explain Smith's reasoning in his approach to the Pratts and others in the summer of 1842, a tactic he admitted was based on "self-defense."[51]

Depressed by the defamation of his wife and heartsick at the conclusions he would have to draw from believing either Sarah or Joseph, Orson grew more despondent. Seated in the church print-

---

48. Qtd. in Bennett, *History of the Saints,* 229-31; emphasis in original.

49. Ibid., 52, citing the *Sangamo Journal,* 1 Aug. 1842; see also Smith, *History of the Church,* 5:137-39; Andrew F. Ehat and Lyndon Cook, eds., *The Words of Joseph Smith* (Provo, UT: Brigham Young University Religious Studies Research Center, 1980), 127-29. Sarah reported to Wilhelm Wyl what Joseph told her: "If any woman, like me, opposed his wishes, he used to say: 'Be silent, or I shall ruin your character'" (qtd. in Wyl, *Mormon Portraits,* 62).

50. Nauvoo City Council Meeting, Minutes, 3 Jan. 1844 (not included in the published version of the minutes; cf. Journal History of the Church, same date), LDS church archives.

51. Smith, *History of the Church,* 5:49.

ing office on the sultry evening of 14 July 1842 and in the presence of George W. Thatcher and perhaps others, the thirty-year-old found himself racked with pain and doubt. He wrote:

> I am a ruined man! My future prospects are blasted! The testimony upon both sides seems to be equal: The one in direct contradiction to the other—[H]ow to decide I know not[,] neither does it matter[,] for let it be either way[,] my temporal happiness is gone in this world[. I]f the testimonies of my wife and others are true[,] then I have been deceived for twelve years past—my hopes are blasted and gone as it were in a moment—my long toils and labors have been in vain. If on the other hand the other testimonies are true[,] then my family are ruined forever. Where then is my hope in this world? It is gone—gone not to be recovered!! Oh God, why is it thus with me! My sorrows are greater than I can bear! Where I am henceforth[,] it matters not.[52]

Reportedly, the document was found the following morning in the street east of Heber C. Kimball's house.

When word spread through the city the next day that the apostle was missing, Smith himself ordered an immediate search "lest he [Pratt] should have laid violent hands on himself." The church president then delivered a stinging public attack on Bennett, whom he blamed for the entire sorry affair.[53] A visibly shaken Pratt returned that night. According to Smith's diary, Pratt "conclud[ed] to do right."[54] Ebenezer Robinson, former editor of the *Times and Seasons,* recalled:

---

52. This document, apparently in Pratt's hand, is in the uncatalogued Orson Pratt Papers, LDS church archives. It has been in the possession of the LDS Church History Department since at least the early 1970s when historian D. Michael Quinn examined it. It is alluded to in Joseph Smith's diary, 15 July 1842, in Dean C. Jessee, ed., *The Papers of Joseph Smith* (Salt Lake City: Deseret Book Co., 1992), 2:398. This may have been the letter that Pratt family legend claims the distraught apostle wrote in his own blood (see England, *Life and Thought,* 80).

53. Alexander Neibuhr, Journal, 15 July 1842, LDS church archives; Smith, *History of the Church,* 5:60-61; Ehat and Cook, *Words of Joseph Smith,* 126; Jessee, *Papers of Joseph Smith,* 2:398-99.

54. Jessee, *Papers of Joseph Smith,* 2:399.

I remember well the excitement which existed at the time, as a large number of the citizens turned out to go in search for him [Pratt], fearing that he had committed suicide. He was found some 5 miles below Nauvoo, sitting on a rock, on the bank of the Mississippi river, without a hat. He recovered from his insanity, but at the next conference, when the vote was called to sustain Joseph Smith as President of the Church, he alone voted, No. He could not at that time conscientiously sustain him in that position.[55]

Two days later, Brigham Young, forty-one-year-old president of the Twelve, wrote to Pratt's older brother Parley, then on a mission in England. After noting that Bennett had been "turned out of the Church," Young explained:

Br Orson Pratt is in trubble in consequence of his wife, hir feelings are so rought up that he dos not know whether his wife is wrong, or whether Josephs testimony and others are wrong and due Ly [do lie] and he dec[e]ived for 12 years or not; he is all but crazy about matters, you may aske what the matter is concirning Sister P[ratt. I]t is enoph, and doct. J[ohn] C. Bennett could tell all about himself & hir—enoph of that—we will not let Br Orson goe away from us[. H]e is to[o] good a man to have a woman destroy him.[56]

A self-avowed traitor to Mormonism, Bennett could be easily condemned, but long-time defenders Orson and Sarah Pratt could not be as facilely brushed aside. One week to the day after Pratt's alleged suicide attempt, Joseph Smith convened a public meeting to counter Bennett's charges. Orson remained conflicted, and when a resolution was presented to the crowd attesting to Smith's good character, Orson's was one of only two or three negative votes out of a thousand. Annoyed, Smith demanded of Pratt: "Have you personally a knowledge of any immoral act in me toward the female sex, or in

---

55. "Items of Personal History of the Editor," *The Return* 2 (Nov. 1890), 11. For most nineteenth-century men, going hatless in sunny mid-July would be seen as evidence of instability.

56. Young to Pratt, 17 July 1842, LDS church archives.

any other way?" By "personally," Smith meant first-hand. According to the *Times and Seasons,* Pratt responded, "Personally, toward the female sex, I have not."[57] The *Sangamo Journal,* which had been serializing Bennett's exposé, editorialized a week later on 29 July: "We do not know what course will be pursued by Mr. Pratt. If he sinks under the denunciations and schemes of Joe Smith—if he fails to defend the reputation of himself and of the woman he has vowed to protect before high heaven—he will fix a stain upon his character which he can never wash out, and carry to the grave the pangs caused by 'the gnawings of the worm that never dies.'"

Two days after the public reaffirmation of his good character, Smith married, with her parents' permission, the seventeen-year-old daughter of presiding bishop Newell K. Whitney. "These are the words which you shall pronounce upon my servant Joseph and your daughter S[arah] A[nn] Whitney," the Lord told her father through the prophet:

> They shall take each other by the hand and you shall say, You both mutually agree, calling them by name, to be each other's companion so long as you both shall live, preserving yourselves for each other and from all others and also throughout eternity, reserving only those rights which have been given to my servant Joseph by revelation and commandment and by legal authority in times passed. If you both agree to convenant and do this, I then give you, S. A. Whitney, my daughter, to Joseph Smith, to be his wife, to observe all the rights between you both that belong to that condition. I do it in my own name and in the name of my wife, your mother, and in the name of my holy progenitors, by the right of birth which is of priesthood, vested in me by revelation and commandment and promise of the living God ...[58]

---

57. Untitled article, *Times and Seasons,* 1 Aug. 1842, 869. Smith, *History of the Church,* 5:70-71, erroneously reports the voting as "unanimous."

58. Qtd. in "A Revelation to N[ewel] K. Whitney," *Essential Joseph Smith,* 165-66.

The young woman's mother later explained: "Our hearts were comforted, and our faith made so perfect that we were willing to give our eldest daughter ... to Joseph, in the order of plural marriage. Laying aside all our traditions and former notions in regard to marriage, we gave her with our mutual consent. She was the first woman given in plural marriage with the consent of both parents. Of course these things had to be kept an inviolate secret; ..."[59]

Sometime after 8 August, a still recalcitrant Pratt received a visit from fellow apostles Brigham Young, Heber C. Kimball, and George A. Smith. All three knew of Joseph's plural marriages, and Young and Kimball had already joined the "patriarchal order." None of the three recounted the visit to Pratt in his diary. Young's manuscript history and autobiography was not compiled until 1856, and the official *History of the Church,* both the manuscript and published versions, does not mention the apostles' visit.[60]

According to Young's autobiography, the three "spent several days laboring with Elder Orson Pratt, whose mind became so darkened by the influence and statements of his wife, that he came out in rebellion against Joseph, refusing to believe his [Joseph's] testi-

---

59. Qtd. in Edward W. Tullidge, *The Women of Mormondom* (New York: Tullidge and Crandall, 1877), 369.

60. Howard C. Searle, "Authorship of the History of Brigham Young: A Review Essay," *BYU Studies* 22 (Summer 1982): 367-74. Young's Manuscript History, currently in the LDS church archives, was serialized in both the *Deseret News* in 1858 and the *Millennial Star* in 1863-64. It was republished by Elden J. Watson in Salt Lake City in 1968. Although Wilford Woodruff was not present because of illness, he wrote a second-hand account in his journal soon afterwards: "There was a Counsel of the *Twelve* held for four days with Elder *Orson Pratt* to labour with him to get him to recall his sayings against Joseph & The Twelve but he persisted in his wicked course & would not recall any of his sayings which were made in public against Joseph & others[,] sayings which were unjust & untrue. The Twelve then rejected him as a member of their quorum & he was cut off ["from the church" added interlinearly]. Dr John Cook Bennett was the ruin of Orson Pratt" (Kenney, *Wilford Woodruff's Journal,* 2:187). Besides being hearsay, Woodruff's report misleadingly implies that the action was taken by the full quorum rather than only three apostles.

mony or obey his counsel." Pratt would not yield, preferring to "believe his wife [instead of] the Prophet." At some point, Joseph reportedly told Orson that "if he did believe his wife and follow her suggestions, he would go to hell." Young, Kimball, and George A. Smith subsequently informed "the Prophet that we had labored with bro. Orson diligently in a spirit of meekness, forbearance and long-suffering," but to no avail. Therefore, Joseph "requested us to ordain bro. Amasa Lyman[61] in bro. Orson's stead," Young would remember. "After receiving these instructions, we met bro. Orson near my house and continued to labor with him. He said to us, there is brother Amasa Lyman in your house, brother Young; he has been long in the ministry, go in and ordain him in my stead."[62] On Saturday, 20 August, the three apostles allegedly "cut [Pratt] off from the church, and according to the Prophet's direction, ... ordained bro. Amasa Lyman in his stead."[63] Surprisingly, no mention is made of any action against Sarah.

In the context of these events, it is interesting that two days earlier Smith had written to his new seventeen-year-old bride and her parents, asking that they meet with him secretly:

I ["know" added interlinearly] it is the will of God that you should comfort ["me" added interlinearly] now in this time of affliction, or not at all[. N]ow is the time or never, but I hav[e] no kneed of saying any such t[h]ing, to you, for I know the goodness of your hearts, and that you will do the will of the Lord, when it is made known to you;

---

61. Pratt had earlier converted Lyman to Mormonism.

62. This statement seems to be what prompted David J. Whittaker, another of Pratt's biographers, to write that, during this time, Pratt "asked that his name be removed from the records of the Church until he could satisfy his questions" ("Orson Pratt: Early Advocate of the Book of Mormon," *Ensign* 14 [Apr. 1984]: 55).

63. "History of Brigham Young," *Deseret News,* 17 Mar. 1858, [1]. This printing is faithful to all three manuscript drafts. Smith, *History of the Church,* 5:120, reports Lyman's ordination without commenting on the traumatic circumstances.

the only thing to be careful of; is to find out when Emma comes[,] then you cannot be safe, but when she is not here, there is the most perfect safty; only be careful to escape observation, as much as possible, I know it is a heroick undertaking; but so much the greater frendship, and the Joy, when I see you I ["will" added interlinearly] tell you all my plans, I cannot write them on paper, burn this letter as soon as you read it; keep all locked up in your breasts, my life depends upon it. ... I think Emma wont come tonight[. I]f she dont[,] dont fail to come to night.[64]

It is not clear from the available documents if Smith personally called for action against Pratt, nor is it clear if Lyman's ordination was intended to temporarily or permanently preempt Pratt's right of office. Joseph, at the time, was hiding from Missouri state officials and courting other potential wives.[65] Somehow, Orson must have communicated his feelings to Joseph the next day. The prophet's diary recorded optimistically for 21 August: "Orson Pratt has also signified his intention of coming out in defence of the truth and go to preaching."[66] Soon afterwards, some 380 men, including Lyman, Young, Kimball, and George A. Smith, were called to preach against Bennett's allegations.[67] If Joseph had expected to see Pratt go with them, he was soon disappointed.

Nine days after Pratt was disciplined, Joseph complained that Pratt had still not publicly recanted. He lashed out at Pratt and other "apostates" during a Monday morning meeting:

> Orson Pratt has attempted to destroy himself—caused all the City almost to go in search of him.[68] ... O. P[ratt] and others of the same class

---

64. Joseph Smith to Newel K. Whitney, Elizabeth Ann Whitney, and Sarah Ann Whitney, 18 Aug. 1842, in *Essential Joseph Smith,* 166-67.

65. Pratt's biographer believes that Smith "assented to Orson Pratt's excommunication," but provides no source for this conclusion (England, *Life and Thought,* 81). Hill documents Smith's courtship of other plural wives during this time (*First Mormon,* 313-14).

66. Jessee, *Papers of Joseph Smith,* 2:421.

67. See Smith, *History of the Church,* 5:153, 160-61, 183, 194.

68. Pratt's descendants "feel that Orson Pratt did not get so depressed as to

caused trouble by telling stories to people who would betray me and they must believe these stories because his wife told him so! I will live to trample on their ashes with the soles of my feet. I prophecy in the name of Jesus Christ that such shall not prosper, they shall be cut down in their own plans. ... I have the whole plan of the kingdom before me, and no other person has. And as to all that Orson Pratt, Sidney Rigdon or George W. Robinson can do to prevent me[,] I can kick them off my heels, as many as you can name, I know what will become of them. ... [T]o the apostates and enemies I will give a lashing every oppertunity and I will curse them.[69]

A tormented Pratt sat directly behind Smith as he spoke these words. It would have been curious to see Pratt on the dais on such an occasion if Smith believed that he had been excommunicated. According to Smith's diary, Pratt "looked serious and dejected, but did not betray the least signs of compunction or repentance."[70]

"Altho' I do wrong," the prophet told the Relief Society about this same time:

I do not the wrongs that I am charg'd with doing—the wrong that *I do is thro'* the frailty of human nature like other men. No man lives without fault. Do you think that even Jesus, if he were here would be without fault in your eyes? They said all manner of evil against him—they all watch'd for iniquity. ... If you have evil feelings and speak of them to one another, it has a tendency to do mischief—these things result in those evils which are calculated to cut the throats of the heads of the church. ... I would to God that you would be wise, I

---

attempt to take his own life and that Joseph Smith is in error as far as this particular statement is concerned" (Watson, *Orson Pratt Journals,* 525n92). Pratt's biographer thinks otherwise (England, *Life and Thought,* 79).

69. Jessee, *Papers of Joseph Smith,* 2:446-47; see also Ehat and Cook, *Words of Joseph Smith,* 128-29; and Smith, *History of the Church,* 5:137-39. Pratt, Rigdon, and Robinson refused to sign the 20 July resolution—Pratt because of Smith's attentions to Sarah, Rigdon and son-in-law Robinson because of Smith's proposition to their daughter and sister-in-law Nancy.

70. Jessee, *Papers of Joseph Smith,* 2:447.

now counsel you, if you know anything, hold your tongues, and the least harm will be done.[71]

The prophet, according to historian and general authority B. H. Roberts, possessed a "too fierce disposition to give way to reckless denunciation when once he really broke the ties of friendship—his anger was terrible, all agree upon that."[72] This was demonstrated when he and other church leaders decided to discredit Sarah Pratt by identifying her as Bennett's paramour, arranging in late August 1842 for publication of three lurid testimonials of her promiscuity.[73] In the first, addressed to Orson, Stephen Goddard affirmed that his wife and he "went over several times late in the evening while she [Sarah Pratt] lived in the house of Dr. [Robert D.] Foster [as a boarder during Orson's mission to England], and were most sure to find Dr. [John C.] Bennett and your wife together, as it were, man and wife."[74] In the second statement, Goddard's wife, Zeruiah, alleged: "On one occasion I came suddenly into the room where Mrs. Pratt and the Dr. [Bennett] were[. S]he was lying on the bed and the Dr. was taking his hands out of her bosom; he was in

---

71. Nauvoo Female Relief Society, Minutes, 31 Aug. 1842, LDS church archives.

72. Roberts, *Comprehensive History,* 2:358.

73. In publishing these documents, church leaders explained: "There are some things among these statements that necessity, for our reputation as a religious society, has compelled us to make public, which decency and humanity would have gladly dropped with the rest of their infamy into their proper receptacle." Similar tactics were adopted in response to other women who rejected Joseph's marriage proposals, especially Jane Law, wife of second counselor in the First Presidency William Law, and Nancy Rigdon, daughter of first counselor Sidney Rigdon. See Van Wagoner, *Mormon Polygamy,* 30-32, 63-66; Stephen Markham, affidavit, 28 Aug. 1842, *Affidavits and Certificates, Disproving the Statements and Affidavits Contained in John C. Bennett's Letters,* broadside, Nauvoo, 31 Aug. 1842, LDS church archives.

74. Stephen H. Goddard to Orson Pratt, 23 July 1842, in *Affidavits and Certificates.* Although presented as a letter, his statement was probably created for this particular publication. Sarah Pratt asserted that the Goddards were forced to sign these statements (Wyl, *Mormon Portraits,* 62-63).

the habit of sitting on the bed where Mrs. Pratt was lying, and lying down over her."[75] The third statement, written by Jacob B. Backenstos, sheriff of Hancock County, "accused Doctor John C. Bennett, with having an illicit intercourse with Mrs. Orson Pratt, and some others," and claimed that Bennett had told him "she [Sarah] made a first rate go."[76] As historian Richard Van Wagoner has shown, these allegations are demonstrably false.[77] Nevertheless, many believed the accusations,[78] and their effect on the Pratts must have been devastating.

While Orson did not function actively as an apostle at the time, he did not consider himself excommunicated. Not quite two weeks after his last meeting with Young, Kimball, and George A. Smith, he refuted allegations that he had left Nauvoo and Mormonism by publishing the following: "Neither have I renounced the Church of Jesus Christ of Latter Day Saints, but believe that its doctrine ... is pure and according to the scriptures [and] of eternal truth, and [that it] merits the candid investigation of all lovers of righteousness. ... There is something in it which seems to whisper that 'God is there' ... The lustre of truth cannot be dimmed by the shadows of error and falsehood." He dismissed the "petty difficulties" separating him from the prophet and other church leaders and proclaimed that the church's "course is onward to accomplish the purposes of its great Author in relation to the happiness and salvation of the human family."[79] Four weeks later, and again in response to Bennett's asser-

---

75. Zeruiah N. Goddard, affidavit, 28 Aug. 1842, *Affidavits and Certificates.*

76. J. B. Backenstos, affidavit, 28 July 1842, *Affidavits and Certificates.*

77. See Van Wagoner, *Mormon Polygamy,* 32-33, 235.

78. See Joseph Fielding's diary, reprinted in Andrew F. Ehat, ed., "'They Might Have Known That He Was Not a Fallen Prophet'—The Nauvoo Journal of Joseph Fielding," *BYU Studies* 19 (Winter 1979): 144: "Some trouble about Orson Pratt arrising from said Bennett's Crime Com[mited] with his Wife." Ehat concluded that Bennett "made sexual advances" to Sarah without Joseph's permission (n20).

79. "Mr. Editor," *The Wasp,* 2 Sept. 1842, 3.

tion that Sarah and Orson were preparing to quit Mormonism, Orson published a second, more emphatic, statement: "We intend to make NAUVOO OUR RESIDENCE, AND MORMONISM OUR MOTTO."[80] By this time, he had apparently succeeded in separating human frailties—his own, Sarah's, and Joseph's—from what he saw as the church's divine mission. Of his emotional and mental state during this trying period, he remained silent. He recorded only: "I remained in Nauvoo about one year, during a portion of which I had the charge of a mathematical school."[81]

Thus matters stood for the remainder of the fall and beginning of winter 1842. In January the next year, a counselor in the First Presidency, Sidney Rigdon, who was himself deeply troubled over Joseph's proposal to his nineteen-year-old daughter Nancy,[82] received a letter from Bennett, addressed jointly to him and Pratt. In it, Bennett asked for their support in publicly battling Mormonism. First, it seems unlikely, if Bennett had committed improprieties with their daughter and wife, he would try to enlist their aid against Smith—unless, for some reason, they had all conspired together to conceal the truth. Second, the response from Rigdon and Pratt belies such collusion. Uncertain at first what to do with the letter, Rigdon gave it to Pratt who immediately handed it over to Smith.[83] By this time, Pratt had concluded that Bennett could not be trusted since many of the rumors about his and Sarah's "disaffection" could be traced to Bennett. Pratt's action confirmed to the prophet that he "had no correspondence with Bennett, and had no fellowship for his works of darkness."[84] Five days later, on 20 January 1843, Smith, Pratt, and other officials convened in Brigham Young's residence to review Orson's standing in the church.

---

80. Ibid., 1 Oct. 1842, [2].

81. Qtd. in Watson, *Orson Pratt Journals,* 186.

82. See Van Wagoner, *Sidney Rigdon,* 294-302.

83. That Rigdon did not immediately give Smith the letter worsened their relationship. See Smith, *History of the Church,* 5:252.

84. Ibid.

TWO

Return to Power and Authority

$\mathcal{U}$nlike the scanty documentation for the action taken against Orson Pratt in August 1842, there are four separate accounts of the apostle's January 1843 reinstatement. These include the official minutes of the meeting, Joseph Smith's diary, Wilford Woodruff's journal, and Brigham Young's manuscript history narrative.[1]

According to the official minutes, the fullest and most contemporary account of the four, Joseph Smith and his older brother, Hyrum, met during the afternoon of Friday, 20 January, with seven apostles: Brigham Young, Heber C. Kimball, Orson Hyde, Wilford Woodruff, John Taylor, George A. Smith, and Willard Richards. Orson Pratt was in attendance as well. The meeting was held in Young's house on the corner of Kimball and Granger Streets in

---

1. Minutes of the Quorum of the Twelve Apostles, 20 Jan. 1843, Brigham Young Papers, LDS church archives; Faulring, *American Prophet's Record*, 293-95; Kenney, *Wilford Woodruff's Journal*, 2:212-13; "History of Brigham Young," *Deseret News*, 17 Mar. 1858, 1.

downtown Nauvoo.[2] Also in the city but not at the meeting was Amasa Lyman, whom Apostles Young, Kimball, and George A. Smith had ordained five months earlier to replace Pratt. After some unrelated business, the prophet announced to the group that Pratt was in fact "still a member" of their quorum and hence of the church.[3] Pratt had not been "legally cut off" because a majority of the quorum (at least seven) had not been present when Pratt's "case came up before."[4]

Smith continued to say that ordination to the apostleship, unlike admission to the quorum, did not require a quorum majority. Therefore, Lyman would remain an apostle.[5] Having "repented in

---

2. The quorum's published minutes of Pratt's reinstatement, unlike the manuscript minutes, list Orson as a member of the Twelve and in correct seniority as the meeting began (see Smith, *History of the Church,* 5:254).

3. Brigham Young's manuscript history makes it clear that the three apostles believed they were expelling Pratt from the church. The accounts of his reinstatement imply that he had been dropped from the Twelve. That Pratt was rebaptized and reordained suggests that whatever the result of the illegal action taken against him, the intent of the three apostles had been to sever him from the church.

4. See Doctrine and Covenants 107:27-29, dated 28 Mar. 1835. Two months after this revelation, Joseph Smith instructed the Twelve: "When the twelve are all together or a quorum of them in any church [branch], they have authority to act independently of the church and form decisions and those decisions will be valid, but where there is not a quorum of them together, they must transact business by the common consent of the church" (Remarks, 2 May 1835, in "A record of the transactions of the Twelve apostles of the Church of the Latter-Day Saints from the time of their call to the apostleship which was on the 14th Day of Feby. A. 1835," bound in "Patriarchal Blessings Book," Vol. 1, LDS church archives). Not all of the apostles agreed that a majority of members was necessary to transact business. Elder George A. Smith opined in early 1847: "I dont believe in 12 men having to get together on every little thing ... suppose some secret plot cuts off 11 of the apostles & only the Junior left—he is he to cry & say oh I cannot ask act because there is not 7 of us? No!!" (qtd. in Willard Richards, Diary, 10 Jan. 1847, LDS church archives).

5. About two weeks later, Smith appointed Lyman to be a counselor in the First Presidency, although not as a first or second counselor since both positions were already occupied (see Faulring, *American Prophet's Record,* 299; Smith, *History of the Church,* 5:138). Brigham Young said in 1867 that Lyman "never was Joseph Smith's Councillor but was a Thirteenth Apostle for a long time" (qtd. in

dust & ashes ... for opposing Joseph & the Twelve,"[6] a humbled
Pratt voiced that "he had rather die than go to preach in any other
standing than he had before." "Let him have the same [apostolic]
calling that Paul had," Smith pronounced. "Let him have the keys
to the Jews. [F]irst unto the Gentiles, then unto the Jews." He then
explained that "Orson by transgression laid himself liable to have
another ordained in his stead." Quorum president Young commented that "all he had against Orson was when he came home he
loved his wife better than David," an allusion to the Old Testament
story of Uriah who, unlike Orson, loved his leader more than he
loved his own wife, Bathsheba (2 Sam. 11-12). Young seems to suggest that Orson (Uriah) should have remained loyal to Joseph (King
David), even if Joseph had been sexually intimate with Sarah
(Bathsheba).[7]

Joseph stressed to Orson that Sarah "had lied about me. I never
made the offer which she said I did." Turning to the Twelve, the
thirty-seven-year-old prophet added, "I will not advise you to
break up you[r] family—unless it were asked of me. [T]hen I would
council you to [get] a bill [of divorce] from you[r] wife & marry a
virtuous woman & raise a new family[,] but if you do not do it [I]
shall never throw it in your teeth.[8] ... Orson," he said, "I prophesy in

---

Kenney, *Wilford Woodruff's Journal*, 6:344). After Smith's death in June 1844, Lyman
returned to the Twelve as a counselor to the quorum. One year later, in October
1845, he was admitted as a regular member of the Twelve. He was dropped from
the quorum in 1867, excommunicated in 1870, and died in 1877. See Quinn,
Mormon Hierarchy: Origins, 562-63; and Loretta L. Hefner, "From Apostle to Apostate: The Personal Struggle of Amasa Lyman," *Dialogue* 16 (Spring 1983): 90-104.
Joseph Smith's decision to sanction Lyman's ordination, though not as a member
of the quorum, justified later church leaders in ordaining their own sons to the
apostleship, presumably in anticipation of joining the quorum in the future.

6. According to Kenney, *Wilford Woodruff's Journal*, 2:212-13.

7. D. Michael Quinn brought this interpretation of Young's remarks to my
attention. See also England, *Life and Thought*, 85.

8. Cf. Brigham Young's later teaching: "The second way in which a wife can
be seperated from her husband, while he continues to be faithful to his God and
his preisthood, I have not revealed, except to a few persons in this Church, and -a

the name of the Lord Jesus Christ that it will not be 6 months before you learn things which will make you glad you have not left us. ... Orson[,] the latter part of your life shall be made joyful thru the former."

A year earlier Smith had publicly said: "If you will not accuse me, I will not accuse you. If you will throw a cloak of charity over my sins, I will over yours—for charity covereth a multitude of sins. What many people call sin is not sin; I do many things to break down superstition, and I will break it down."[9] His position with regard to Pratt's reinstatement echoes this sentiment. At 4:00 p.m., an hour after the meeting broke, Orson and Sarah stepped into the Mississippi River to be rebaptized. Although Sarah had not been formally disciplined, the rebaptism symbolized their continuing commitment to the church. Rebaptism was a relatively common practice in Nauvoo at the time.[10] Following the ritual, the prophet placed his hands on Orson's head and told his friend and follower to "receiv[e] the priesthood & the same power & authority as in former days."[11] "It is expected by the Twelve," Smith's personal secretary, William Clayton, recorded, "that Orson will be restored to his

---

few have received it from Joseph the prophet as well as myself. ... If ~~she~~ a woman can find a man holding the keys of the preisthood ~~and holding~~ with higher ~~in~~ power and authority than her husband ~~holds~~, and he is disposed to take her he can do so, otherwise she has got to remain where she is" ("'A few words of Doctrine' Given by President Brigham Young in the Tabernacle in Great Salt Lake City Oct 8th 1861. A.M. Reported by G. D. Watt," Brigham Young Papers). Remember, too, that Smith married Orson Hyde's wife, Marinda, in early 1842, apparently without first asking Hyde to divorce her.

9. Qtd. in Smith, *History of the Church*, 4:445.

10. See D. Michael Quinn, "The Practice of Rebaptism at Nauvoo," *BYU Studies* 18 (Winter 1978): 226-32. Quinn notes that "[s]urviving certificates of baptism from Nauvoo indicate that from 1843 to 1844 many members of the Church in good standing were rebaptized 'for Remission of Sins'" (229). A third person, Lydia Granger, who was not previously excommunicated, was rebaptized with the Pratts.

11. Joseph Smith's journal for the day adds "all the authority of his former office" (Faulring, *American Prophet's Record*, 295). Wilford Woodruff recorded: "Jo-

standing in the quorum."[12] Smith clearly considered the matter closed, forgotten even, and declared at a churchwide general conference less than three months later on 6 April, "I do not know any thing against the Twelve. If I did I would present them for trial."[13] By contrast, Elder Kimball insisted several weeks earlier on 8 March that "O[rson] Pratt was stiff and had to be cast off the [potter's] wheel and A[masa] Lyman put on it."[14]

Pratt received his endowments that December and his second anointing—the highest ritual the church conferred—the following January 1844. This probably fulfilled the promise Smith had made

---

seph ... ordaind *Orson Pratt* to the *apostle*ship & his former standing which caused Joy to our hearts" (Kenney, *Wilford Woodruff's Journal*, 2:212-13; original emphasis; Woodruff misdated this meeting to 19 January). Brigham Young's manuscript autobiography says: "Orson Pratt ... confessed his sins and manifested deep repentance, which resulted in his baptism and re-ordination by the Prophet to his forming [sic] standing in the Quorum of the Twelve" ("History of Brigham Young," *Deseret News,* 17 Mar. 1858, [1]). Pratt biographer T. Edgar Lyon claimed that Young's view that Pratt did not need to be rebaptized since he had not been legally excommunicated ("Orson Pratt—Early Mormon Leader," M.A. thesis, University of Chicago Divinity School, 1932, 160-62), but no contemporary source supports this.

12. William Clayton, Diary, 20 Jan. 1843, LDS church archives.

13. Qtd. in Faulring, *American Prophet's Record,* 344. The next day Smith publicly referred to Pratt's defense of the resurrection. Critics who deny the resurrection had said that "flesh and bones are constantly changing, completely new in 7 or 10 years." To this, Pratt had countered that "[no] more than 3/4 of our bodies is comprised of animal organization, but is purely vegetable," and that at the end of our lives, "one or two parts" of the animal composition "will be the same original. ... the same body" (qtd. in ibid., 353). Smith agreed that there are "fundamental principle[s] belonging to a human System" that never become part of another human being "in this world or in the world to come'" (ibid., 355). His diary adds: "[T]he principle of Bro[ther] Pratt was correct" (ibid.). As recounted in the *History of the Church* (5:339), however, Smith's comments read like a correction and would be treated as such by Brigham Young (see his 8 October 1875 general conference discourse, *The Resurrection* [Salt Lake City: Deseret News Co., 1884], 2-3, 15-16).

14. Qtd. in Smith, *Intimate Chronicle,* 94. Clayton said the room where Kimball spoke was "crowded to suffocation."

to Pratt that he would learn things that would make him glad he had not left. It foreshadowed Smith's promise several months later to William Clayton, then involved in a plural marriage, that if Clayton were exposed, Smith would give him "an awful scourging and probably cut you off from the church and then I will baptise you and set you ahead as good as ever."[15] Sarah, on the other hand, presumably still ached over the church's treatment of her. She was either unwilling or was not invited to participate in the temple rites until after Smith's death more than a year later.[16]

Orson's changing status in 1842 and 1843 reflects, in part, the evolution of the church's disciplinary tribunals and punishments. In the early 1830s, most cases of misconduct were argued before a court of elders, also called a bishop's council, or before a group of high priests. With the organization of a stake high council in 1834 in Ohio, jurisdictional lines shifted; tribunals convened by stakewide high councils began to take the place of the elders' and high priests' courts.[17] In 1838, to give an example of jurisdictional uncertainties, the presiding bishop argued that charges against the stake presidency in Missouri should be brought before the entire stake, not just the high council. The council was divided on the issue but overruled him, and proceeded to excommunicate two of the stake presidency and then the stake president. This was done over the stake president's objection that the council did not have the authority to do so. When put to a vote of the general congregation, one of the members expressed doubt that the council had the proper authority and

---

15. Qtd. in ibid., 122.

16. David John Buerger, "'The Fulness of the Priesthood': The Second Anointing in Latter-day Saint Theology and Practice," *Dialogue* 16 (Spring 1983): 23; Ehat, "Joseph Smith's Introduction of Temple Ordinances," 103.

17. For elders' courts, see Smith, *History of the Church*, 1:354, 355, 469; 2:2, 218, 228; 3:327. High council courts are recorded in the *History of the Church*, 2:225, 235, 276, 442, 444. For a fuller treatment, see Edwin Brown Firmage and Richard Collin Mangrum, *Zion in the Courts: A Legal History of the Church of Jesus Christ of Latter-day Saints, 1830-1900* (Urbana: University of Illinois Press, 1988), 25-47.

was consequently disfellowshipped "for speaking against the authorities of the Church." Joseph Smith endorsed the action.[18]

Jurisdictional issues were as unclear in the case against ranking Mormon Oliver Cowdery. Assistant president of the church, Cowdery was tried in April 1838 before a joint bishop's council and high council, a meeting which Joseph Smith attended but did not conduct.[19] Three months earlier, a revelation had stated that if the First Presidency were tried by a stake high council, its decision would be valid only in that stake and that for such a ruling to be binding throughout the church, it would have to be made by a majority of the stake high councils or by a majority of the general membership.[20] Perhaps Smith considered Cowdery's case an exception. It may be that he saw Cowdery as an informal member of the First Presidency or thought that the joint council in Missouri, where the majority of the church was now located, met the requirements or that one could temporarily suspend the rules in such a case.[21]

By the early 1840s, more and more cases of alleged misconduct were being heard by the Nauvoo Stake high council,[22] and it could be argued that this group should have tried Orson Pratt. The Twelve had only the authority to drop Pratt from membership in the coun-

---

18. See the relevant entries in Donald Q. Cannon and Lyndon W. Cook, eds., *Far West Record: Minutes of The Church of Jesus Christ of Latter-day Saints, 1830-1844* (Salt Lake City: Deseret Book Co., 1983), 138-39, 140n6, 147, 149, 151, 176-78.

19. Ibid., 162-70.

20. Unpublished revelation to Joseph Smith, Sidney Rigdon, Vinson Knight, and George W. Robinson, 12 Jan. 1838, Kirtland, Ohio, in "Revelations Collection," LDS church archives.

21. Smith similarly set aside established, revealed protocol in 1844 in removing William Law from the First Presidency. See Lyndon W. Cook, *William Law* (Orem, UT: Grandin Book Company, 1996), 17-20.

22. While the high council was able to resolve most cases, it referred especially troublesome matters to the First Presidency. For the First Presidency's dismissal of all charges against a defendant, see Nauvoo Stake High Council, Minutes, 28 Nov., 12, 13, 20 Dec. 1840, LDS church archives.

cil, according to precedent. Prior to Pratt's case, the Twelve, acting as a solitary priesthood quorum, had never disciplined even one of its own members. However, Joseph Smith, whose authority trumped all others, had concluded by this time that some cases should be determined either by himself or by the Twelve, particularly those which might bring embarrassment or condemnation to the church at large.[23] In June 1842, Smith unilaterally withdrew church fellowship from two Tennessee Mormons for teaching false doctrine. When they were reinstated as members in good standing early the next year, it was not by Smith but by the Nauvoo high council.[24] Four months after Pratt's reinstatement, when Brigham Young recommended that a particular case be turned over to the high council, Smith ruled that high councils should only try cases that directly concerned their stake.[25] In Pratt's case, the charges against him concerned activities that occurred in the Nauvoo stake.[26] Perhaps the view was that the apostle's public posture and personal animus jeopardized the prophet's reputation throughout the church.

And what of Smith's assurance that Sarah had lied about him—

---

23. The 1844 excommunication of William Law would be one such example.

24. See "Letter from Tennessee" and the editor's response, *Times and Seasons,* 15 June 1842, 820-22; Nauvoo Stake High Council, Minutes, 8 Jan. 1843; "Notice," *Times and Seasons,* 16 Jan. 1843, 80.

25. See Minutes of the Quorum of the Twelve Apostles, 27 May 1843; Smith, *History of the Church,* 5:410. The previous month Smith seems to have suggested that charges against the Twelve should be resolved by the entire church membership. He said if he knew "any thing against the Twelve," he "would present them for trial" (see n13). Four months later the First Presidency's intervention in a case before the Nauvoo high council resulted in the defendant's acquittal. See Nauvoo Stake High Council, Minutes, 1 Sept. 1843.

26. Before year's end, Smith brought charges before the Nauvoo high council against a member for "trying to seduce a young girl, living at his house," and for "using my [Joseph's] name in a blasphemous manner, by saying that I tolerated such things in which thing he is guilty of lying &c. &c." The high council took no action against the member since he already had been "corrected by President Joseph Smith." See Nauvoo Stake High Council, Minutes, 25 Nov. 1843; cf. Smith,

"I never made the offer which she says I did"? Smith may have been trying to conceal his involvement in polygamy. He was not opposed to lying in self-defense.[27] At Pratt's reinstatement, there were brethren in attendance who had not yet been introduced to plural marriage—most notably Joseph's own older brother, Hyrum, the church patriarch. Joseph may have felt that he could not risk the censure of such uninitiated brethren.[28] Using Smith's own definition of lying, Sarah Pratt was the liar since she had not been authorized to reveal Joseph's secret proposal to her and had thus violated a confidence. Perhaps Joseph was telling the truth: John Bennett had seduced Sarah and the two carried on a *ménage à deux* while Orson was abroad. Yet, Richard Van Wagoner, Sarah's biographer, noted that her name was not mentioned in any of the Nauvoo high council meetings that investigated sexual irregularity. No disciplinary action of any kind was ever initiated against her. Joseph Smith reported a revelation in January 1841, while Bennett would have been involved in the affair with Sarah praising Bennett: "I have seen the work which he hath done, which I accept if he continue, and will crown him with blessings and great glory" (Doctrine and Covenants 124:17). Smith appointed Bennett acting

---

History of the Church, 6:81. The man's wife was not as easily convinced and charged her husband before the First Presidency and Twelve, who referred the matter of "the abominable doctrine of Spiritual wives" back to the high council. It ruled that the complaint had already been resolved. See Nauvoo Stake High Council, Minutes, 13 Apr. 1844.

27. "What a thing it is for a man to be accused of committing adultery, and having seven wives," Smith would say in May 1844, "when I can only find one" (qtd. in Smith, *History of the Church*, 6:411). By this time, the prophet had married more than thirty women. Seven months earlier he had instructed his secretary: "No man shall have but one wife" (qtd. in Faulring, *American Prophet's Record*, 417). See also Carmon B. Hardy, "Lying for the Lord: An Essay," in his *Solemn Covenant: The Mormon Polygamous Passage* (Urbana: University of Illinois Press, 1992), 363-88.

28. For Hyrum Smith's reluctant acceptance of polygamy, see Van Wagoner, *Mormon Polygamy*, 52-53. Hyrum would not fully accept his younger brother's doctrine for another four months.

assistant church president three months later in April. There is no record linking Sarah's name with Bennett that predates Orson's confrontation with the prophet.[29] It is possible that Smith was telling the *literal* truth. He might not have made the precise proposal that Sarah and Bennett asserted. This scenario is speculative, but Joseph may have admitted to Orson sometime after August 1842 but before late January 1843 that he had in fact invited Sarah to become his plural wife in order to "test" her virtue.[30] Sarah's negative reaction would have only reinforced Smith's decision to treat such a proposal as a test.[31]

Whatever the case, less than four months after his reinstatement, Orson wrote to a cousin that "J[ohn] C. Bennett has published lies concerning myself & family & the people with which I am connected. His book I have read with the greatest disgust. No candid honest man can or will believe it. He has disgraced himself in [the] eyes of all civilized society who will despise his very name."[32] Thirty-five years later, and only three years before his death, Orson publicly declared that during the time of his difficulties in Nauvoo, he, Orson, "got his information from a wicked source, from those

29. See Richard S. Van Wagoner, "Sarah M. Pratt: The Shaping of an Apostate," *Dialogue* 19 (Summer 1986): 81.

30. "[I]f Joseph Smith did speak to Sarah [Pratt] about plural marriage, he probably did so to test the Pratts," theorized Mormon historians Allen et al., *Men with a Mission,* 279n19.

31. The strangest reason given for Pratt's reversal is the claim that Bennett tattooed "the mark of the beast" on the abdomens of the women he seduced and that when Pratt found this on his wife, he knew that Smith had been telling the truth (see Nels B. Lundwall to T. Edgar Lyon, 9 Apr. 1947, microfilm, Lundwall Papers, L. Tom Perry Special Collections, Harold B. Lee Library, Brigham Young University, Provo, Utah; hereafter BYU Library). See also England, *Life and Thought,* 78, who attributes this story to "Pratt family legend." Presumably Pratt would have found the mark upon his return from England and would have been immediately reconciled to Smith.

32. Pratt, postscript, in Parley P. Pratt to John Van Cott, 7 May 1843, Parley P. Pratt Papers, LDS church archives.

disaffected, but as soon as he learned the truth he was satisfied."[33] According to one contemporary report, Orson came to believe by the end of 1845 that Sarah had lied about Joseph's propositions to her.[34] Sarah herself testified otherwise years later: "[I] know that the principle statements in John C. Bennett's Book on Mormonism are true."[35]

Was Orson expelled from his quorum and from the church on 20 August 1842? The original working notes and the subsequent narrative drafts based on the rough notes for Joseph Smith's manuscript history—books D-1 and D-2, housed in the LDS church archives—as well as the first published versions of the history in the *Deseret News* and later in the *Millennial Star,* all describe Orson as having been "cut off." Today the term would imply "excommunicated," but in the nineteenth century it could have referred to a lesser punishment of disfellowshipment or suspension.[36] These same manuscript and printed sources are unanimous that on 20 January 1843 Joseph Smith pronounced the previous action illegal and void.

The earliest manuscript history account, and hence the most contemporary, is from the original working notes, apparently dictated by Brigham Young on 22 December 1845. It was reworked and recorded by apostle and official Church Historian Willard Richards almost immediately after it was dictated.[37] It relates that Pratt had been:

> cut off from the Quorum ["of the Twelve" added interlinearly] for

---

33. "Report of Elders Orson Pratt and Joseph F. Smith," 788; see also "Orson Pratt's Testimony," 230. When referring to "a wicked source," Pratt undoubtedly meant Bennett.

34. Sidney Rigdon's account of his interview with Pratt in "Tour East," *Messenger and Advocate of the Church of Christ* 2 (Dec. 1845): 401.

35. Undated statement, qtd. in Arthur B. Demming to C. F. Gunther, Mormon Collection, Chicago Historical Society.

36. "History of Joseph Smith," *Deseret News,* 9 Apr. 1856, 1; 3 July 1858, 423.

37. See Brigham Young, Diary, 22 Dec. 1845: "I went to G[eorge] A Smith's

neglect of duty, and Amasa Lyman had been ordained an apostle in his place. I [Joseph Smith] told the council that there was not a quorum present when Orson Pratt's case came up before, that he was still a member[,] that he had not been cut off legally, and that I would find some other place for Amasa Lyman ["to which the council agreed" added interlinearly]. President Young said there were but three present when Amasa was ordained. I [Joseph Smith] told them that was legal when no more could be had.[38]

The earlier of the two manuscript narratives, Book D-1, was recorded by church scribe Thomas Bullock with some involvement from Apostle George A. Smith. It was drafted sometime after 22 December 1845 but apparently before 15 January 1846.[39] The second narrative, Book D-2, is a duplicate and in some instances was revised and corrected by George A. Smith in 1856 in Salt Lake City. By then, Smith had replaced Willard Richards as Church Historian.[40] To Bullock's original sentence in D-1, "... the case of Orson Pratt who had previously been cut off from the quorum of the Twelve, ..." Smith added two words: "for disobedience." This was written into Book D-1 interlinearly. However, Book D-2 and the two published versions read simply, like the original notes, "for neglect of duty." The correction to D-1 may have been made after the published versions appeared. In addition, "disobedience" could mean either that Orson declined to give Sarah to Joseph or that he

---

room & found my clerk [Thomas Bullock] there making notes for History. I dictated the following to be placed therein viz the expulsion of Br O Pratt & ordination of Br A Lyman in his place which was forwarded to the Historian [Willard Richards]."

38. Original draft notes to Manuscript History of the Church, under date, LDS church archives; see Howard C. Searle, "Willard Richards as Historian," *BYU Studies* 31 (Spring 1991): 47-48. An account of Pratt's "expulsion" did not figure in Smith's manuscript history because Smith was out of town when it occurred.

39. See Dean C. Jessee, "The Writing of Joseph Smith's History," *BYU Studies* 11 (Spring 1971): 441.

40. Ibid., 472. Willard Richards died on 11 March 1854.

refused to accept Joseph's explanation. "Neglect of duty" could similarly mean one of two things: either that Pratt was unwilling or unable to function as a member of the Twelve or, again, that he neglected to obey Joseph Smith. Like Willard Richards in the original working notes, Thomas Bullock in Book D-1 wrote that Pratt "was still a member[,] that he had not been cut off legally." This was later crossed out in D-1 but appeared verbatim in D-2 and in the published versions. Again, it is not known why the correction, presumably made by George A. Smith, was not transferred to D-2 unless it occurred after the published versions appeared. Finally, all five accounts agree that Pratt's reinstatement returned him to his "former office and standing" in the Twelve.

This vacillation between "disobedience" and "neglect of duty" may indicate that even those who were eyewitnesses did not fully understand or recall the implications of the events. It is clear that prior to the first publication of the two events in Joseph Smith's official history in 1856, if not after, ranking church authorities and historians viewed Pratt's 20 August 1842 expulsion as illegal and his 20 January 1843 reinstatement, including his seniority in the quorum, complete. According to the official histories as well as all contemporary documents, the 1842 action was at most a temporary suspension of duties within his quorum. If Pratt had been excommunicated, the record would have read differently.

Some fifty years later, LDS church president Lorenzo Snow commissioned Elder B. H. Roberts, under the immediate supervision of Apostle and Church Historian Anthon H. Lund, to reedit Joseph Smith's *History of the Church* for publication beginning in 1902.[41] Roberts's new edition made no mention of Pratt's 1842 "excommunication"; but when he came to Pratt's 1843 reinstatement, he favored George A. Smith's emended account in Book D-1 over the rough working notes and wrote that Pratt had been "cut

---

41. Anthon H. Lund, Diary, 22 May 1901, LDS church archives.

off" for "disobedience." He ignored the comment that Joseph Smith considered Pratt to have been a member of the Twelve throughout the ordeal and reported only that Pratt had been reordained to his "former office," not his "former office and standing."[42] Twenty-one years later, in the seventh and final volume of his edited *History of the Church* by Joseph Smith, Roberts acknowledged in a footnote that Smith had declared the action against Pratt "illegal" (7:295). Evidently, the intervening twenty years had brought additional materials or insights to bear on Roberts's interpretation.

However, by not drawing the reader's attention to the different versions of Pratt's reinstatement, Roberts, who had published a biography of church president John Taylor ten years earlier, may have hoped in 1902 that he could harmonize the different accounts of the incident, including Taylor's own 1881 rendition. This avoided questions about the pattern of presidential succession, something that Roberts himself defended in a book he had published eight years earlier.[43] In his apologetic eyes, he found a public airing of Pratt's reinstatement unnecessary since it would raise questions about Taylor's succession in 1880 and about the entire succession process. At the same time, Roberts was known for his objectivity, and it is significant that he revisited the question. Unfortunately, his belated admission in volume seven of the *History of the Church* would not offset the impact of his portrayal in an earlier volume. Apostle and Church Historian Joseph Fielding Smith made later use of Roberts's fifth (1909) volume because, in part, it legitimized Brigham Young's 1875 interpretation of Orson Pratt's difficulties.

Following his 1843 reinstatement, Orson received a new church

---

42. Smith, *History of the Church*, 5:255-56. This volume first appeared in 1909.

43. See also Howard Searle, "Early Mormon Historiography: Writing the History of the Mormons, 1830-1858," Ph.D. diss., University of California, Los Angeles, 1979, 327-28; B. H. Roberts, *Succession in the Presidency* (Salt Lake City: Deseret News Publishing Co., 1894), expanded in 1900.

assignment to New York. His brother Parley had arrived in Nauvoo from England only days after Orson's rebaptism, and kept abreast of his younger sibling's struggles. He later wrote to a non-Mormon cousin:

> Bro. Orson Pratt is in the church and always has been & has the confidence of Joseph Smith and all good men who know him. ... As to [John C.] Bennett or his book[,] I consider it a little stooping to mention it. It is beneath contempt & would disgrace the society of *hell* & the *Devil*. But it will answer the end of its creation viz: to delude those who have rejected that pure & glorious record the book of Mormon. There is not such a thing named among the saints as he represents [spiritual wifery]. & his book or name is scarcely mentioned. & never except with perfect disgust. [H]is object was vengeance on those who exposed his iniquity.[44]

Orson returned to Nauvoo from the East shortly after Joseph's and Hyrum's violent deaths on 27 June 1844. Sometime that fall, he married his first plural wife, twenty-year-old Charlotte Bishop, apparently with Sarah's permission. (Charlotte would leave Orson the next year.) Sarah gave birth on 27 October to a daughter, Sarah, who died the following year. Less than a month later on 22 November, Orson and Sarah were invited to be sealed by Brigham

---

44. Pratt to Van Cott, 7 May 1843. Orson, as already noted, added his own postscript to this letter affirming his commitment to Mormonism.

Parley's rocky experience with plural marriage deserves mention. According to Andrew F. Ehat ("Joseph Smith's Introduction of Temple Ordinances," 66-71), Parley and his civilly married wife, Mary Ann Frost, were sealed by Hyrum Smith on 23 June 1843. But when Joseph Smith learned of the ceremony performed in his absence, he canceled it. (Reportedly, Joseph wanted Parley to marry his wife's sister, Olive Grey Frost, whereas Parley was courting Martha Elizabeth Brotherton.) The following month, on 24 July, Joseph sealed Parley to his deceased first wife, Thankful Halsey, for eternity, with Mary Ann acting as proxy; then he sealed Parley to Mary Ann, possibly for time only; and then to Martha Brotherton. It is possible that Mary Ann wanted to be connected to her own deceased husband, Nathan Stearns, but she was instead sealed for eternity as a plural wife to Joseph Smith (deceased) on 7 February 1846 in the Nauvoo temple.

Young for time and eternity, evidently recognizing Sarah's support of plural marriage. On 12 December Sarah was voted into the anointed quorum and received her washings and anointings; the next day Orson married his second plural wife, eighteen-year-old Adelia Ann Bishop, sister of his first plural wife. Early the next year on 27 March 1845, Orson, now thirty-three, took his third wife, twenty-five-year-old Mary Ann Merrill. He then left for another church mission to New York that summer and fall.[45] "He told me," Sarah reported years later, "that he believed it was his duty to take other women besides myself to wife, and at first he said that this would make no difference in his affection for me, which would continue pure and single as it had ever been."[46]

Prior to departing Nauvoo on the Western exodus, Orson Pratt and Parley Pratt tangled in a public disagreement that would leave the two brothers estranged for the next several years.[47] On 20

---

45. For Pratt's marriage dates, see Lyon, "Orson Pratt—Early Mormon Leader," 171-72.

46. Qtd. in "The Utah Theocracy," *New York Herald*, 18 May 1877.

47. Parley's temper is evident in an exchange of letters (Parley P. Pratt Collection, BYU Library) with senior apostle Orson Hyde regarding polygamy while both were in England. In the first letter, dated 2 November 1846, Hyde cautioned:

> The Spirit whispereth me that you are preaching things in Manchester which you ought not. The union of man and wife hereafter, or if they are dissatisfied with their present companions[,] they are not bound to be united for Eternity, but are at liberty to choose others.
>
> I hope I am mistaken, but I fear I am not. It is the spirit of lust that teaches the above doctrine in *this country*, and not the spirit of God, for such principles [en]gender evil and create anxieties that cannot be relieved without going into an explanation of things that ever has been forbidden, and if the churches are to be taught such things[,] I would rather they would not be taught at all. We were not sent to teach any such things as noted above, or even to know any thing about them. It is casting pearls before swine and giving holy things to dogs. ...

Offended, Parley responded a week later on 9 November:

> Your "Dreams[,]" your "Whisperings of the Spirit[,]" your "hopes," "fears," and "doubts"—Your false insinuations, your "disgust"—Your entire want of Confidence in those holding the "Keys of the Holy Apostleship, and of

November 1844, Parley secretly married his fourth plural wife, Belinda Marden, apparently without telling his first wife, Mary Ann
Frost. Thirteen months later on 1 January 1846, Belinda gave birth
to a son, Nephi.[48] Orson did not know that Belinda was his brother's plural wife but discovered the two together when he replaced
Parley as the church's representative in New York in late 1845.
Orson seems to have told Sarah that his brother was courting or

---

the Kingdom of God" in common with yourself—your railing accusations,
and insults against that Priesthood as manifested in certain letters writen to me
of late, altogether manifest a spirit so false—so foreign from the true spirit
ofyour high and responsable office that I am constrained to Exhort you to repent and Return again to the Spirit of Charity and Truth.

And, not only so, but if you Continue in the same spirit of Railing,
false-hood, and Insult, as manifested towards me in those "Letters," Take heed
lest you are removed out of your place, and sent home, to answer for these
things before the Council: For, be assured that spirit shall never preside over
me, nor over the Interests of the people of God in this Land so far as I have
power by the help of God, and by the Cooperation of Brother [John] Taylor
and the saints here, to prevent it.

You, Elder Hyde, Do not hold the keys of siting in Judgement upon my
soul, by your dreams, visions, Whisperings of the Spirit or fears, or by any other
means. This belongs to a united quorum, and they Can only do it by testimony,
according to the Laws of the Kingdom.

I care not a fig for your dreams, nor for the whisperings of the spirit about
me, or my teachings[,] for I know and so does the Holy Ghost, and all that hear
me, that the spirit that whispers to you bears false witness. As I have taught
nothing about Marriage, Wives, covenants, or Choosings either for time or
eternity, in England. And furthermore, it [should be known to] another, of the
same quorum, without being told. They aught to know it by the Holy Ghost
or if they do not know it, they aught, at least to believe nothing to the Contrary
without they were compeled to believe.

Br. H. Let me tell you that the spirit that whispered to you had *Lips* of flesh
and Blood, and a tongue to *"set on fire of Hell."* And next time a spirit of that
kind whispers to you, Pray, handle them and see. …

No doubt, Orson experienced firsthand his older brother's penchant for sarcasm.
Parley would marry two English converts (ages twenty-three and seventeen) five
months later on 28 April 1847.

48. For Parley's marriages, see Parley P. Pratt [Jr.], ed., *Autobiography of Parley P.
Pratt* (Salt Lake City: Deseret Book Co., 1938; 1st ed., 1873), 429-31. For an account of Belinda's marriage to Parley, see Watson, *Orson Pratt Journals*, 496.

had married another wife, unless Sarah suspected the baby's pater-
nity on her own. In any case, Sarah told Mary Ann Pratt what she
believed, and Mary Ann was evidently furious. She left Parley several months later in 1846. Parley confronted Sarah in the Nauvoo
temple on 11 January 1846, accusing her of "influencing his wife
against him, and of ruining and breaking up his family," as well as
of "being an apostate, and of speaking against the heads of the
Church and against him." Orson intervened to defend Sarah. In
the intervening quarrel, two brothers argued so loudly that they
were asked to leave the temple.[49]

Parley had not defended himself by disclosing the plural marriage. The next morning, Orson, still unaware that the liaison had
been authorized by Brigham Young, wrote a heated letter to the
acting church president in which he explained his actions, defended
his wife, and criticized his brother:

> With all the light and knowledge that he [Parley] has received
> concerning the law of the priesthood [plural marriage], and with all
> the counsels that he has received from our quorum, if he feels at lib-
> erty go into the city of New York or elsewhere and seduce girls or fe-
> males and sleep and have connexion with them contrary to the law of
> God, and the sacred counsels of his brethren, it is something that does
> not concern me as an individual. And if my quorum and the church
> can fellowship him, I shall find no fault with him, but leave it between
> him, the church, and God. But when it comes to that, that my wife
> cannot come into this holy & consecrated temple to enjoy the meet-
> ings and society of the saints, without being attacked by his false accu-
> sations and hellish lies, and that too in the presence of a large assembly,
> I feel as though it was too much to be borne. Where is there a person,
> that was present last evening, that heard my wife say the least things
> against him or his family[?] ... And yet she was accused by him, before
> that respectable company, in the most impudent and malicious man-

---

49. Orson Pratt to Brigham Young, 12 Jan. 1846, Brigham Young Papers.
Pratt's letter is discussed in Watson, *Orson Pratt Journals*, 495–97.

ner of whispering against him all over the temple. Under these circumstances, brethren, I verily supposed that I had a perfect right to say a few words in defense of my much injured family. I therefore accused him of false accusations and lying. It was my belief at that time, that there was no place nor circumstances, in heaven, on earth, or in hell, too sacred to defend the cause of my innocent family when they were publicly attacked in so unjust and insulting manner.

Now with regard to confession; After I learned that it was my duty to stand and hear my family abused in the highest degree without the least provocation, and yet not open my mouth in her defense, I immediately confessed my fault to the counsel, but my confession was rejected. Now brethren, I stand ready and willing to make any further confessions to the council, necessary to my restoration from banishment to the enjoyment of your meetings, which you in your wisdom may dictate.[50]

Apparently Young viewed Pratt's letter as sufficient and may even have tried to soothe Orson's feelings by explaining that he had personally sealed Belinda to Parley. The next day Orson "was [re]-anointed a King & a Priest unto the Most High God in the church of Jesus Christ of Latter Day Saints & to all Iseral," while each of his three wives—Sarah, Adelia Ann, and Mary Ann—was anointed a queen and a priestess.[51] Four days later on 17 January, Pratt took his fourth plural wife, twenty-three-year-old Sarah Louisa Chandler.

---

50. Pratt to Young, 12 Jan. 1846.
51. "Book of Anointings," entry no. 7, copy in my possession, original in LDS church archives.

THREE

Perfectly Submissive

*F*our months after the arrival of the first wave of Mormon pioneers in the Great Salt Lake Valley in mid-1847, Orson Pratt returned to the church's temporary settlement in Winter Quarters, Nebraska. There he met with fellow Apostles Brigham Young, Heber Kimball, Willard Richards, Orson Hyde, Wilford Woodruff, George A. Smith, Amasa Lyman, and Ezra T. Benson. Quorum president Young had summoned the group, in part, to urge a formal reorganization of the three-man First Presidency, automatically dissolved at the death of Joseph Smith three and a half years earlier on 27 June 1844.

Beginning shortly after Smith's assassination, Young had assumed *de facto* presidency of the church by virtue of his position as president of the Quorum of Twelve Apostles. Now he wanted to consolidate his position by reconstituting the highest governing council, thereby allowing him to remain at church headquarters in the West while the Twelve gathered the elect to Zion. As historian D. Michael Quinn has noted, throughout the previous year, Young,

Kimball, and Richards had already been functioning "in council meetings as if they were an ecclesiastical unit."[1]

Not everyone—in particular, Orson Pratt—concurred with Young's precedent-setting plan. Orson was satisfied for the time being in allowing the Twelve to lead.[2] Brigham cited Joseph Smith's example, his revelations, and the practical realities of church governance, all of which, he felt, mandated such a move. The following three exchanges in November and December 1847[3] highlight what seemed to be irreconcilable differences over authority and doctrine dividing Young and Pratt, both strong-willed and opinionated. Their interaction and the eventual resolution presaged in many ways the soul-wrenching conflicts that would engulf both men and their quorum in the 1860s.

At the first meeting, held in Winter Quarters on 16 November, Young began:

The subject before us—Av[4] I been out of the way or does this

---

1. Quinn, *Mormon Hierarchy: Origins,* 247. For a discussion of Young's reorganization of the First Presidency, see Richard E. Bennett, *Mormons at the Missouri, 1846-1852: "And Should We Die ..."* (Norman: University of Oklahoma Press, 1987), 199-214; and Richard E. Bennett, *We'll Find the Place: The Mormon Exodus, 1846-1848* (Salt Lake City: Deseret Book Co., 1997), 287-92.

2. On 12 October 1847, as they and others were returning to Winter Quarters from the Salt Lake Valley, Young asked Apostle Woodruff "what my [Woodruff's] opinion was concerning one of the Twelve Apostles being appointed as the President of the Church with his two Councellors." Woodruff replied that, regarding "[a] quorum like the Twelve who had been appointed by revelation & confirmed by revelation from time to time[,] I thought it would require A revelation to change the order of that quorum." Even so, the apostle added sometime later, "What ever the Lord inspires you [Young] to do in this matter I am with you" (Kenney, *Wilford Woodruff's Journal,* 3:283).

3. "Minutes of Councils, Meetings, & Journey," 16, 30 Nov., 5 Dec. 1847. D. Michael Quinn provided the initial transcription; Ron Priddis helped to decipher and interpret problematic passages.

4. Thomas Bullock abbreviated words. In some instances, missing letters have been supplied within brackets to facilitate readability. In other cases, words such as the following have been left incomplete: ad = had, altho = although, as = has, av = have, blest = blessed, bro = brother, diff = different, is = his, presy (also precy,

Council[5] want to dictate my conversation. ...[6] [T]he question is am I biassed [influenced] by men or women, or is my conduct right or wrong—I want this council to say whether I abuse my bre[th-re]n—or whe[the]r are they satisfied—[H]ere is a Quorum of the Twelve[,] let them dictate my course. ... I mean good shall come from this, & so does the Lord—[B]r Orson [Pratt] stated yesterday there is no difference bet[wee]n me & the 12 only on acc[oun]t of my age[7]—[I]f that's the case[,] I will take back my age & put some one else to preside[. M]y course has been [steady],[8] [and] since Spring 1840 (in England) this Quo has never [h]ad a difficulty from that time to this—[N]ow I want to see some man who has the brain, & I am willing some of the rest of the brethren sho[ul]d. try. Are you willing that this shall be the understanding—& that there is no other preemi-nance than 16 days of age[?]

H[eber] C K[imball:] Since the Organizat[io]n of this Quo, ...[9] [I believe] there has been a rev[elatio]n from the Lord appointing bro Brigham as Pres[ide]n[t].

O. Pratt[: I]t is true we av ad no difficulty in this Quo. since we went to England—I dont consider this a difficulty—but I do say that every member has a right to express his sentiments—& if I am in-correct[,] I stand ready to be corrected by the authority of the

---

prescy) = presidency, quo = quorum, r = are, stept = stepped, straiten = straighten, wipt (also whipt) = whipped, yrs = years. Readers will also encounter contrac-tions and possessives without apostrophes, such as: aint, cant, dont, Im, its, Ive, thats, theyd, theyll, theres, weve, whos, wont, and Youngs. Bullock uses the amper-sand for "etcetera" (&c) and for "and." Speakers sometimes use archaic forms such as "shew" for "show." Simple misspellings have been retained where an "s" replaces a "c" or two "l"s are utilized in place of one and so on. Terminal punctu-ation and initial capitalization have been added within braces to indicate sentence breaks.

5. The seven apostles present constituted a functioning quorum.

6. The rest of the sentence reads: "some alluded to Joseph—that is nothing to me." The meaning is unclear.

7. Seniority in the founding Quorum of the Twelve was determined by year of birth.

8. The word "steady" is implied by context.

9. The text replaced by the ellipses reads: "Joseph sd. in Prison—since then."

Ch[urch]—the Twelve—[T]here is no authority higher in decision than 7 of the 12—the highest decision is the united authorities of the Ch[urch]—[B]ut if in my views I am wrong & [I] am willing to be corrected—I ought to av the confidence of the Quo. [I]f I come out bef[ore] the Ch[urch] & proclaimed in public ag[ain]st any member of the Quo[,] I sho[ul]d be doing wrong—We all hold equal offices in this Quo. [T]here is no diff. in the Quo. from the Pres[iden]t to the last admitted—but of necessity there must be one to regulate them—I dont think the decision of Pres[iden]t Young is equal to the decision of 7 of this Quo. [I]f one man decides a question[, does] ... the man [have] ... a right to appeal to this Quo[rum?][10] I sho[ul]d appeal to the Quo. for them to decide which is correct. I dont know any rev[elatio]n which requires me to give implicit confidence to every decision that one man might give. [T]hey av a Pres[iden]t in the Senate—but his decision does not overrule the Senate—[T]hat body av a right to appeal to the Senate—[T]hat is all I claim—I av submitted in every decision to Pres[iden]t Young & this is the 1st. time I av differed from him—[and] I av appealed to this Quo. In regard to age—the rev[elatio]ns say that age as something to do [with it]—the oldest man of the 1st 12 [that were called]—& it is Pres[iden]t Youngs place because he is the oldest—& he has a right to chastise us in this Quo—but I do not think we ought to be bound to av our names bro[ugh]t bef[ore] the public for chastisement—[I]f a member of this Quo does wrong openly—why sho[ul]d one man av the right to bring his name befo[re] the public—without first consulting the Quo[?] I consider this Quo. [to be]—the President of the Church— & this Quo has a right to regulate the Pres[iden]t as much as to regulate me or any other member—[T]here is no subject but this Quo has a right to decide, & I consider it is superior on acc[oun]t of being a majority—than the decision of the President.

B. Young[: T]hen if this Quo. ~~who~~ will not decide—why[,] I shall do as I av a mind to. [I]t is right for us to av a social chat & get

---

10. The full passage reads: "if one man decides a question & if the man has not a right to appeal to this Quo. I shod appeal to the Quo. for them to decide which is correct."

things right—I av not tried any one of the Quo since I av been a
Pres[iden]t. [W]ell[,] let this be a Social chit chat[;] let it be on the
minutes so. I wo[ul]d sit a week & hear all speak bef[ore] I spoke—I
made a statement yesterday & was very broad—the nature of the calling of a man in the Priesthood[. Y]ou may suppose all the cases on record—& even where they cast lots for Kings—he was King was not
he?—& if the lot is in me & I av the case! & if 14 days difference is
all—my case is longest—but like Joseph I will not be trammelled—I
wo[ul]d rat[her] av to be shot in Carthage Jail than to be under the
necessity of aving to run to my bre[thre]n before I can speak bef[ore]
the public—[M]ust man be eternally grumbling because my stick is
the longest[?]—[H]ow much fault av I found with T[homas] B
Marsh, Jos[ep]h Smith[,] or S[idney] Rigdon[?] I never opened my
mouth when they lammed[11] it on to me—[I]f my lot is to preside
over the Ch[urch] & I am the head of the Quo—I am the mouth
piece & you r the belly—[N]ow tell the [occasion] where I failed—I
chastised bro. Parley [Pratt]—I asked the Quo if I ad a right to chastise & I co[ul]d not get a man to squeak—[B]ut I knew it & I told
them—before we left here—[that] Parley & J[ohn] Taylor[12] ought to
av taken a Wagon & a Stove & gone with us—[B]ut they wo[ul]d
not—[B]ut when we were gone[,] they stuck up their nib[13] & you
may take the privilege & lam it on to me as much as you please—but

---

11. "Lam" means "to beat soundly: thrash, strike, whack," as in, "[He] lammed
out wildly at them" (*Webster's Third New International Dictionary,* s.v., "lam").

12. Twice before, Apostles Parley P. Pratt and John Taylor had performed unauthorized plural marriages for each other. The first occurred in the Nauvoo temple in early 1846 after Brigham Young and the rest of the Twelve had left Illinois.
The second took place in late April 1847 while the two men were stationed in
Winter Quarters. Before leaving Iowa, Young forbade the apostles to take additional wives. For their disobedience, he felt that they had technically committed
adultery (see his explicit charge on p. 58). Young was also unhappy that they had
not joined the initial pioneer company, that they interfered with the organization
of the second company, brought too many settlers with them, failed to consult him
about changes, and delayed the second company's progress. See Journal History of
the Church, 4 Sept. 1847. See also Bennett, *Mormons at the Missouri,* 306n31; and
Bennett, *We'll Find the Place,* 270-72, 278nn57, 61.

13. "Nib" refers to a "bill, beak" (*Webster's,* s.v., "nib").

if you do wrong[,] I will straiten you—[A]ny of you may take the responsibility if you please—I s[ai]d in this room the other day that I wo[ul]d pledge that hand (striking the table) that P[arley] P[ratt] had committed adultery—[I]t was shewn to me in the valley—[T]hey committed an insult on the Holy Priesthood—& I say again[,] I will chastise you when ~~you~~ I please, & how I please, & say what I please—[P]ut some one else in my room—& I will do as Orson Pratt has done, teach my children, & suck my thumbs—& let you do all your load yourself—[B]ro. Orson never felt the burden of the Pres[iden]t—he had never had any care on his mind—[E]very horse might av been stolen every night for all the care of Orson Pratt—[N]ow to the subject[:] O[rson] P[ratt][14] came to this place & insulted me, & my Quorum, & the Priesthood—& insulted the Almighty—I told it right out in bro Spencer's Co[mpany]—[I]t was written before me. I told the Saints [how to travel] & by the [authority of the] Pres[iden]t.[15] [T]he very roads on the Prairie show how they were led—[D]id P[arley] Pratt le[a]d that body[?]—No—the Devil led it—I shall never av any rest until I get in that Valley & P. P[ratt] & J. T[aylor] bow down & confess that they r not B. Y[oung]. [T]hey r devoid of the auth[orit]y— [W]hen they ret[urne]d from England[,] they got the Big Head & s[ai]d I am the Twelve—[D]id I ever say so[? N]o never—[W]hy don't some of you get up & tell me the nature of my office[? B]ro Orson is as ignorant of it as he was 10 yrs ago. I wonder if I am not hurt[? Y]es I am. ... What is bro [John] Taylor's course[?]—I know it [and] I tell you a few points—[H]e tried to gull[16] every Sov[ereign] & Shil[ling] in England—& let the rest of the 12 come home naked—[J]ust as quick as he was in the Quo—he s[ai]d you r my niggers & you shall black my boots & he [would] ride you all the time (several— thats a fact[17]). [H]e will throw burdens on

---

14. The reference is probably to Parley P. Pratt, not to Orson.
15. Bullock writes "prest" for "president" throughout the document, but in this case it may refer to "priesthood."
16. To "gull" is "to make a dupe of" or "deceive, cheat," as in, "a subtle trick intended to gull the unwary and naive" (*Webster's*, s.v., "gull").
17. Bullock indicates short interjections, gestures, interruptions, and editorial clarifications within parentheses. In this case, "(several—thats a fact)" indicates that

this Ch[urch] & I will tell of it when I please—I feel Independent, &
if you dont like it[,] just try [my] titles[18]—[W]hen I make decisions,
the Sp[irit] tells me to do so, & if you dont like it—well[,] just wrestle
for it & see who is right—[Y]et I feel my nothingness as much as any
of you & if the Lord dont lead us—we shall go wrong—[W]e should
all go to the Devil—What does O P[ratt] do[? W]hy[,] sit in his
house all the time—[N]o man runs to him for a yoke of oxen, or any
thing—[B]ut you see me running all the time—If I av to be mouth
Piece—I av to be so in councilling, in dictating, [and] just tie me [up]
in one instance & I [will] tell you an[othe]r instance—just tie me
up[,] I am ready—& I will thro[w] the responsibility upon you—&
tie you up by the uplifted hands to Almighty God & I will av it recorded with a Diamond & hide it up until the day it is required—
[B]ut you r not going to run a red hot iron into my side without my
heating the other end for you—I know my standing before God &
bef[ore] the p[eo]pl[e]—[If you were me,][19] then you will feel &
know things that you never knew before—[B]ut as the lot is mine—
dont quarrel with it—[I]f it is a man's lot to draw 1 [million] ...[20] & all
the rest get nothing—dont say you av as much money as I av—[B]ut
I av a carriage & can ride over you—but I will be untrammelled
too—[T]he question is [one] I want the bre[thre]n to decide—[B]ut
I sho[ul]d av told Parley[,] bro. P[ratt,] you av done wrong & you av
insulted me [and God][21] as well as bro Brigham—[I]f you tie me up[,]
you will all just go down into darkness—[I]f the same feeling was allowed to take place in the Salt Basin[,] they might [as well] go to remove that city 50 miles somewhere else—It will never do. Who does
wrong[,] I will put it to them—[T]hey will av to bow & confess that
they have done wrong. Brigham never did so— [T]here never has

---

others voiced approval. Other examples are: "(striking the table)," "(reads page
102, par[agraph] 11)," "(several amens)," and "(in England)."

18. This could mean to "try [on my] titles."

19. The added clause is a guess.

20. The full clause reads "if it is a man's lot to draw 1000000 of money & all
the rest get nothing."

21. The bracketed "and God" is an assumption about this missing portion of
the sentence.

been a decision but it has been decided by the Quorum—If you organize this Ch[urch,] you will all run against a Snag & I shall av to help you out too—I am going to go it [with] the Lord being my helper[;] but without the Lord I am nothing—I will be free[,] but if you tie me up[,] you will se[e] the whipple trees & chains fly—[Y]ou r free—& if I see you going to the Devil[,] I will head you & prevent you—I carry the oracles when I av a Quorum around me—but I will make the same decision now as I did then—Gent[leme]n[,] I will chastise you when I please & how I please & now help yourselves. ... If any of you get the Big Head & think of trampling upon this Quo. you will find me behind & before you—If you do a thin[g] that ought not to be know[n]—I shall know it—yet it may be as secret as the Grave with me—[T]here r things that r treasured in my bosom that I am as secret [about] as the Grave—Brethren[,] If I dont do right[,] tell me who there is that does right—I never saw a day [but] that[,] if I was wrong[,] I could drop upon my knees & say Brethren[,] will you forgive me[,] & any man who wants to stand where I am[,] he must be a Lion—& he would be trammeled—& if he does wrong[,] God will remove him out of the way. I love my brethren so much that I want to be with them all the time. ... Joseph's instructions were if one of the 12 were to go & do wrong—just go & get him home & smother it up—[B]ut I talk to them because I want them to live—[I]t is not because I want bro Parley [Pratt] & [John] Taylor to die—but to live—& the only way to save those men is to talk as I do—[B]ut If I were to say all they av done is right[,] they wo[ul]d be our enemies & apostates in 5 yrs[,] if not in 3. I believe I am able to classify what is right & what is wrong—[I]f two persons come bef[ore] a Council to blaze their faults abroad[,] I say hush it up. ... It is the right of one man to chastise this Church & if I av a right—[i]s not my lot higher than any one[? I]f a lot falls on a man to be King—is he not King? I just will be perfectly untrammelled. ...

O. P.[:] I consider that the regulating power lies in this Quorum. ... I consider the decision of 7 men as superior to the Pres[iden]t.

B. Y.[:] You cant speak [of] the time or thing that I ever decided without having a Quorum with me. Do you O. P. hold the Sealing Keys of the Priesthood?

O. P.[:] Bro. Young has!—[Y]et this Quo has to sit on judgment on every revelation—[I]f we get a rev[elatio]n—the Quo has to say whether it is right or wrong.

B. Y.[:] I bel[ieve] when the Pres[iden]t [speaks,] if he was absolutely wrong[,] God wo[ul]d disown him & the Church wo[ul]d disown him too—[H]as 11 men the right to say—If I receive the Will & mind of the Lord—that it is wrong[?]

O. P.[:] I say that the decision of 7 men wo[ul]d be right—they wo[ul]d not decide that a thing is a rev[elatio]n if it is not a rev[elatio]n. ...

B. Y.[:] There is not a set of men on the Earth who can say that a rev[elatio]n from the Lord is wrong—I am God's freeman. ... I am the Pres[iden]t of the 12—[and] they r the head of the people. I am mouth—I will say as I please & do as I please &—if I am right[,] all lift up the right hand

[U]p—Kimball, Richards, Smith, Woodruff, Benson, Lyman, Phelps, & Bullock

B. Y.[:] Those who say Orson is right[,] lift up the right hand— Orson held a hand up

Brigham[:] That is 9 to 1—I mean to improve by my tongue & guard it more—but I mean to improve—[W]hen I feel any thing by the Sp[irit] of the Almighty—there is no flinch here—

O. Pratt[:] I have unburdened my mind—I feel free in my mind—I state I consider br Young to be the best calculated to stand at the head of the Ch[urch] & I am perfectly submissive & receive all chastisements either private or public—& when I am wrong[,] I want you to right me—

B Young[:] A man knows when he does wrong—I do mean that my tongue shall not offend my brethren—I shall & do want to grow with you. ...

Pratt left the meeting unconvinced of Young's arguments. Over the next two weeks, he turned to Joseph Smith's revelations on church government in the Doctrine and Covenants. It was with this studied perspective that he met two weeks later, again in Winter Quarters, with several other apostles, including Young, joined by two members of the Seventies quorum. The meeting was convened to consider some unrelated business, but Pratt predictably raised his concerns about Young's bid for the presidency:

> The First presy. has not the power of choosing his two councillors—by the D[octrine] & C[ovenants] (page 102-11 Sec[tion]). [T]he three r chosen by the body [of Melchizedek priesthood holders].[22]
>
> B[righam] Y[oung:] That does not touch the point at all—the Pres[iden]t chooses his 2 Co[unselor]s & they r upheld by the p[eo]pl[e]—
>
> O[rson] P[ratt:] The Bishops choose their Councillors &c &c.—the Pres[iden]t might suggest so & so for Co[unselor]s.
>
> B. Y.[: I]f the Ch[urch] upholds him [as a counselor,] he belongs to him[, to] B[righam] Y[oung] as his Co[unselor,] & the Church has not [the] right to nominate. ...
>
> O. P.[:] Would the Church be required to take the 2 next men by age or whom they please[? S]uppose for instance bro. B[righam] is appointed 1st Pres[iden]t—& if the Ch[urch] had the power to put in 2 of the P[residency] of the 70[,] wo[ul]d it be right? [S]till it wo[ul]d be out of joint to do so. ...
>
> B. Y.[:] Go back a little further to the time of the 3 Wit[nesses]: when O[liver] Cowdery had nearly as much power as Joseph [Smith. H]e [Joseph] went & bap[tize]d a man & then s[ai]d I want you to be my 1st Co[unselo]r—that was (Fredrick Gee [Williams]). ... It is just B[righam] that can put B[righam] out—or Heber that can put Heber out. ...
>
> O. P.[: S]uppose the Ch[urch] sho[ul]d app[oin]t 3 [in the] first presy.—they av a ri[gh]t to do any thing else[. W]o[ul]d that 1st P[residency] av the same power over the 12 that Jos[eph] & his 2 Co[unselors] had[? O]r sup[pose] 3 of the 12 sho[ul]d be ap[pointe]d a 1st P[residency]—wo[ul]d that decision be as valid as the Quo of the 12[?] ... I wont consider they co[ul]d be add[ed] to a greater power. ... If they av that power[,] there is something in the dark yet—if 3 men need an ord[inatio]n to be app[oin]t[ed] Pres[iden]ts[,] who will ordain them[?]

---

22. See Doctrine and Covenants 107:22.

B. Y.[:] It dont convey that Idea—

O. P.[: T]he B[ook] of [Doctrine and] Cov[enan]t[s] say[s] that 7 is required in all things—

B. Y.[:] If men r elected by this Ch[urch,] it is by Election—Joseph [Smith] was ord[aine]d an Apostle—but the Ch[urch] elected him as a Pres[iden]t[,] Prophet—Seer & Rev[elato]r—[B]ut he never was ord[aine]d to that office[.] Jos[ep]h was ord[aine]d an apostle by O. Cowdery—they rec[eive]d their ord[i]n[ation] by Peter James & John bef[ore] there was a Ch[urch]. [T]hey r taken & selected & up-held by the Ch[urch] & therefore elected—

O. P. (reads page 102 par[agraph] 11 [of the Doctrine and Covenants]).

B. Y.[:] Aint I the Pres[iden]t of the 12[?]—Yes—Aint the 12 the Pres[iden]t of the Ch[urch?] Yes. [T]here it is—they r appointed & upheld—it presupposes their ordinat[io]n. BY (reads it). [I]t explains itself. Joseph was ord[aine]d an Apostle[,] so was O. Cowdery. O[li-ver] C[owdery] is gone by the board—J[oseph] S[mith] is gone to [the] grave leaving the 12—O[liver] C[owdery] was the Junior Apos-tle—[N]o man has the ri[gh]t to regulate the Ch[urch] unless he is an apost[le]—Joseph has stept out of the way—[W]e take 1 step in ad-vance—& I ask—if there is an Apos[tle] in the Church—[are not] all the keys 4 [leadership] teetotally vested in him[?]—Peter was the Pres[iden]t & he chose James & John & they gave the power to Joseph & they were only Apostles—if the Ch sh[oul]d sa[y] take 3 men from the Quo of the 12[,] their dec[isio]ns wo[ul]d be as legal of necessity[. W]e must av 3 men to preside in the Stake—[O]f necessity we must av 9 more to preach the Gospel to the nations of the Earth & of ne-cessity we must [have] the 70 to assist—[I]f any man thinks he has as much power as I have[,] wrestle with me & see where he will go—[I]f the Quo. of the 12 sa[y] to the 3 men—decide[, good;][23]—[or] if the Quo decide a point[, good]—& I will stand up & contend ag[ain]st them if I know them to be wrong[.] I shall throw the 11 men & the Lord will help me up—

---

23. The context seems to indicate this meaning.

O. P.[: S]uppose 7 men of the 12 say to a man[,] go home—& 3 ... say come, ...[24] which shall he submit to?

B. Y.[:] If I had not confidence in the 3[,] I wo[ul]d never go a preaching—

O. P.[:] I wo[ul]d like to see the 12 hold tog[ethe]r perfectly & unitedly—& 7 to decide in all decisions. ...

B. Y.[:] Which is better[,] to untie the feet of the 12 & let them go to the nations—or always keep the 7 at home[?] ...

O. P.[:] It is my feelings there sho[ul]d not be a 3[-member] first Presy. but the 12 be the First Presy.—[I]n the ancient order ther[e] was no 3 first presy—neither were there any high councils. ...

B. Y.[:] If the glory of God is to be carr[ie]d over all the nations of the Earth[,] I wo[ul]d as soon go as stay—or stay as go[. B]ut if our hands r tied—it lies upon those who tie our hands—

O. P.[:] I certainly sho[ul]d av more confidence in the decision of 7 men, than in the decision of 3. ...

By the end of that week, Pratt's resistance was softening, though he continued to ask how three men could be removed from the Twelve, leaving an incomplete quorum to transact business. Young summoned the apostles to a private council on 5 December at Orson Hyde's cabin across the Missouri River in recently settled Kanesville (later renamed Council Bluffs), Iowa. He wanted to resolve the thorny issue once and for all. In what proved to be a marathon meeting, any who had questioned the wisdom and necessity of forming a new First Presidency changed their minds. By meeting's end, the Twelve voted unanimously to sustain Young as president of the church and to allow him to organize a First Presidency and select his two counselors:

B[righam] Young[: A]s we are now as many of the Qu[orum] of the 12 as can be gathered tog[ethe]r I feel disposed to open my minds and feelings in a regard to a question we av talked over, & I want to av a decision—1st. on the death of Jos[eph,] the 12 ad to step forw[ar]d

---

24. "& 3 at home say come home."

to lead the Ch[urch.] & I felt then as now as, when duty prompts me[,] I mean to do it[,] let consequence be what they ma[y]—[C]onsequently[,] I acted as I did—& so did those of this Co[unci]l of 12—[25]and [matters] have been conducted satisfactorily—[A]t [that] time[,] 12 stept forw[ar]d & follow[ed] in t[he] steps of [the] prophet[. A]t that time & since[,] Ive ad but one mind to the whole affair & I tho[ugh]t I knew what angle to be done & do now. [W]e stept forw[ar]d in [the] midst of opposit[io]n[,] calamity[,] & trial of every kind & was sure [the] Lord wo[ul]d bear us of[f] conque[r]or over all our Str[ong] foes. [A]t the time[,] I ad become understand[in]g as to [the] organ[izatio]n of its perfect [design].[26] I never mouthed it till lately[. I]t was not time to broach the subject until I felt it [my] duty & I knew the L[ord] wo[ul]d not [yet] let me do it—[F]rom [the] time I ad been in G[rea]t Sa[lt] Lake City till now[,] the tap[pin]gs of the Sp[irit] to me is[,] the Ch[urch] ou[gh]t to be now org[anized.] & frames [itself] to the Ch[urch as a question] if there is a God in Mormonism—that is[,] in [the] 12[. W]e are [tried and have] proved to [the] L[ord] & Devil & men that we r just [as] willing to do what [the] L[or]d wants us to do—[N]ow is [the] time [that] this quest[io]n is to be sett[le]d—if all r going into [the] valley[,] let it be there—[I]f that qu[estion] can be settled by 9 of 12[,] then it can be carr[ie]d bef[ore] the] auth[oritie]s of [the] Ch[urch] & it can be settled in their own minds[.] & then—the feel[in]g that I av & the Sp[irit] that guides leads & protects me is—if this is not right[,] right it—[B]ut [the] Sp[irit] prompts me to take these steps. If [the] Ch[urch] continues to stand as now—if 12 stand as [the] Presy[,] the Ch[urch] may [j]udge whe[th-e]r it w[an]ts [the Twelve to go abroad] to teach [or if the] 12 [will stay] at home to preside. ...[27] If the] L[or]d requires & manifests that it be wisdom to av [a] 1st Precy. & liberate 12—[or][28] 12 to stand as now & not sep[arate]—but stay with [the] Ch[urch] & preside over [the]

---

25. Three illegible words appear here.

26. "Design" may or may not convey the exact nuance of Young's sentiment.

27. The full passage reads: "If Ch. continues to stand as now—if 12 stand as Presy. the Ch may gudge wher. it wts to teach 12 at home to preside, & if I dont no."

28. The bracketed "or" replaces "&" in the original.

Ch[urch] as [now—I] say[,] I hold [the] pre[ro]gative [in either case]—I am going to roll that responsibility of[f] my shoulders & roll it on these my live [brethren.][29] [W]e can organize [a] 1st. Prescy. [I]t [i]s [time]—[I]f they r disposed to do it[,] well & good[. I]f not, the responsibility is on you. I feel I dont so much [see the objection.][30] [T]here's a [w]rong concep[tio]n regard[in]g organizing [a] 1st. Prescy. [A]s there [is] nobody here but [the] 12 & our clerk[,] Im going to tell you—[W]e av ad talk—& bro O. P's arguments were singular to me talk[in]g of divid[in]g [the] 12[.] I dont understand[. I]f one man is taken as Pres[iden]t & is 2 co[unci]l[or]s—I understand the 12 stand as [they do] now—[T]he [rest] of [the] 12 can be foot loose [and] can carry the K[ingdom] to [the] world—[W]hen the 12 sit [together,][31] they sit as now—[I]f we r not 1[,] we cant suppose we r the L[or]d[']s or his Serv[an]ts. [Othe]rs will not take our places[.] Jos[ep]h [Smith] always wanted 12 to transact with him as 1 Co[unci]l—[T]his wo[ul]d not stop us—but wo[ul]d give us an org[anizatio]n filling up [the] D[octrine] & C[ovenants] & [the] org[a]n[ization] of [the] Ch[urch] & wo[ul]d be no more than does this Ch[urch] now. J[oseph] S[mith,] he [called his] 1st. Pres[iden]cy[,] sec[retary, and] co[u]n[cilors with the authority of an apostle]. [T]hats settled—thats all the ord[i]n-[ation,] election[,] & ap[point]m[en]ts [that were needed].[32] [H]e was an Apostle[,] thats all we can sa[y] ab[ou]t it— [W]herever his lot is cast[,] there act & in all faithfulness—[T]he question ought to be decided—[T]he future acts of the 12 will be accord[in]g to [the] decision of the council in this respect[:] whos going to [the] mountains, E[ast], or [to] England—[M]y conversat[io]n has hitherto been independent to rouse his [Orson's][33] feelings—[I]f [the] 1st. Prescy is to be[,] it falls on me[. I]t cant fall on any one else. I wo[ul]d be glad if it did—[A]s to going forw[ar]d [only] to be trammeled[,] I wont do it.

---

29. The missing word may be "quorums."
30. The bracketed words are conjecture.
31. The passage reads, "when the 12 sit logg. they sit as now."
32. Presumably these lines convey the same sense as what follows: "he was an Apostle thats all we can sa abt. it." Without interpretations, the original reads: "J. S. he 1st Prescy. Sec'. Con'. thats settled—thats all the ordns. election & apmts."
33. The referent seems to be Pratt.

I mean to do right—ri[gh]ter & rightest—[I]f we dont do it[,] we r down—I want every man to go with [the] convi[ctio]n of [the] L[or]d. [J]ust learn which wa[y] that [the Lord] goes & go with that—that will carry out [the] designs of [the] Al[mighty] in giving P[lace] unto us. [A]n El[der] who [resists the][34] current of [the] Sp[irit] will spit in his own face. I dont want any of you to grieve [in] the Sp[irit.] I want it decided that we now [k]no[w] our future movements. I mean to be free & justified bef[ore the] L[or]d in the matter—[W]hen Sidney [Ridgon] came back[,] I walked up to the meet[in]g alone[.] I asked L. White[35] if he w[a]n[te]d [to] go. [H]e s[ai]d no—A man that wo[ul]d [be as] [Ca]llow [as][36] S[idney] R[idgon,] I dont care a damn. I did not ask the like if I might speak[.] I just spoke as I did. [I]n my days[,] God knows I wo[ul]d not consent to any such measures[. I]f a man does wrong[,] we can correct him. ... You ma[y] hasten your remarks or deliberate on them[.] I want you to manifest your feelings in regular order.

H[eber] C. K[imball:] I suppose the matter bef[ore the] house is ab[ou]t appoint[in]g [a] Prescy—I am perfectly satisf[ie]d concerning such a matter[.] I av no hesitation nor av not ad a long time—I feel its right—I am satisfied it wo[ul]d be accord[in]g to [the] will & mind of God & wo[ul]d hur[r]y [the] cause instead of [the] checking of it. & I dont consider it wo[ul]d give any more power [to the presidency] than they av now. I av all the power I can handle & [that] God is willing to give me. I bel[ieve] the heavens will be rent some day & [we] will behold [the] L[ord]. I am subject [to the president][37] & intend to be from this time forth inasmuch as I can.

O[rson] H[yde: I] feel perfectly to accord with [the] views of bro Y[oung] & [Brother] K[imball]—[W]e av fought the battle disorganized & now we av wipt the enemy in a disorganized state[. W]hat can we do when org[anize]d[?]—& now [let's] go to work & org[an-

---

34. I have substituted "resists" for "meets" in "an El who meets current of Sp will spit in his own face."
35. Lyman Wight.
36. Or perhaps "A man that wo[ul]d [fo]llow ..."
37. Instead of "president," the word may be "priesthood" or perhaps "the Lord."

ize]: but [do it the Lord's way][38]—[W]hat his p[eo]pl[e] do under the influence of the Sp[irit] of [the] L[or]d is [the] voice of God—I claim [authority][39] from the cong[regatio]n. [I]f theyd give me all power in heaven & earth[, it] w[oul]d [be] a good [thing,] & [if] they gave it me & 3 men [who] can manage the Ch[urch] & K[ingdom] of God & the quicker it is brought to bear—I am in favor of it. I bel[ieve] Bro Y[oung] is the man[. I]t is his natural in[stinc]t—[I]t is his priv[ilege] to nominate his Councillor[s]—[W]e ma[y] as well commence [the] work & do it up to[o] right [now] as any [other] time. ...

O[rson] Pratt[: T]his is [the] 1st. time that the subj[ec]t of [a] 1st. [presidency] is [formally] bro[ugh]t bef[ore the] Co[unci]l. [In the past,] it as been thrown in incidentally in conversat[io]n. [B]oth out of Co[unci]l & in our Co[unci]l there were some ob[jec]tions in rel[a-tio]n to [the] subj[ec]t.—[I]ts a subject I av for some few weeks re-flected on—I av meditated on it considerably—~~when~~ I did hear of it some 2 or 3 yrs ago that there wo[ul]d be a drive to av a 1st. Presi-dency. I av tho[ugh]t the time w[oul]d soon be, that it was necessary for me as well as the rest of this Quo to get all the li[gh]t [possible] upon the subject. I dont dispute the r[igh]t of the Ch[urch] to app[oin]t a 1st. Prescy. [T]he only question in my mind is the expedi-ency of the thing, not whe[the]r the Ch[urch] has [the] power—but what is rightest[,] that is what we want—[U]nder the Council of this Quo the Ch[urch] has prospered—the Ch[urch] has been led & in-structed right[. T]he question is[:] is it not more expedient to con-tinue this Qu[orum] as it is instead of making 2 sep[arate] Quo[rums? I]t wo[ul]d make 2 sep[arate] Quo[s] out of this Quo—the decision of 3 wo[ul]d be equal to the decision of 9—I question the decision of this Ch[urch] whe[the]r the dec[isio]n of 3 sh[oul]d be equal to 9[,] for this wo[ul]d be the case accord[in]g to the D[octrine] & C[oven-ants. I]f 6 of this Quo sho[ul]d be abroad & decide on a subject—& the [presidency of] 3 at home, it wo[ul]d be in their [the presidency's] power to decide diff[eren]t[ly] with d[ou]bl[e] the no. [objecting. I]f 3 [are] app[ointe]d—it will be by election—there needs [to be] no ad-

---

38. In the next line, "what his ppl do," the pronoun "his" seems to refer to the Lord; therefore the antecedent, "do it the Lord's way."

39. "Authority" seems to be the issue Hyde addresses.

ditional ordination—& consequently our decisions r now all equal—
[B]ut it is the Pres[iden]ts right to Preside by virtue of his age & to
decide any little ma[tter]s[. B]ut if the Pres[iden]t & 5 men decide one
thing—& 7 decide the [opposite,] the 7 wo[ul]d carry. I bel[ieve] the
Ch[urch] will app[oin]t a 1st. Presy. but I want to express my mind. I
bel[ieve that] following the current of the Sp[irit] is for me to decide
accord[in]g to the li[gh]t I av upon it—that I wo[ul]d [otherwise not
be] deciding by the Sp[irit]—[I]f I give up my judg[men]t & views[,]
that wo[ul]d not decide bec[ause] the Ch[urch] ma[y] av diff[eren]t
views—I dont think we sho[ul]d act right in the sight of God with-
[ou]t we exercise our jud[g]ment—[I]n all matters[,] I intend to act as
independently as if there was no Quo—[I]f this is not right[,] there is
no necessity for Councillors—I [k]no[w] we have often been whipt
by bro Joseph, & urged by bro Young[,] if we av any views to let them
out. Ill bear the Coolishness. I do [fer]vently bel[ieve] from the bot-
tom of my heart that there is no occasion for [a] 3[-man] first
Pre[sidenc]y. [B]y appoint[in]g 3 [for a] first Presy—we sho[ul]d be
just as disorganized as we r now unless the vacancies r filled out—
[A]ccord[in]g to [the] D[octrine] & C[ovenants, the] 3 [in the] first
Presy. r [a] sep[arate] Quo—the 12 ano[the]r. [I]f the 3 [in the] 1st
Presy. r a part of the Quo—its no pattern to us—[I]n ancient days [the
presidency was] Peter and Ja[me]s & John[,] but we av nothing to do
with [the] ancient organizat[io]n—[I]n ancient times they ad no
Hi[gh] councils & we av—[I]f we organize according to the D[oc-
trine] & C[ovenants]—the Quo wo[ul]d av to be filled up or there
wo[ul]d be a lack—[C]annot we say as a Quo—to 3 men—you go
over into the valley [and] take charge of the affairs in that reg[io]n[?
D]oes not that liberate 9[? C]ertainly it does. [C]ant we say to 1
man[,] go & act—but when we return[,] we act with you[? I]f there is
a 3[-man] first Presy. they act whe[the]r we r present or absent—
[S]ince the days of Joseph[,] 3 men went to England[;] we gave them
power to do it—[W]e backed them up & the L[or]d blest them to as
great an extent as if we ad conferred on them the [rights of] 3 [in a]
first Presy. [T]his Quo can all decide that we stay here & delegate 1 2
3 or 4 men & set them apart to go into the valley & preside[,] that the
blessing of heaven wo[ul]d be with them as much as if he [we] had
delegated to them the 3[-man] first Presy. [I]f we app[ointe]d a

3[-man] first Presy[,] we dont hold an equal right with them. I av an idea there will be a 3[-man] first Presy. app[pointe]d[.] I dont think the L[or]d will bless this Ch[urch] if it is done[,] as much as if they cont[inue]d [as] the 12[-man] first Presy. & in the midst of a number of Councillors[,] there is safety. I will say[,] if there is a decision on the subject[,] & the Ch[urch] decides there shall be a 3[-man] first Presy[,] I shall be ab[jec]t to them[.] I will acquiesce in the decisions—I remember that in ancient days they requested a King & the L[or]d gave them a King & Samuel says in order to convince of you the wickedness of this thing[,] the L[or]d will send thunder & lightning in harvest time—[T]he whole Ch[urch] went wrong[,] yet Samuel was convinced it was wrong—[T]his Ch[urch] av no restraints on them[. T]here is nothing to prohibit this Ch[urch] from appoint[in]g a 3[-man] first Presy[,] but according to my present sight[,] I sho[ul]d say it is not expedient.

B. Y.[:] I was precise to follow the current of the Sp[irit] of the L[or]d & not of the current of the p[eo]pl[e].

O. P.[:] I av remarked we av hitherto acted too much as machines[,] heretofore—instead of as councillors—[A]s to following the Sp[irit], we have been machines. T]hat is what I believe in—He [a counselor] sho[ul]d decide upon the best wisdom & jud[g]m[en]t he has got—I will confess to my own shame I av decided contrary to my own feelings many times. I av been too much a machine—[B]ut I mean hereafter not to demean myself as to let my feelings run contra[ry] to my own judg[men]t. [I]f I am wrong[,] am I not willing to be corrected by this Council[?] I wo[ul]d be an hypocrite to say [something and not believe] it—[I]t wo[ul]d be so much beneath my feelings that I dont intend to do it.

O. H.[:] My feelings wo[ul]d be to fill up the Quo[rums] of the Ch[urch.]

B. Y.[:] That will be for me to speak [to] hereafter ~~that is my~~[. I]f we are not [of] a mind to fill up the Quo[rums]—thats none of their [the apostles']⁴⁰ bus[iness,] if there's a 1st. Presy. who as any bus[iness]

---

40. Instead of "the apostles," Young may have meant "the church members."

with it—[the presidency will decide. W]e av met the defect of a 1st. Presy. & we can meet the defect of not hav[in]g a full Quo of 12.

H. C. K.[:] I av my doubts if we co[ul]d get 3 or 4 more horses to draw the 12 as we av done.

W[illard] R[ichards:] I dont [k]no[w] that [it] is necessary to sa[y] much[.] I concur freely with the 1st. 3 that av spoken—[I]n regard to bro Pratt[,] he thinks it best to let 7 av the power—[I]f that wine is good[,] now I cant see why it [would] not always [have] be[en] so[41]—I cant see why our Heavenly Fa[the]r saw best to av a Presy. of 3 instead of 7. [M]y feelings [are] 4 those [truths] that av originated from a Sp[irit] to me & which [were] manifested to me bef[ore] it was mouthed to me—[T]his is manifest to me clearly[,] & that is an end of all controversy & that is the end of the law to me—[I] Saw by that Sp[irit]—[that th]is i[s] w[he]n there sho[ul]d be a 1st. Presy. [Of] the individual who as the ri[gh]t[,] I av no doubt— [Of] the verasity of it[,] I av no doubt—& if we dont organize this Ch[urch] from this time[,] I bel[ieve] we shall see a waning in this Ch[urch]—[I]f we go for[war]d[,] we shall prosper as hitherto & more abundantly— [T]here r [other] things that might be spoken of[,] but it is not necessary now—[I]n regard to filling up the Quo[,] I am also prepared to act upon that object[,] but I do not think there is the occ[asio]n [today,] as there is [only] the 1st. W[ord] of the subject.

W[ilford] Woodruff[:] I view it to be of great importance to us as a p[eo]pl[e]—[I]n regard to all matters of this kind—if they come [before us] without reasons [that] r given[,] they come in a different view to [us than] what they are after the reasons r given—[M]y feelings r now[,] whatever the will of God is[,] that is my will[,] let it come in what shape it may—[I]n the 1st. place[,] a query came[:] will the Quo be filled up[? I]f 3 [or] 4 [are] taken out to form a 1st presy[,] it seemed like sev[e]ring a body in two. [T]here were no reasons given me & I desired [that] the Quo sho[ul]d continue as it was. I felt if the Quo of 12 were to surrender their power unto 3[,] I sho[ul]d be totally opposed to it. [T]ho there 4 [therefore] some things r bought up

41. The line reads, "if that wine is good now I cant see why it did not always be so."

ag[ain]st it—my feelings r on [the side of the] Pres[iden]t who stands at our lead[. A]s [he] s[ai]d[,] he was moved upon by the Sp[irit] to speak to us. [O]ur Pres[iden]t seems to be moved upon by the Sp[irit]—[H]e stands bet[wee]n us & God & I for one dont want to tie his hands. I dont care what the Al[mighty] wants—his will is my will—I am perfectly willing that sho[ul]d be the case—[W]ith re-g[ard] to [the] Quorum remaini[n]g as it is[,] 3 men holding the keys can ordain any man in the Church—Bro Y[oung and his councilors should] go forw[ard] & anoint whom they please—[I]f the 3 [in the] first Presy. hold their station among the Quo of the 12[,] agreed. I dont want to stand in his way & tie up his hands[. H]e is nearer God than I am & I wo[ul]d ra[the]r untie his hands—[I]f the 3 first Presy. were sep[arate] from us[,] Iv ad some feelings [against this,] but [it] ma[y] be a selfish feeling. As the Pres[iden]t seems to be moved on by the Sp[irit,] Im reconciled to it—If I had the disposit[io]n to hedge up his wa[y,] I co[ul]d not do it—but I sa[y,] God speed him.

B Y to W. W.[: T]hank you for your submissive feelings. [D]ont you feel contracted[! If you do,] then feel ag[ai]n. [W]ell go thro[ugh] the world & preach the gospel to every creature—[H]ow do you feel bro W.[?] ([al]right.) [W]ill you tie me up[?]—I feel as If I wo[ul]d pull up mountains. I sa[y,] bro O P[,] if you tie me up[,] you seek your own downfall. [W]eve fought the battles & you cant get awa[y] from me[,] if youl ownly feel the Sp[irit]—[Y]ou cant get rid of me—I [k]no[w] what God wants with this p[eo]pl[e]—[I]f you dont sa[y] Go ahead & preach the Gospel[,] Ill thro[w] the load on you & it will sink you to hell—[T]hats the wa[y] I feel (full of Spirit & Shout).[42] I feel right all the time—[S]et O Pratt at the head of this Ch[urch] & he [will] lead them to hell—[Y]ou cant give me any power[;] I got it myself—[Y]ou cant get rid of me[,] Orson (P).

O P.[:] I dont intend to.

B. Y.[:] I see some things run to a point & ag[ai]n I see [say] Glory Hallaluyah (Shout & sing). I foresee things—Ive stood up & only

---

42. Brigham shouts here and two paragraphs later: "Glory Hallaluyah (Shout & sing)." Orson comments on the "roaring," to which Brigham adds (five paragraphs after his first shout): "it is in my like 7 thunders rolling—I wod not av alloed tonight but its in me." By "alloed," he means "hollered."

Death is no difference to me. [B]ro Orson[,] I dont attach any blame to you, but I know where the Spirits lead to.

O P.[:] If I ad the priv[ilege] of roaring[,] I co[ul]d roar too. I bel[ieve] every man who stands as a Councillor sho[ul]d not express one thing out of doors & ano[the]r in. I dont consider it a narrow contracted Sp[irit]—I want this Quo to know it.

G[eorge] A. Smith:] Ive chatted with O P on this subject—[I]n a matter of importance that comes bef[ore] me—I go to pray upon it until I see it—[B]ut blast the thing[,] I feel two [too] tormented bad about it to talk. I dont want to be pulled apart—& pulled locomotive fashion—I dreamed some dreams ab[ou]t it & understood it all—I want to do the thing that wo[ul]d build up the K[ingdom] of God the most—[I]f there was 3 of the Quo—Good heavens[,] theres an end of the matter. I want to stick together as we av done—I av felt as tho I wo[ul]d fly—& if I [coul]d blow [my stack,] I wo[ul]d let off the Steam with good grace. I calculate to keep on it. I dont want to see this Quo. divided—we r good fellows & better having [unity]—[I]f 3 r picked out[,] there might be jealousies—[W]e av acted under the 1st. Presy. I dont want the app[ointme]n[t] on my necks—[M]y head aches most blastardly & I wo[ul]d like to sleep on it. I am such an intolerant gab-bler[.][43] I wont make any pledges—[T]his K[ingdom] will roll ahead[,] just take what course you please—[I]f its the will of the L[or]d that this course sho[ul]d be taken, Ill twist myself to it[,] but its not my will tonight. Im not prepared ab[ou]t it, on acc[oun]t of my health.

B. Y.[: M]y feelings r precisely like yours—I wo[ul]d not be div[ide]d in our feelings or sep[arate]d no more than you wo[ul]d. [I]t is in my [head] like 7 thunders rolling—I wo[ul]d not av [h]alloed to-night but its in me. I love this Quo as I love my eyes, but if you con-tract this K[ingdom,] you will throw us out—[B]ut the K[ingdom] will roll on. I [k]no[w] what it is to av a 1st. Presy. God as brought us where we r & we av got to do it[.] & if the Devil can get us to decide that we will not av a 1st. Presy—if you throw the K[ingdom] into the Quo of 50[,][44] they cant manage it & the 70 cant do it. ...

43. A "gabbler" is one who "talk[s] fast, idly, foolishly, or without meaning" (*Webster's*, s.v., "gabble").

44. The Council of Fifty was founded by Joseph Smith in 1844 as a political

G. A. S.[:] Im perfectly satisfied with Pres[iden]t Young's course. I av no objections only my private feelings—this K[ingdom] will roll even if it rolls us out. I cant find I am perfectly ready to act in any place as one of the 12 or any thing that ma[y] be necessary. ...

A[masa] L[yman:] I will state my present feelings—& views in relation to the apostleship—[I]f my notions r incorrect[,] I want the Pres[ide]n[t] to put light on me. I expect some time or other to exercise the duties of an Apostle [either] a great wa[y] from here or [in] the Council. I am not going to say what may be the feelings if & if & if 3 were a first Presy. I am satisfied what they will be if they are as they av been. [W]e will be glad to get together again (B Y: & fall on each o[the]rs necks). [T]he door for the wider spread of the work upon a larger scale is doing [it] in the [other lands. T]he time for a man to go on an 18 mo[nth]s mission is about to be toed off. [T]he int[erests] of Zion r to be watched over in the valley[,] States[,] Europe[,] & all o[the]r parts of the world. & now it is nec[essar]y to see what is to be done[. T]he Quo has to be spread abroad[. T]he Presy. has not fully s[ai]d what is the nature in reg[ar]d to a sep[aratio]n by 3 of the Quo being taken to preside & where [their] residence is to be at—Head Quarters. ...[45] [T]here's a business to be done here[. T]his is to carry out a work that has already been begun by ano[the]r. [I]f one man is not to stand in any [other] mans place[,] he wo[ul]d stand as Pres[ident] of [the] Quo of 12—[H]ow much Fas[te]r will they be sep[arate]d from the Quo of 12—than I sh[oul]d be if I was sent as an apostle to England[,] Scotland &c—I am the rep[resentative] of the Quo of 12 & in doing my duty as an Apostle[,] my work is as good & as strong as if all the 12 were there—[I]f I am wrong[,] I am where I can be corrected. I go if with the faith of the Quo & the Ch[urch] & Im an almighty great man—but here[,] the work is not here for us to do—[K]e[e]p here 2 [or] 3 of the 12—they av already got all the

---

organization. It was active through the settling of the Great Basin and existed in some form until about 1890 (see Klaus J. Hansen, *Quest for Empire: The Political Kingdom of God and the Council of Fifty in Mormon History* [East Lansing: Michigan State University Press, 1967]).

45. The omitted line reads: "if they wad. me into any shape or form to hinder Presn Young being the same relation to us."

Power that God ever gave[,] & that man is the head of the body—
[W]hen the Pres[iden]t goes up to lead[,] he can blow off the Church
according to the order of the P[riesthood. E]very Quo of the
Ch[urch] is a body—& to every body there is a head—& the head is
the biggest member bec[ause] it knows the most & as the most responsibility—[I]f you see my arm[,] it is as perfect a member of my
body as my head—[A]int the head accountable where my arm is not
accountable[? T]hat is true even when you carry it down to any individual member—[T]hen my view is relative to the responsibility of
the head in the power & right to dictate that the head has over the
member[.] & the power & admonition is in the head & not the
body—[T]he head [is] who made it—[D]id the body? Then I say[,]
the body has no right to dictate [to] the head—[A] bigger body made
the head & was placed above the body & is accountable for all—
[T]hen who can reprove me[?] I dont feel that I am dishonored in my
Station—[I]f I was the head[,] I co[ul]d see as far as him—[W]hen
the head sees a thing & tells me to do it—if I am wrong[,] I can be
corrected that I may tell somebody what is right & the truth—
[T]here are 2 m[a]ny reasons that the head of this Ch[urch] is
[above], has more responsibility than any member of the Quo—[I]f
not[,] I wo[ul]d like to have one that did (Brig Amen, Hyde Amen). If
I retain the heart or the foot[,] they r all pretty much intelligent & I
want my Pres[iden]t [and] head to know as much more as my head
does than my toe & try to prevent it being mashed up—[W]hen the
head says to the arm[,] go & do so & so[,] go & exercise yonder in the
power of Apostleship in disseminating truth or [e]nj[oi]n[in]g Saints—
then Im a big man[,] as big as the 12. Im plenty big enough & as big as
any Or[dained] Apostle (BY: I wish you ad 1/2 day to preach). I let
you know what my feelings r—[I]f my head says Im wrong[,] tell
me— [I]ts enough to know what my feelings r in regard to what [re-
lation a] member bears to the head—& the prin[ciple is] that [of
whether] the int[eres]ts of the p[eo]pl[e] wo[ul]d be safer in the hands
of 7 men than 3—[I]t does not appear so to me. ...[46] [I]t takes 7 men
to comprehend as much as 3 in [their] place—[I]t appears to me in

---

46. The ellipses replace "in a caln. Reln."

the nature of circumstances that [a] Quo of 12 can reasonably entertain the act[io]n of being together as they av been since the death of
Jos[ep]h. [S]omebody as to preside. I presume 3 will go to valley [and]
there they [will preside] & watch over the int[erests] of Zion & they
may send me to preside over Gentiles & S[ain]ts. I sho[ul]d preside
over Gentiles whe[the]r they acknowledge me or not. [T]he 3 apostles co[ul]d not get any bigger howev[e]r. I suppose God ad[min-
istere]d that Pres[iden]t Young sho[ul]d be born so many years be-
f[ore] me. At any rate[,] I dont remember it. I av got to act in my place
& I dont bel[ieve anything] as to the matter of what will happen to
the Quo of 12—[T]hats not a matter of business for to night—
[W]hen I think of [someone] being taken out—my mind is [on] what
bearing will that be to the Quo of 12—Ive supposed a sep[aratio]n of
3 or [and] they co[ul]d not belong to the Quo of 12. [T]heyl either
belong to it—or not.

B Y [47] [T]heyl either belong to [the] Quo of 12—or [the] 12 belong to them—If we get all our way here[,] I consider it the poorest
kind of pay, [but] by & by I expect a rew[ar]d for our past labors &
burdens[. T]he changes that may be made here will not av a bearing
to sep[arate] us any more than if the subject had not be[e]n agitated[.
I]t wont make a bit of difference—[S]up[pose the] Quo [calls] bro
Amasa [Lyman to] go to England—Ezra [T. Benson] to ano[the]r
[land, and Orson] Hyde to ano[the]r. [A]ll r sent[,] all r [equals][48] in
relation to the bus[iness they are] sent to do—& they r just the men to
do it—[T]here is no load so big but they can grapple it. [S]uppose the
Ch[urch] says [that] bro B[righam] shall preside over the affairs of the
Ch[urch]—[I]f we stay 15 years—we'll av an almighty big K[ing-

---

47. Although credited to Brigham Young, this paragraph may belong to Willard Richards. The last lines of the paragraph read: "I expect the Prest. will tell all
abt. the particulars. the end of the law was with me when he sd. the whispering of
the Sp told him to do this. when the Sp taps him it is right. if I was error the Sp
wod tap me." In determining who "he" is—allowing for the possibility that Young
might refer to himself in third-person as "the Prest."—it is Young's statement
about "the tapgs of the Sp to me" that is endorsed, and the speaker uses Richards's
previous wording: "that is the end of the law to me."

48. Bullock writes "=s" for "equals."

dom]—& they ma[y] be an enormous big drove & army—[A]s to the Presidency[,] I feel ab[ou]t it as when the 12 assumed the responsibility of the Ch[urch]—I felt then & now—that when the circumstances of the p[eo]pl[e] require it—then is the time to be concerned ab[ou]t it—[W]henever it come[s] to the time for me to know[,] when I sho[ul]d feel [if something is right,] I av always been perfectly satisfied. I expect the Pres[iden]t will tell all ab[ou]t the particulars. [T]he end of the law was with me when he s[ai]d the whispering of the Sp[irit] told him to do this. [W]hen the Sp[irit] taps him[,] it is right. [I]f I was [in] error[,] the Sp[irit] wo[ul]d tap me. ...

E. T. Benson[:] I can offer my feelings [that] whe[the]r right or wrong[,] thats the course I av always taken—I only know how to dispose of matters [as they occur and no better] than as [the] Sp[irit] guides me from da[y] to da[y]—I av not exchanged a word with bro Brigham on the matter. I feel now as the o[the]r day[,] when some things were talked over[,] that every thing is right & its hard to get it wrong[.] & if any help is wanted[,] I wo[ul]d help to will down a mountain[.] I av ad testimony that he is called of God—[M]y conscience is perfectly clear & my feelings r the same as they ever av been & [I] am willing to lift him up a [little] hig[her]—thats my private & public feelings[. T]he arguments that av been used r good—the time is come that it may as well be done now as any o[the]r time[.] I can act as well tonight as any o[the]r time[. A]s the rev[elatio]n says[,] it is of necessity—I av thought more about it—to understand the order of God[. I]t is as plain to me as the nose on my face. I av as much power as I can feel wield—I will not carry any burden that grinds in here (bosom). [T]he K[ingdom] of God is a K[ingdom] of light & power & we av enough—theres crowns & kingdoms & people enough in the world[.] I want to act as I wish to—[T]he L[or]d says it is of necessity—[W]ill that take away my power[?]—[N]o[,] it will give me almighty power—[W]herever the head is[,] let the power be—[I]f my head tells my hand to murder a man—my head suffers for it—[I]f my head is cut off[,] theres a possibility of some of the [other] members sprouting—I want a chance to spread myself & I want to be about it—[B]ro Orson[,] the Valley is not big enough for us 12. I wanted to [k]no[w] of the L[or]d concerning the auth[orit]y of the Holy P[riesthood]—I came in not from the testimony of man—I came in like Abram—going from his home not knowing what I came [for]—I was tapped on the head like a shock of electricity—[I]f I did not keep watch ahead[,] as J[ohn] E. Page s[ai]d[,] its hell & damnation all around—I am in torment all the while if I do not do right—I co[ul]d not get it into my mind that God wo[ul]d send an angel [to] call on his servants & then suffer an ignoramus to lead away the p[eo]pl[e] to the devil. I wo[ul]d not worship such a God & I bel[ieve] God wo[ul]d remove our head out of his place. I am here & am willing to act. I am a machine in the mill. & if the L[or]d throws a belt over me[,] I will be a dram.[49] I will be propelled—and am like clay in the hands of the Potter[.] I want to help with the Quo of the 12 & I mean to stick to bro B[righam]. I love him as well as I do any o[the]r man. I am perfectly willing you sho[ul]d take 3 & they govern & control me as the L[or]d wo[ul]d av it[,] for I consider they av some burdens & av feelings for us[,] & may God call out the honest of the heart & gather his elect from the four corners of the Earth (Several Amens).

Orson Pratt arose to correct some ideas & to state wherein he differs from them—[W]herein the Ch[urch] of God has a head for its Gov[ernment,] no one of this Quo wo[ul]d sa[y] that the Ch[urch] needed no head. I av too much confidence in the good sense of this Quo to maintain any such thing—altho [I also say that] the head is governed as well as the arm[,] & I intend to expose my [belief in the] follies [of what has been said][50] before this Quo in all subjects—I cannot with my present light view all things in the same light with Bro Amasa & bro Benson—[I]f we were to act as machines[,] there is no need of this Council. We acknowledge that bro Young has more ~~ins~~ & superior wisdom to any one single individual of this Quo—[N]ow[,] to say ~~bro~~[,] as when he says[,] that the Sp[irit] of the Lord says thus &

---

49. A "dram" is a wooden cart that coal miners pulled along a narrow-gauge rail, also the miner or donkey pulling the cart. The "belt" Benson refers to is the leather harness (see, e.g., www.pitwork.net/history1.htm; www.welshcoalmines.co.uk/Glossary.htm).

50. Since Pratt proceeds to point out the fallacies, as he saw them, in what Elders Lyman and Benson said rather than his own "follies," the original line ("& I intend to expose my follies before this Quo in all subjects") must be incomplete.

so—I dont consider we sho[ul]d act as machines—[that] all we
sho[ul]d do is to say let it be so—[I]f we r to be governed in all cases
in that way—we av no room in the least degree to look at a thing together—Paul says [the] Apostles r set in the Church [to counsel to-
gether]—not one individual of the Apostles, without councilling on
the subject[. I]f all acquiesced[,] where wo[ul]d be the use of Councilling—[I]f a man supposes he has the Sp[irit] of God—& the
o[the]rs unitedly think he is mistaken[,] I feel they overrule the
first—I do not acquiesce with the sentiments of bro Amasa—in another thing—[If] I [do not] misunderstand[,] the D[octrine] & C[ov-
enants] points out that the 1st Presy. with the 12 shall do so & so[,] &
there is where I consider the highest power lies[,] in the Quorum of
the apostles—[Y]et if the Pres[iden]t told me to do thousands of
things[,] I wo[ul]d go & do it[,] but I do not consider it in the light of
the Quo doing it—[T]he necessity of having a Pres[iden]t is seen in
thousands of instances where it is not expedient that all should av to
decide—[E]ven the Gentiles do not act as a body—[T]he majority of
the House of representatives decide & not the Speaker who sits as a
Pres[iden]t—& I consider that our Pres[iden]t does not control the
Quorum.

B Y.[:] I say again[,] Orson[,] start [at] a [particular] point & see
where it carries you too [to.][51]

O P.[:] I brought that up to shew what the D[octrine] &
C[ovenants] says that it requires 7 to control. ...

B. Y.[:] Orson[,] you have feet[,] arms[,] legs[,] eyes—what puts
them in motion[?]

O. P.[:] The Spirit that is in that part.

B. Y.[:] Every particle of the body is moved by the principle of
Will. You admit all the time that Joseph [Smith] is still the 1st. Presy
of the Ch[urch]. Who stand[s] next to [the first] El[der]? (Benson &
K[imball:] you.) [F]or any man to teach me is an imposition on
me—[W]hen you undertake to dictate & Council me[,] it insults
me[. W]hen I want a man to go to Nauvoo—a new 40 Elders to

---

51. From Pratt's response, this line seems to be sardonic rather than serious
advice.

preach—then is the time for you to assist me & you wont do it. [B]ut you want to get between me & Joseph—[Y]ou cant get there—[H]ere is business going nearer to the Celestial K[ingdom]—[I]ts of importance now to organize the Ch[urch]—that this Quo may do as bro Amasa says—there ought to be 1 in England—an[othe]r in Germany—an[othe]r in France—2 in Canada—&c [E]very man ought to be distributed all over the world—[B]ut your Sp[eech]⁵² now wants to say you are apostles & you can never be any bigger—[W]e r to grow—[W]hy[? B]ecause it is of necessity—I must either stop following my file leader or I must follow him—[T]he premises you would give me is no more than you give any one—[Y]ou cant make me Pres[iden]t bec[ause] I am [already] Pres[iden]t. [Y]ou cant give me power because I av it—[Y]ou wont even give us the power that you av got yourself. I want to advance. [Y]ou want your mind to expand wide as Eternity. [W]e must either ascend or descend. [N]ow is the time to take another stride—[H]ere's the nations of the Earth to be gathered. [C]ut your heart strings and let them expand. [L]et a man put his hand on the history where I av snubbed a man[.] I have scolded a man but no more. [A]v I ever manifested any thing that wo[ul]d cause the bre[thre]n to lose confidence in me[? I]f I dont grow[,] you cant [either. J]ust let human nature rule[,] & what does it lead to[?]—I see where one thing leads to & where the o[the]r thing leads to. [W]e r now commencing a bigger thing than ever you did before. [W]hat we av done is a mere patching to what we av to do—[I]f you tie us up[,] we cant do any thing—[B]ut only go out with the word of life[,] & he gathers up a K[ingdom] bigger than we av now.

H C K made a simile of a currant bush being planted [first] in a cluster & [then] spread out—[I]f we r hampered up together[,] the less chance there is to spread.

O. H.[: S]uppose we decide a thing. Bro B[righam] puts his vote upon it. & we carry it bef[ore] the p[eo]pl[e] with the veto bef[ore] our face—[W]e sho[ul]d be thrown [out by his veto]. [H]e has the power now & why not concede to it. ...

---

52. Or "Sp[irit]."

B Y.[:] I dreamed the o[the]r night a personage came to me & told me I ad contemplated the planets—[T]his cha[racte]r said he co[ul]d shew me in 2 min[utes] what now takes days & weeks—[H]e showed me the rule & shewed me how simple it is—I bel[ieve] the L[or]d God will give me revelations as plain as he ever told Joseph[,] & when it comes to you[,] you will see just as plain.

O Hyde[:] I move that bro Brigham Young be the President of the Church of J[esus] C[hrist] of L[atter] D[ay] S[aints] & that he nominate his two councillors who will constitute a First Presidency.

W. Woodruff seconded—[A]ll hands up—B. Young[,] H. C. Kimball[,] O. Hyde[,] O. Pratt[,] W. Richards[,] G. A. Smith[,] A. Lyman[,] W. Woodruff[,] & E. T. Benson & T. Bullock. ...

O. Pratt[:] I suggest that bro Young appoint his two Councillors tonight.

B. Y.[:] I should nominate bro. Heber C. Kimball as my first councillor.

O Pratt[:] I second it[. A]ll hands up again.

B. Y.[:] I nominate brother Willard Richards as my other councillor.

O. Hyde[:] I second it. All hands up again. ...

Nineteen days later, on 24 December, Orson Pratt publicly addressed at length "the policy of electing a First President":

God had saw proper to govern the Church by the Twelve since the death of Joseph the Prophet and that he could govern it by whatever authority he saw proper even by teachers and deacons. There was a time when this church was governed by the Lesser Priesthood[.] But now the Lord had manifested by his Spirit that it was best to appoint a First Presidency again[,] that the organization of the Church might be perfected and the Twelve have a chance to spread abroad again to the Nations &c.

"His discourse," wrote one observer, "was very interesting and was recieved with breathless silence."[53] The following Monday the local

---

53. Qtd. in *On the Mormon Frontier: The Diary of Hosea Stout*, 2 vols., ed. Juanita

church faithful, assembled in the recently completed 65-foot-by-40-foot log tabernacle in Kanesville, voted unanimously to sustain Young, Kimball, and Richards as their new First Presidency. (The action would be reconfirmed by a general conference of the church the following 6 April 1848 in Kanesville.)

It is doubtful that Young resented for long Pratt's opposition to him during the intense three-week period at Winter Quarters/Kanesville. Although Young was clearly annoyed with the delays, Pratt was not alone in expressing reservations about forming a First Presidency.[54] Still, a pattern emerged that would be repeated. Pratt would continue to feel the need, or the responsibility, to question Young, who for his part would respond in kind to Pratt. Fourteen months after these momentous meetings, now in relation to filling the vacancies in the Twelve resulting from the organization of the presidency, Young expressed some begrudging appreciation for Pratt's forthrightness:

> [W]hen I came to Nauvoo [in 1844 after the death of Joseph Smith,] I knew by [a] vision of the Spirit [that] from [out of] the 12 there would be a first Presy. ... I never told the story, but got so full that when I left W[inter] Q[uarters], I leaked out & said so & so & suggested so & so. I look[ed] round a year ago[,] saw the 12 completely shackled up[, and] says I[,] this must not be. [It] came to me like thunder that this shackling must be loos[e]d. [T]hey have got to go to all the nations. Orson Pratt would dip into everything a perfect gauger. [H]e would enquire & [find out if] it is the Disposition of some [to think one way or another and say,] I want to know about this. & that—a great deal [was] said[:] Here is 12 apostles[. D]o they not hold keys equally[?] No & Yes[. P]rove both[. W]hen a man [is] ordained an apostle of J[esus] C[hrist, he has all authority] & can receive no more keys, but he may not be made King [and] Pres[iden]t.[55] [W]e

Brooks (Salt Lake City: University of Utah Press/Utah State Historical Society, 1964), 1:292.

54. See Quinn, *Mormon Hierarchy: Origins,* 247. For a contrary view—that Young's resentment did fester—see England, *Life and Thought,* 265.

locked horns[,] Orson & I—but all to bring things out. ... Am I not an apostle[?] Yes. [V]iz. Bre[thren] of the 12 [who] may yet be called to other places. I am called to another place. I am an apostle. [A]s to the Bre[thren] of the 12 having lived in love round each other[,] I have loved them as much as they all have loved one another. No man can tell how the harness [Elder] K[imball] speaks of feels till its on. [Y]ou are in the harness, but let there be one particle of variation in your movements [and] I will cuff you. ... I do leave the 12[, yet] I do not. I want other men to take our place. I want the body to be perfect that there may be no [dissension] nor discord in the building.[56]

For the remaining thirty-two years of his life, Pratt would devote himself wholly to the church. This would include his private practice and public defense of polygamy. He would cross the Atlantic Ocean on sixteen European missions. He would also serve seven terms in pioneer Utah's territorial legislature and win election as speaker of the house. He would prepare new editions of the church's scriptures—the Book of Mormon and Doctrine and Covenants—arranging them for the first time into chapters and verses, with footnotes and references. Despite his initial reluctance to approve the formation of a new First Presidency, and despite subsequent, protracted doctrinal disagreements with Young, Pratt would remain forever committed to the church and its teachings, even at the expense of his own welfare and that of his several families.

---

55. Although Bullock has written "Prest" to abbreviate "president" throughout, in this case it may mean "priest."

56. Minutes of the Quorum of the Twelve Apostles, 12 Feb. 1849. The four called to be the new members of the Twelve were Charles C. Rich (age thirty-nine), Lorenzo Snow (thirty-four), Erastus Snow (thirty), and Franklin D. Richards (twenty-seven).

FOUR.

Preaching Salvation and Eternal Truth

By mid-1852, LDS officials had finally decided to proclaim plural marriage to what they perceived to be a godless world and embark on an ambitious program to counter anticipated public outrage. Carefully selected leaders, usually trusted apostles, were assigned to populous cities in the West, Midwest, and East to publish pro-Mormon newspapers. The purpose, according to fifty-one-year-old Brigham Young, was to offer non-Mormons a more favorable view of such misunderstood activities and doctrines as polygamy. John Taylor was called in 1854 to New York City where he would found *The Mormon* (1855-57); that same year, Erastus Snow was sent to St. Louis to edit *The St. Louis Luminary* (1854-55); and George Q. Cannon went to San Francisco to publish *The Western Standard* (1856-57).

The first to receive an assignment was Orson Pratt who was called to Washington, D.C., at the close of a special missionary conference in Salt Lake City. By late August 1852, the church had just officially declared to the world its practice of "Celestial Marriage," one of the West's better known secrets. At Brigham Young's request, Pratt delivered the formal announcement, which itself was evidence of the esteem Pratt had come to hold among the hierarchy and general membership.[1] (Pratt had taken his fifth plural wife, Marian Ross, six months earlier on 19 February.) Colleague Wilford Woodruff, moved by his associates' millennial fervor, proclaimed to his diary four months later that Pratt's mission would be "to preach Salvation & Eternal truth to Presidents Senators & Legislators that they might be left without Excuse" at the Second Coming.[2]

The calling to be a spokesman for the church in the nation's capital was a logical step. The irony of the articulate apostle's role in defending polygamy given his devastating experience with it ten years earlier went unnoticed.[3] Among the best educated and most intellectually minded of Mormonism's leaders, Pratt had emerged as a formidable apologist, perhaps second only to his brother Parley.[4] His prowess in defense of his religion was evident as early as January 1834, three and a half years after his conversion, when a reporter for the *Brookville* (Iowa) *Enquirer* wrote: "If a man may be called eloquent who transfers his own views and feelings into the breasts of others—if a knowledge of the subject, and to speak without fear—are part of the more elevated rules of eloquence, we have

---

1. Orson Pratt, "Celestial Marriage," 29 Aug. 1852, in *Journal of Discourses*, 1:53-66. Also see David J. Whittaker, "The Bone in the Throat: Orson Pratt and the Public Announcement of Plural Marriage," *Western Historical Quarterly* 18 (July 1987): 293-314. "[E]ven a cursory examination suggested that [Pratt's address] was not a spontaneous presentation as he implied at the beginning of his presentation," observed Whittaker (302).

2. Kenney, *Wilford Woodruff's Journal*, 4:155.

3. The previous month on 24 July, the "History of Joseph Smith" was serialized in the pages of the *Deseret News*, with reference to Pratt's "stubborn spirit" fifteen years earlier during a minor confrontation with Joseph Smith over Hebrew pronunciation (see chap. 1, n1). Pratt felt that the prophet's scribe had maligned him in Smith's diary, the source of the history. Pratt must have felt gratified to be able to exhibit publicly his loyalty to the church.

4. For a selection of some of Parley Pratt's most important writings, see *The Essential Parley P. Pratt* (Salt Lake City: Signature Books, 1990).

no hesitancy in saying ORSON PRATT was eloquent; and truly veri-
fied the language of Boileau: 'What we clearly conceive, we can
clearly express.'"[5] This blend of fearlessness and eloquence was undoubtedly what made Pratt so appealing yet dangerous to Joseph
Smith in the summer of 1842 and to Brigham Young in the late fall
of 1847.

"The lucid reasoning, and powerful arguments displayed in the
many pamphlets you have written," Mormons in England testified
of Pratt's influence in early 1851, "have already won thousands from
their superstitious ignorance, to the knowledge and favor of God."[6]
"If sound reason coupled with revelation would convince a man of
the error of ... a doctrine," church stalwart William Clayton added
as he accompanied Pratt east to Washington, D.C., "one discourse
from Brother Pratt would settle the question."[7] As an adolescent in
territorial Utah, James Henry Moyle recalled: "I would not have
missed ... the discourses of Orson Pratt for anything. I remember his
sermons as being magnificent, and believe many of them will someday be honored and glorified. ... When it was advertised that Orson
Pratt would preach in any ward, however far away, I attended no
matter how far I had to walk. ... We thought nothing of walking; it
was the only thing to do, especially to hear Orson Pratt."[8] The
apostle's devotion to Mormonism, biographer T. Edgar Lyon explained in 1932, "extended to the point of mild fanaticism. He was
as zealous in his efforts to establish, strengthen and expand the

---

5. Reprinted in the *Latter Day Saints' Messenger and Advocate* 1 (Feb. 1835),
5:77.

6. "Testimonial Presented to Elder Orson Pratt, ..." *Millennial Star,* 1 Feb.
1851, 43.

7. William Clayton to Brigham Young, 4 Oct. 1852, Brigham Young Papers.

8. Gene Sessions, ed., *Mormon Democrat: The Religious and Political Memoirs of
James Henry Moyle* (Salt Lake City: Historical Department of the Church of Jesus
Christ of Latter-day Saints, 1975), 55; see also Gene Sessions, ed., *Mormon Democrat: The Religious and Political Memoirs of James Henry Moyle* (Salt Lake City: Signature Books in association with Smith Research Associates, 1998), 45.

Mormon Church as Innocent III had been toward the Medieval Church in the thirteenth century. ... Today, fifty-one years after his death, most of the older generation in the Mormon Church still believe that he did not have a peer in the world of thought and science."[9]

Nor has time diminished Pratt's reputation as one of the church's foremost thinkers. When in 1969 future LDS Church Historian Leonard J. Arrington asked some fifty Mormon scholars to identify the most eminent intellectuals in LDS history, Pratt ranked second, ahead of Joseph Smith and such venerable twentieth-century writers as Apostles James E. Talmage and John A. Widtsoe. Only Brigham H. Roberts ranked higher. Orson also outranked his brother Parley.[10] Twenty-four years later an update of Arrington's survey found that Pratt still ranked second overall.[11] According to LDS historian David J. Whittaker, Pratt "contributed significantly to Mormon thinking and was revered by rank and file Utah Mormons as their foremost thinker."[12] His "contributions remain unequaled in volume and scope," another biographer enthused; "his ingenious attempt to bring together a unified theory of nature, God, and humanity, his deeply affirmative vision of man as a noble truthseeker and son of God bring to mind a Mormon Aquinas; a Mormon Aristotle; a 'philosopher apostle'—hence a Mormon

---

9. Lyon, "Orson Pratt—Early Mormon Leader," 114, 116.

10. See Leonard J. Arrington, "The Intellectual Tradition of the Latter-day Saints," *Dialogue* 4 (Spring 1969): 13-26.

11. Stan Larson, "Intellectuals in Mormon History: An Update," *Dialogue* 26 (Fall 1993): 187-89.

12. Whittaker, "The Bone in the Throat," 294. Elsewhere Whittaker clarified: "In most of his work, however, Orson was an 'elaborator,' a systematizer, and popularizer of Mormon thought, not an innovator nor an originator" (David J. Whittaker, "Early Mormon Pamphleteering," Ph.D. diss., Brigham Young University, 1982, 121). While Pratt no doubt would have agreed, in those areas where he did innovate, his contributions to Mormon theology were as important as they were controversial. For a selection of some of his most crucial writings, see *The Essential Orson Pratt* (Salt Lake City: Signature Books, 1991).

Paul."[13] "Pratt was an important theologian," concluded American religious scholar Craig James Hazen, "not because of the form of his arguments but because of their content. Pratt had an especially deep and uncompromising commitment to proclaiming and defending ideas that a century earlier were pillars of the Enlightenment in America, and he fought for those ideas in the context of a new and popular American religious movement."[14]

For several years prior to leaving Salt Lake City in mid-1852, Pratt had contemplated the doctrinal insights he hoped to share with readers. Particularly taken with Joseph Smith's theology of multiple gods, universal materialism, and the possibility of progressing from mortality to divinity,[15] he hoped to supply a biblical cachet and the philosophical underpinnings he thought were lacking in the prophet's teachings. His intellectual ambitions are evident in a series of four essays he published in 1845, a year after Smith's untimely death: "Questions on the Origin of Man"; "Mormon Philosophy: Space, Duration, and Matter"; "Questions on the Present State of Man"; and "Angels."[16] His developing ideas postulated a materialistic universe brimming with the basic, indivisible elements from which all matter is organized. These elements, "atoms," contain the perfect intelligence, which he defined as "attributes," that animate all life. Over time the intelligent, self-directed combinations of these attributes may develop into pre-mortal embodied spirits, into flesh-and-bone human beings, and eventually into gods. This was not the first time Pratt had aired these innovations for

---

13. England, *Life and Thought*, 299.

14. Craig James Hazen, *The Village Enlightenment in America: Popular Religion and Science in the Nineteenth Century* (Urbana: University of Illinois Press, 2000), 16.

15. See Joseph Smith, "I Now Call the Attention of This Congregation," 7 April 1844, in *Essential Joseph Smith*, 232-45. For a discussion of this seminal sermon and its doctrines, see the entire Winter 1978 issue of *BYU Studies*, especially the articles by Donald Q. Cannon, Stan Larson, and Van Hale.

16. Rpt. in *Essential Orson Pratt*, 29-47.

which he would later be censured,[17] but his four short, somewhat breezy articles hinted at the direction his theology would take.[18]

Less than two years after the appearance of these essays, during the Saints' exodus west, Pratt publicly applied his theory of "particles of intelligence" to the "original formation of the first God." Notes on his sermon were recorded by his colleague, Apostle Wilford Woodruff:

> As eternity was filled as it were with particles of intelligence who had there Agency, two of these particles in process of time might have joined their interest together[,] exchanged ideas[, and] found by persueing this course that they gained [double?] strength to what one particle of intelligence would have[,] & afterwards were joined by other particles & continued untill they formed A combination or body though through a long process.
>
> Yet they had power over other intelligences in consequence of their combination, organization[,] & strength[.] And in process of time[,] this being[,] body[,] or God[,] seeing the Advantage of such an organization[,] desires company[,] or A companion[,] And Having some experiance goes to work & organizes other beings by prevailing [on] intelligences to come to gether & [in the hope they] may form sumthing better than at the first. And After trials of this kind[,] & the most perfect way sought[, a]ught it was found [that] ... the most expeditious & best way to recieve there formations or bodies[,] either spiritual or temporal[, was] through a womb.[19]

---

17. Five months earlier Pratt delivered a sermon on the subject of "the Gods." The next speaker was Brigham Young, who responded by observing, "Those to whom the word of God came were called 'Gods' because they knew more than anybody else" (qtd. in Watson, *Orson Pratt Journals,* 229). Young seems to be agreeing with Pratt that divinity, at least in part, is a function of the attribute of intelligence.

18. England, *Life and Thought,* 100–105. Although not as fulsomely developed as Orson's, Parley's theology shared a similar radical materialism. See especially his pamphlets on *The World Turned Upside Down, Or Heaven on Earth* (Liverpool, Eng.: Millennial Star Office, 1842?), *Immortality and Eternal Life of the Material Body,* and *Intelligence and Affection* (Milwaukee, WI: W. T. Courier, 1841).

19. See Kenney, *Wilford Woodruff's Journal,* 3:216–18.

The following March 1848 after the reorganization of the First Presidency, Pratt again "preached on the combination of intelligent atoms & producing an organization of God. [A]lso the intelligent atoms of the Holy Ghost combining with the intelligent atoms of a human's spirit."[20] By the end of that year, he had developed these ideas further in a pamphlet on *The Kingdom of God*. He wrote:

> The Holy Spirit being one part of the Godhead, is also a material substance. It exists in vast immeasurable quantities in connexion with all material worlds. ... [I]t extends through all space, intermingling with all other matter ... It must exist in inexhaustible quantities, which is the only possible way for any substance to be omnipresent. ... Each atom of the Holy Spirit is intelligent, and like all other matter has solidity, form, and size, and occupies space. ... If several of the atoms of this Spirit should unite themselves together into the form of a person, then this person of the Holy Spirit would be subject to the same necessity as the other two persons of the godhead [the Father and the Son], that is, it could not be everywhere present.[21]

"If the process of decomposition were carried to its fullest extent," he added in early 1851,

> we should find, no doubt, that all the ponderable substances of nature, together with light, heat, and electricity, and even spirit itself, [are] all originated from one elementary simple substance, possessing a living self-moving force, with intelligence sufficient to govern it in all its infinitude of combinations and operations, producing all the immense variety of phenomena constantly taking place throughout the wide domains of universal nature. ... All the organizations of worlds, of vegetables, of animals, of men, of angels, of spirits, and of the spiritual

---

20. Qtd. in Church Historian's Office Journal, 19 Mar. 1848; see also Journal History of the Church, 19 Mar. 1848.

21. Orson Pratt, "The Kingdom of God. Part I" [1848], rpt. in *Essential Orson Pratt*, 54. Pratt refined his views two years later in "The Holy Spirit," *Millennial Star*, 15 Oct., 1 Nov. 1850, 305-309, 325-28; and again as "The Holy Spirit" in *A Series of Pamphlets* (Liverpool, Eng.: Franklin D. Richards, 1852), rpt. in *Essential Orson Pratt*, 198-217. See also England, *Life and Thought*, 147-55.

personages of the Father, of the Son, and of the Holy Ghost, must, if organized at all, have been the result of the self combinations and unions of the pre-existent, intelligent, powerful, and eternal particles of substance. These eternal Forces and Powers are the Great First Causes of all things and events that have had a beginning.[22]

For Pratt, the defining attributes of godliness—love, mercy, justice, knowledge—not only fill the universe but deserve veneration wherever they are found. "When we worship the Father," he explained the following year,

> we do not worship merely his substance, but we worship the attributes of that substance; so likewise, when we worship the Son, we do not merely worship the essence or substance of the Son, but we worship because of his qualities or attributes; in like manner, when we worship the Spirit, we do not merely worship a personal substance or a widely diffused substance, but we worship the attributes and qualities of this substance[. I]t is not then the essence alone which is the object of worship, but it is the qualities of the essence. These attributes and qualities, unlike the essence, are undivided; they are whole and entire in every part. A truth is not two truths because it dwells in two or more beings, but we worship it as one truth wherever we find it. Hence if the qualities and attributes are the principal cause of our

---

22. Orson Pratt, *Great First Cause, Or the Self-Moving Forces of the Universe* (Liverpool: R. James, printer, 1851), rpt. in *Essential Orson Pratt,* 196; see also the excerpt published in the *Millennial Star,* 1 Feb. 1851, 44-47. In 1855 Parley Pratt echoed:

> This substance [i.e., the Holy Spirit], like all others, is one of the elements of material or physical existence ... Like the other elements, its whole is composed of individual particles. ... This substance is widely diffused among the elements of space. This Holy Spirit, under the control of the Great Elohim, is the grand moving cause of all intelligences ... [T]hese tabernacles [of the Gods] are quickened, or animated by a fulness of that holiest of all elements, which is called the Holy Spirit, which element or spirit, when organized, in individual form, and clothed upon with flesh and bones in the highest possible refinement, contains, in itself, a fulness of the attributes of light, intelligence, wisdom, love, and power. (*Key to the Science of Theology* [Liverpool, Eng.: F. D. Richards, 1855], 39, 45.)

worship, we worship them as one and the same, wherever they are found, whether in a million of substances or one. If these qualities and attributes dwell in all their fulness in every substance of the universe, then one and the same God would dwell in every substance, so far a[s] the qualities are concerned.[23]

Pratt's writings reflect an interesting combination of Platonic, Newtonian, and humanistic influences. He conceived of a universe containing pure essences—attributes and qualities of perfection—in material form, and intelligences that develop from primitive to more complex states over time and may mirror the attributes and qualities of perfection. The attributes and qualities themselves do not progress. In Pratt's theory, if an intelligence attains a fullness of a particular quality—for example, knowledge—that quality cannot increase. "The Father and the Son do not progress in knowledge and wisdom," he would write in 1853, "because they already know all things past, present, and to come."[24] This limit on "eternal progression," together with the idea of unembodied divinity, and the ramifications of these ideas, would prove to be the most controversial aspects of Pratt's philosophy.

In late 1852, Pratt and his traveling companions began their trek east and exchanged theological ideas along the way. One camp member remembered the content of Pratt's remarks on the evening of 30 September, less than two weeks after leaving Salt Lake City. Pratt's topic was

> on the subject of the resurrection of the dead, that they are to come out of their graves, but [he] said that he did not know how the power of God would operate to raise them up from their graves. Also he did not believe that Father Adam had flesh and bones, when he came to

---

23. Pratt, "The Holy Spirit," *Millennial Star*, 308. "He [the Supreme] is in every person upon the face of the earth," Brigham Young seemingly agreed in mid-1852. "The elements that every individual is made of and lives in, possess the Godhead" *(Journal of Discourses*, 1:93).

24. *The Seer* 1 (Aug. 1853), 8:117.

the garden of Eden, but he and his wife Eve were spirits, and that God formed their bodies out of the dust of the ground, and the[y] became living souls. He also said that he believes that Jesus Christ and Adam are brothers in the Spirit, and that Adam is not the God that he [Pratt] is praying unto.[25]

The camp scribe, William Clayton, added:

> He advises the Elders never to advance an idea before the world, which we cannot substantiate by revelation; and also to respect each others views and sentiments however much we may differ in opinion; inasmuch as it is but reasonable to suppose that every brother entertains his opinions honestly; and if we know anyone to be in error, and cannot convince him of his error by sound argument and revelation, not to ridicule him for his opinion, but treat him with respect ...[26]

Three days later, camp members attended a Sunday morning service at which Chaplain Orson Spencer and Orson Pratt addressed the role of Adam. Spencer spoke of

> our father Adam coming to this earth in the morning of creation with a resurrected body and &c. ... He [Spencer] was followed by Elder Orson Pratt on the same subject. ... [Pratt] takes the literal reading of the scriptures for his guide, and maintains that God took the dust of the earth, and moulded a body into which he put the spirit of man just as we have generally understood from the scriptures; while Brother Spencer endeavors to substantiate the position taken by President [Brigham] Young viz. that Adam came to this earth with a resurrected body, and became mortal by eating the fruits of the earth which was earthy. The subject was finally left in so much difficulty and obscurity as it has been from the beginning. The Brethren are evidently getting tired of arguing on a subject in regards to which so little is known, or satisfaction desired; and on which there is so great a difference of opinion. Elder Pratt advised the Brethren to pray to God for knowledge of the true principles and it appears evident that when

---

25. Thomas Evans Jeremy, Journal, 30 Sept. 1852, LDS church archives.
26. William Clayton, Journal, 30 Sept. 1852, in Smith, *Intimate Chronicle,* 431.

ever the question is decided, it will have to be [by] revelation from God.[27]

The brethren's debate was prompted by Brigham Young's recent, surprise announcement—six months earlier at the church's semi-annual general conference: "When our father Adam came into the garden of Eden, he came into it with a *celestial body*, and brought Eve, *one of his wives*, with him. He helped to make and organize this world. He is MICHAEL, *the Archangel*, the ANCIENT OF DAYS! about whom holy men have written and spoken—HE *is our* FATHER *and our* GOD, *and the the only God with whom* WE *have to do*" (emphasis in original).[28] According to Young's emerging Adam-God teaching, LDS scholar Boyd Kirkland explains, Adam was known as Michael in a pre-earth existence. As Michael, he helped to create the earth and fathered all human spirits, as well as the physical body of Jesus Christ. Michael/Adam is thus, as Young taught, both the father of all humankind and, in the pantheon of gods, its reigning deity.[29]

---

27. Ibid., 433-34. In his letter to Brigham Young, 4 Oct. 1852 (see above), Clayton added, "On this subject[,] brother Pratt and myself, have rather locked horns, ... but there can be no difficulty between us, as he is my superior and I shall not argue against him; but if it [I] were an equal[,] I should be apt to speak my feelings in full. There are difficulties on both sides, take it which way we will, and he is unwilling to express anything more than *his opinion* on the subject" (emphasis in original). For Pratt's public opposition to Young's teachings on Adam, see *Journal of Discourses*, 1:55-65, 282-91.

28. Brigham Young, "Self-Government—Mysteries—Recreation and Amusements, Not in Themselves Sinful—Tithing—Adam, Our Father and Our God," 9 Apr. 1852, in *Journal of Discourses*, 1:50; see also 3:80-96, 6:275. Young's fullest statement on the subject may be found in Brigham Young, "I Propose to Speak upon a Subject That Does Not Immediately Concern Yours or My Welfare," in *The Essential Brigham Young* (Salt Lake City: Signature Books, 1992), 86-103, portions of which are quoted in the next chapter.

29. Boyd Kirkland, "The Development of the Mormon Doctrine of God," in Gary James Bergera, ed., *Line upon Line: Essays on Mormon Doctrine* (Salt Lake City: Signature Books, 1989), 38-39. See also David John Buerger, "The Adam-God Doctrine," *Dialogue* 15 (Spring 1982): 14-58.

Another, somewhat less divisive, topic was the status of children after death. "The brethren," Clayton wrote, "have learned to keep cool in their discipline, and to respect each others views and sentiments." He referred to the discussion Pratt's comments engendered about whether children continue to grow after the resurrection. Pratt believed they would.[30] Clayton probably disagreed since nine years earlier he had recorded Joseph Smith's teaching that in the resurrection "we shall receive them [children] precisely in the same state as they died[,] ie no larger. They will have as much intelligence as we shall[,] but [they] shall always remain separate and single. They will have no increase [offspring]. [However,] children who are born dead [stillborn] will have full grown bodies being made up by the resurrection."[31] While some of the Saints came to espouse the idea, others—including Pratt and Young—were skeptical.[32]

The men in the camp continued debating such doctrines, including the possibility that after the Judgement resurrected beings will continue to progress from lower degrees to higher levels of exaltation,[33] until Pratt finally cautioned his companions that

when they attempted to reason on the person of God, to be careful

---

30. Clayton to Young, 4 Oct. 1852.

31. Qtd. in Smith, *Intimate Chronicle*, 104. "Eternity is full of thrones," Joseph Smith also proclaimed, "upon which dwell thousands of children reigning on thrones of glory, with not one cubit added to their stature" (qtd. in Journal History of the Church, 7 Apr. 1844, 5).

32. "I very much doubt," Pratt would say twenty years later in 1873, "whether the Prophet Joseph, at the time he preached that sermon [on the resurrection of infants] had been fully instructed by revelation on that point, for the Lord has revealed a great many things to Prophets and revelators, and among them to Joseph Smith, the fullness of which is not at first given" (*Journal of Discourses*, 16:335). By the end of the nineteenth century, most LDS general authorities had concluded that "all spirits before appearing in the flesh [in mortality] are of adult age, and that after the death of the body they appear in their natural adult sizes[,] but that such spirits, if death occurs in childhood, again enter the child bodies, which grow to the full stature of their spirits after the resurrection" (in Journal History of the Church, 2 June 1898).

33. See Smith, *Intimate Chronicle*, 442.

not to indulge in levity, nor to speak of God irreverently. He [Pratt] brought forth proofs sufficient from revelations already given to satisfy any reasonable mind, that the Gods do not eternally progress in knowledge, or wisdom, but shewed that when they arrive at a fulness they have learned all th[ere] is to learn. He then referred to the peace of union and the desire [to seek] after knowledge [that] there is in this camp; and also demonstrated that the Lord is pleased to see us search after the mysteries of his kingdom, for this is eternal life[,] to know God and Jesus Christ whom He has sent.

The apostle hoped to minimize differences between his views and those recently expounded by Brigham Young:

> He further showed that there is no difference in opinion between him and President Young in regard to the Gods progressing in knowledge, but the apparent difference arises from our not taking time to connect the ideas. When President Young speaks by the power of the spirit there is frequently such a flood of revelation that he has not time to explain every particular, and unless we have the spirit of God resting upon us, it is easy to get wrong ideas.[34]

However genuinely Pratt may have believed that any differences stemmed from the president's and the audience's inability to "connect the ideas," he clearly hoped the brethren would conclude that he and President Young were fundamentally in agreement on these—meaning Pratt's own—teachings. In fact, two days later Pratt again broached his ideas on the "nature and character of the God we worship," perhaps reading from the long treatise on the topic he would begin publishing early the next year, "[s]howing that he is the same God who is worshipped by all the millions of worlds besides this. That it is not the person of God we worship, but the attributes or properties which constitute the Godhead. He also proved that there is a substance which fills all the elements of eter-

---

34. Qtd. in ibid., 444-45.

nity called the Holy Spirit, separate from the personage of the Holy Spirit."[35]

Reaching the nation's capital in December, Pratt immediately began negotiations for printing *The Seer*, named in honor of the martyred Joseph Smith. He also finalized a series of articles on the pre-existence of man and the nature of God.[36] His brainchild was not a hastily written or superficial conceit but represented the fruition of years of study, and he harbored high hopes that his theology would be positively reviewed. But after the first sixteen-page paper appeared the last week of December, he wrote discouragingly to Brigham Young:

> I have tried to get subscribers for the Seer wherever I could hear of any saints; but, as yet, I have only o[b]tained a little less than 200 East of the Rocky Mountains. I have taken the Seer to seven different book Stores and periodical depots in this city, and left them for sale on commission, but I have not heard of even one copy being sold. In order to call the att[e]ntion of the people I had large hand bills about 2 feet square handsomely printed on good paper to be posted up in front of the book stores; many are so prejudiced that they would be ashamed to have such a bill before their door; while other booksellers, after reading the Seer[,] refused to offer them for sales and requested me to take them away, and the people generally dare not enquire for a Mormon paper, because they are ashamed to do so.[37]

Much of the Washington book trade's apprehension stemmed no doubt from Pratt's confrontational approach. His prospectus left no room for question as to his intentions: "The view of the Saints in regard to the *ancient Patriarchal Order of Matrimony, or Plurality of Wives*, as developed in a Revelation, given through JOSEPH the SEER, will be fully published."[38] Ever true to his word, Pratt printed

---

35. Qtd. in ibid., 447.
36. See Clayton to Young, 4 Oct. 1852.
37. Pratt to Young, 31 Dec. 1852, Young Papers.
38. "Prospectus," *The Seer*, Dec. 1852.

in the inaugural number Joseph Smith's 1843 revelation on "celestial marriage," appending to it an extended commentary by Pratt himself.[39] The unapologetic affront to conventional morality would have scandalized most readers.

Issues two through eight of the first volume (February–August 1853) featured, in addition to Pratt's meticulous, carefully reasoned defense of polygamy, his speculations on the "Pre-Existence of Man." That the zealous apostle was perhaps more interested in eschatological themes than in defending plural marriage is suggested by the fact that the former always preceded the latter in each of the seven issues in which they appeared together. The series afforded Pratt an opportunity to embark on the most detailed—detractors might say tedious—presentation yet of his views, including several veiled rebuttals of Young's Adam-God teaching.[40] "All these Gods," he wrote in the second issue about resurrected and exalted men "and their wives," "are equal in power, in glory, in dominion, and in the possession of all things; each possesses a fulness of truth, of knowledge, of wisdom, of light, of intelligence; each governs himself in all things by his own attributes, and is filled with love, goodness, mercy, and justice towards all. The fulness of all these attributes is what constitutes God" (p. 24). "[T]here will be no Being or Beings in existence that will know one particle more than what we know," he added in the eighth issue. He continued:

[W]hen they [the Saints] become one with the Father and Son, and receive a fulness of their glory, that will be the end of all progression in knowledge, because there will be nothing more to be learned. ...

[T]here are none among them [the Gods] that are in advance of the others in knowledge; though some may have been Gods [for] as many millions of years, as there are particles of dust in all the universe[. Y]et there is not one truth that such are in possession of but what every other God knows. They are all equal in knowledge, and in

---

39. See *The Seer* 1 (Jan. 1853): 7–16.
40. For these, see issues for Feb. (pp. 17, 19), Mar. (37), May 1853 (65, 68).

wisdom, and in the possession of all truth. None of these Gods are progressing in knowledge; neither can they progress in the acquirement of any truth. (August 1853, p. 117.)

"All these names [of God] as well as the personal pronouns He, His, and Him," Pratt continued in the final installment:

are applied to the FULNESS OF TRUTH, wherever it or He may dwell, whether in one tabernacle or in unnumbered millions. This Great God—the FULNESS OF TRUTH, can dwell in all worlds at the same instance—can be everywhere present—can be in all things, and round about all things, and through all things. He is in the personage of the Father; He is in the personage of the Son; He will be in the personages of all His Saints when they receive of his fulness; and in fine, He is the only living and true God, and besides Him there is no God; He is the only God worshipped by the righteous of all worlds; for He exists in all worlds, and dwells in all his fulness in countless millions of tabernacles. He has no beginning, neither have His works a beginning, but each of His organized tabernacles had a beginning; each personal spirit was organized out of the elements of spiritual matter. ...

The Fulness of Truth, dwelling in an endless succession of past generations, would produce an endless succession of personal Gods, each possessing equal wisdom, power, and glory with all the rest. In worshipping any one of these Gods[,] we worship the whole, and in worshipping the whole, we still worship but one God; for it is the same God who dwells in them all; the personages are only His different dwelling places. After the resurrection, when the Fulness of Truth or God dwells in us, it can then be said of us, as is now said of Christ, that we are "from all eternity to all eternity"; it can then be said [of] us, that our "works have no end, neither beginning"; it can then be said of us, that we are "in all things, and through all things, and round about all things"; it can then be said [of] us, that the number of worlds which we have created are more numerous than the particles of dust in a million of earths like this; yea, that this would not be a beginning to the number of our creations; it can be said of us, that we are there in all these infinity of worlds, and that our bosom is there. (September 1853, pp. 131-32.)

The time and effort involved in writing, editing, and publishing the monthly *Seer* was considerable, and since Pratt had other responsibilities as the east coast representative of the church, he found the weight of his calling onerous. "You will realize," he wrote to Young early the following March:

> that I have been very dilligent when you learn that I have already published the first 6 Nos. of the Seer, and shall have the proof sheet of the seventh No. tomorrow. Every item yet admitted into the Seer has been new matter of my own composition. It is no small task to write 112 pages of printed matter as large as the Seer. I am confident that I will have to rest my mind a little and exercise my body more in order to preserve my health. ...

"I get letters constantly from all parts of the United States and British provinces," Pratt continued, trying his best to be positive,

> stating that they had seen in the public prints that we had started a paper at the capital and wishing to see a speciman copy. The seer is doing great good among the scattered saints; half-hearted Mormons are awaking out of a deep Sleep and are beginning to take fresh courage and the great enquiry by letter is "how shall we get to Utah;" many old apostates are also beginning and really begin to think that "Mormonism" is true. ... My subscription list is gradually on the increase; I have now between four & five hundred subscribers in all. I still keep the Seer in five of the most prominent Book stores in Washington; but it is unsaleable or nearly so. The Seer is not without honor save it be in its own native city, where it is published. The sale of the Seer is so limited, and the expense of board & printing so great, that I shall probably lose a few hundred dollars the first year, but should you consider it wisdom for me to continue the publication, it may in the course of a year or two cover expenses & perhaps more.[41]

"It is truth your reception at Washington was evil and forbiding," consoled Brigham Young in reply,

---

41. Pratt to Young, 4 Mar. 1853, Young Papers.

but we observe that your subscription list is increasing and you must be aware, without our particularizing, that Washington is the very place for you and your operations to hail from. ... I am aware that the "let alone" policy would tend to try the feelings of a person of your zeal and temperament when your appointments have no hearers, and your publications met with so dull a sale, but never mind and do not be in a hurry, it is all right, and all will be well. We were not at all surprised, nor disappointed that you did not take Washington by storm, but on the contrary we can see the hand of the Lord for our good in letting so prominent an item of our public doctrines strike ears of the people at large with so little of bitter opposition; this affords us much pleasure, indicating that your main trial at present is simply to use patience, and exercise that perserverance ... that you speak of in your letter ... and continue so to do as long as the spirit dictates or until wisdom may otherwise dictate.[42]

By this time, Pratt was some four months ahead of printing schedules and decided to take a working vacation to England, his earlier and much loved field of missionary labor. He remained there until September. While abroad, he took his sixth plural wife, Sarah Louise Lewis, on 21 June 1853.[43]

Following his return, he wrote at least six letters to his older brother, Parley. The two had not yet reconciled since their December 1845 feud in the Nauvoo temple. "I embrace a few moments to write a few lines to you," Orson began timidly. "First, I will beg pardon for having been so backward in writing to you; you may be assured that it has been through carelessness and for no other reason that I have been thus negligent. I hope you will forgive me."[44]

"I rec'd your Letter of March 10th, with great joy," replied Parley. "I will be compelled to pardon your former neglect for so many

---

42. Young to Pratt, 1 June 1853, Young Papers.
43. While in England, Pratt would read again of his "stubborn spirit" in the 27 August issue of the *Millennial Star,* then reprinting the "History of Joseph Smith."
44. Orson Pratt to Parley P. Pratt, 10 Mar. 1853, Parley P. Pratt Collection.

years, although it was strange indeed, and appears to me unnatural and unkind in a brother. As I could never obtain a line from you, or even an acknowledgement of the Receipt of any of my letters,[45] I had ceased to correspond with you[,] and as I had supposed[,] forever unless, recommenced by yourself."[46]

"There are no writings in the church with the exception of the revelations" to Joseph Smith, Orson quickly answered, "which I esteem more highly than yours." He encouraged his brother to continue publishing, seemingly voicing his own ambitions and hopes in doing so:

> I think[,] were you to give your time more to writing and publishing[,] it would not only be a blessing to millions, but would render great assistance to you in a temporal point of view. ... Oh, my dear brother, do, in some way, burst these shackles and send forth your theological Works by thousands among all languages and nations till the whole earth shall be enlightened with the light thereof. Soon old age will be upon us, and our span of life ended for this mortal career! Oh, improve it, for God has given you abilities, in some respects, far greater than the most of other men. All nations might be made to rejoice by your exertions. Must abilities like yours slumber, because poverty seems to compel you to hard toil? O may God our heavenly Father look with compassion upon his servant Parley, and set him free, that his voice may be heard in high places, and the nations be made glad because of him & his writings.[47]

Two months later Orson added:

> Writing has always been tedious to me, but seeing the good that may be accomplished, I have whipped my mind to it, till I am nearly bald-headed, and grey-bearded, through constant application. I almost envy the hours as they steal away, I find myself so fast hastening to old age. A few short years, if we live, will find us among the ranks of

---

45. See, e.g., Journal History of the Church, 8 July 1849.
46. Parley P. Pratt to Orson Pratt, 25 May 1853, Orson Pratt Papers.
47. Orson Pratt to Parley P. Pratt, 12 Sept. 1853, Parley P. Pratt Collection.

the old men of the earth; and how can I bear to have it so without doing more in this great cause? I wish to accomplish something ere I die, that shall not only be esteemed great by good & holy men, but shall be considered great in the sight of God. What have we yet done, and to what blessings have we yet attained? when compared with many of the ancient men of God. It seems to me that we are as nothing, and that our faith is hardly worthy to be called faith. Oh, that we could rend the veil and obtain power with the heavens, and be taught of God as the brother of Jared [in the Book of Mormon] was. But you would no doubt counsel me to be patient, but I would remark, that I sometimes fear that while I am waiting with *patience*[,] that the day of my probation will be past and that I may be called away before I have prevailed with God as did the ancients. I will try, my dear brother, to be patient, but sometimes my anxieties are so great that it is hard to wait.[48]

In his role as defender of the faith, Orson would prove to have few equals. Yet, by the end of the decade, these same gifts would earn him another near-expulsion from the church he loved.

One of the first inklings he had of Young's growing disapprobation surfaced in a sermon the president delivered on 10 July 1853. Pratt was still in England. Alluding to Pratt and his doctrinal speculations in the *Seer,* Young told listeners:

Suppose I ask the learned when was the beginning of eternity? Can they think of it? No! And I should very much doubt some of the sayings of one of the best philosophers and writers of the age, that we call brother, with regard to the character of the Lord God whom we serve. I very much doubt whether it has ever entered into his heart to comprehend eternity. These are principles and ideas I scarcely ever meddle with. ... Suppose we say there was once a beginning to all things, then we must conclude there will undoubtedly be an end. Can eternity be circumscribed? If it can, there is an end of all wisdom, knowledge, power, and glory—all will sink into eternal annihilation.[49]

---

48. Orson Pratt to Parley P. Pratt, 2 Nov. 1853, Parley P. Pratt Collection.

49. *Journal of Discourses,* 1:352-53. When Young's sermon was printed two

A more direct warning followed by mail four months later in early November. Dated 1 September 1853, Young's letter emphasized the president's annoyance with some of the content of the *Seer*—items that "are not *Sound* Doctrine, and will not be so received by the Saints."[50]

Absent from the letter was mention of any specific teachings that Young found troublesome. At the same time, Pratt had heard from a close friend at church headquarters who, privy to a less reticent president, had alerted him to Young's more pointed accusations. Pratt hurriedly wrote the president a six-page letter, to which he attached a short confession—the first of several which would follow during the next twenty years.

Apparently Young disagreed with Pratt's theory of godly attributes and unembodied nature of divinity. "By an item dropped in a letter from an individual in the valley," Pratt explained to Young,

> I am led to conclude that the argument I have used to sustain the *Unity* and *Plurality* of God in an article headed *The Pre-Existence of Man*, is not received as sound Doctrine. I have there argued that each of the saints who entered into the fulness of Celestial glory, and became God, would receive a fulness of all truth as prom[i]sed in the book of [Doctrine and C]ovenants, and that they would be, as the vision [section 76] states, "equal in power, and in might, and in dominion;" and that the Unity, Eternity, and Omnipresence of God, consisted in the oneness, eternity, and Omnipresence of the attributes, such as *"the fulness of Truth,"* light, love, wisdom, & knowledge, dwelling in countless numbers of tabernacles in numberless worlds; and that the oneness of these attributes is what is called in both ancient & modern revelations, the One God besides whom there is none other God[,] neither before Him[,] neither shall there be any after Him. I have still further argued that the Plurality of God only had reference

---

years later in England, it ironically was preceded by an undated Orson Pratt sermon on many principles that Young condemned (see ibid., 328-34).

50. Young to Pratt, 1 Sept. 1853, cited in Pratt to Young, 4 Nov. 1853, Young Papers.

to the number of persons or tabernacles wherein this one God, or in other words, the fulness of these attributes dwells. These arguments, and these alone, most perfectly and effectually reconcile the doctrines of the United, Plurality, Eternity, and Omnipresence of God as set forth so abundantly and clearly in both ancient & modern revelations.[51]

Pratt hoped that his efforts would harmonize the teachings on the godhead found in the Bible with Mormon thought. "Without these arguments[,] I have not the most distant idea how to reconcile them," he lamented.

[W]ithout these arguments[,] I could not stand one moment before arguments brought by our opponents; without these arguments, it would be entirely vain for me to try & enlighten the world upon this subject by reason. I could only bear my testimony that there was but one God as clearly declared in our revelations, & that there were many Gods as asserted in the same revelations, and there I should have to leave it, as a stumbling block before the world and as a stumbling block before many that are honest, though uninformed. It is true, when I was in Utah I heard Elder Kimball advance the idea that all God[s] would be forever progressing in knowledge, but then I supposed that it was merely thrown out, without much consideration, as a mere conjecture, and [I] was not aware that it was his *real permanent & settled* views upon this subject.[52]

Pratt's sympathies, which in many ways reflected a more literalistic and absolutist approach to scripture than Young's dynamic theology, lay with those who struggled with the contradictions in Mormon teachings. It was his desire that theology be amenable to human understanding and reasoning, especially his own, rather than a "stumbling block." The majority of his writings stressed the rationality of Mormon doctrine. At the onset of the *Seer's* publication, he challenged non-Mormon readers: "Convince us of our errors of

---

51. Pratt to Young, 4 Nov. 1853.
52. In ibid.

doctrine, if we have any, by reason, by logical arguments, or by the word of God, and we will be ever grateful for the information."[53] His logical treatment of plural marriage, for instance, was founded on the premise that it existed among the prophets and kings of ancient Israel.

Clearly, Pratt thought that Young's teachings needed to meet similar standards of rationality and consistency. "Neither can I persuade myself, even now," he wrote, "that minds accustomed to severe thought and meditation as yours have been these many years, can, after due reflection, and reading the vast number of revelations which seem most clearly to teach differently, still believe in a doctrine which appears to be so contrary to what is revealed."[54] He added:

> It is not through self-will or stubbornness that I have published what I have upon this subject. I have published, whether right or wrong, what I verily and most sincerely believed to be the true doctrine revealed. ... If this be one of the many points of Doctrine urged by me, which you consider unsound, I am willing, and feel it my duty, to let my tongue & pen be silent upon this subject hereafter, until the Lord shall show you, & through you, the church, a still greater fulness of information, that we may be corrected in our errors & instructed more perfectly in the right way. I am also still willing to make any sati[s]faction that you or the saints may require of me. And if I am willing to do this, I hope that you will grant me as an individual the privilege of believing my present views, and that you will not require me to teach others in the temple, or[,] in any other place[,] that which I cannot without more light believe[,] in regard to the eternal progression of all Gods in knowledge. I do not ask any one else to believe as I do upon this subject. I will not use any influence either in public or in private, verbally or by writing[,] to make the people believe differently from what you do. I desire that you & all the saints forgive me

---

53. *The Seer* 1 (Jan. 1853), 1:15.

54. The specific teaching to which Pratt refers is probably the Adam-God doctrine.

for having published any thing which is in the least derogatory to your settled views; and had I been persuaded that you did in *reality* entertain permanent views contrary to what I have published, I should have kept my views away from the public, for it is not my prerogative to teach publicly that which the president considers to be unsound. It may be that this is not one of the unsound points to which you refer, although it has been thus stated to me in a letter.[55]

As a postscript, Pratt added:

By a close and careful re-examination of the articles published in the Seer, I find that in treating upon the Pre-Existence of Man, I have quoted extensively from the new translation of the Bible [by Joseph Smith] & the book of Abraham. These quotations are in direct opposition to what I have heard Elder Kimball teach; they were not brought forward, however, to prove a different doctrine from what he taught; but the quotations were made as being evidences of another subject, foreign from that, and upon which I am not aware that there is any differences in our views[.] I will observe, however, that my own individual belief is in accordance with those quotations[. A]nd with those revelations before me[,] I do not see any possible way for me to believe otherwise than that man's body was made out of the dust of the ground, and that a rib was extracted from his body in the formation of Eve; but as brother Kimball and perhaps others teach, as appears to me, somewhat differently, I do not feel disposed to publicly teach different, though my own sentiments upon that subject are directly the reverse.[56]

Pratt enclosed a carefully worded confession for publication, at Young's discretion, in the Salt Lake City *Deseret News*. Never printed, the disingenuous statement was no doubt greeted with a mixture of relief and uncertainty. His disclaimer read:

I have been informed by letter from our Beloved President Young, that in several of the Seers, "there are many points" urged by me in

---

55. Pratt to Young, 4 Nov. 1853, Young Papers.
56. Ibid.

my reasoning, "that are not *Sound* Doctrine, and will not be so received by the Saints." What those points are is not explained in the
letter. This is, therefore, to acknowledge my weakness & liability to
err, without the immediate inspiration of the Holy Ghost which
leads into all truth. How great is the weakness of man! and how little
can his teachings or writings be depended upon without revelation
from the great fountain of truth! I do most earnestly hope that the
Saints throughout the world will reject every unsound doctrine
which they may discover in the "Seer" or in any of my writings.
Whatever may come in contact with the *settled & permanent* views of
our president should be laid aside as emanations of erring human wisdom. God has appointed him as our president, and it is his province to
correct us; and we should sustain him by our faith and prayers, that
God may, by revelation, unfold unto us, in due time, the truth of all
"things as they are, and as they were, and as they are to come;" for
without revelation[,] human wisdom will err. With the most anxious
desire for the welfare of the saints, I subscribe myself their most humble, though erring servant. Orson Pratt.[57]

The cautious, double-edged tone of Pratt's apology set the stage
for further confrontation with Young. Pratt would simultaneously
submit to the demands of his president yet tenaciously retain the
right to think freely. In the absence of a binding declaration, he
considered it his privilege to arrive at conclusions through any
means available. His reluctance to renounce error would be the
most significant cause of Young's continued criticism. "Pratt was
obstinate," wrote Craig James Hazen,

> when he thought reason and scientific thinking were being chal-
> lenged. He was not always an apologist for the pronouncements of
> Mormon leaders; he was a defender of what he saw as the truth. ... To
> defend Joseph Smith's revelations, Pratt thought it best to show how
> they made better sense of the cosmos than any other system did.
> Smith's inspired words concerning the materialistic nature of the

---

57. "Confession," attached to Pratt to Young, 4 Nov. 1853, Young Papers.

cosmos were especially important to Pratt. Although he may have believed it, Pratt never made the case that revelation in and of itself could settle any question simply because it was a message from an omniscient being. The truth of the revealed message had to match other obvious truths.[58]

Pratt's conversion to Mormonism had resulted from independent thinking which had led to disaffection from traditional creeds. Young's acceptance of Mormonism followed from his own careful weighing of the church's claims in terms of his experience and understanding. Some two years passed between Young's initial contact with missionaries and his baptism in 1832. As he later recalled, "I wished time sufficient to prove all things for myself."[59] Privy to the private conversations of church leaders since his appointment to the hierarchy in 1835, Young knew well the consequences of extravagant doctrines. He realized that for many Saints, their first attraction to the church came through similar intellectual questioning. Yet he viewed this basic impulse from a fundamentally different perspective. As president, he feared the potential danger of an unbridled quest for logical theology, while Pratt saw only the positive aspects of reasoned faith. Theologically, despite his speculations, Pratt tended toward absolutist interpretations, while Young favored a more dynamic, finitist approach, except when it came to obedience to authority. Yet neither man seems to have disapproved of creative theology—doctrinal speculation—at least as far as his own thinking was concerned. Their differences, mostly matters of emphasis, would become increasingly polarized in a battle of wills between two strong, opinionated minds.[60]

---

58. Hazen, *Village Enlightenment*, 23, 40.

59. *Journal of Discourses*, 3:91.

60. For more on Pratt's and Young's approaches to scripture, see Philip L. Barlow, *Mormons and the Bible: The Place of the Latter-day Saints in American Religion* (New York: Oxford University Press, 1991), 81-94. Pratt's literalism was not unqualified, nor was Young's preference for modern revelation. In October 1855, Young publicly worried that Pratt's defense of Joseph Smith's revelations might

Although Pratt continued publishing the *Seer*, it never achieved the success he hoped for. "The Seer is circulated in the United States with a loss of about $500 per year," he wrote to Parley early the next year, "and were it not for the reprint in England and the circulation thereof[,] I should be obliged to stop it. The world will not subscribe for nor read the Seer, and all but one or two of the exchange papers have been withdraw[n]. The subscribers are not so many this year as last. The whole United States and British Provinces take a few over four hundred, and yet the printing and board costs me about $1000 per year."[61]

The failure of the *Seer* was particularly disheartening to Orson, perhaps more so than Young's criticisms of his theology. Blaming his own writing ability, he confessed two months later to Parley: "I shall postpone writing my own biography until I can see you, for I feel incapable of framing together my words and sentences in that interesting, easy, flowing stile which characterizes your writings. Through your counsel and assistance and the dictations of the Holy Spirit[,] I am in hopes to write something that shall hereafter prove a blessing to our brethren."[62]

---

cause some to "scarcely think a Bible worth picking up and carrying home, should you find one in the streets" (*Journal of Discourses*, 3:116; Pratt's sermon, to which Young responds, was never printed).

61. Orson Pratt to Parley P. Pratt, 12 Feb. 1854, Parley P. Pratt Collection.

62. Pratt to Pratt, 4 Apr. 1854, Parley P. Pratt Collection.

FIVE

A Great Mystery

Orson Pratt returned to Great Salt Lake Valley from Washington, D.C., to deliver his homecoming report to church leaders on 3 September 1854. Two weeks later to the day, Brigham Young took the opportunity during a private prayer meeting of general authorities to reproach the apostle. He warned Pratt that his continuing embrace of God's absolute omniscience "was a fals doctrin & not true[,] that there never will be a time to all Eternity when all the Gods of Eternity will scease advancing in power knowledge experience & Glory[,] for if this was the case[,] Eternity wood seease to be & the glory of God would come to an End. But all of [the] celestial beings will continue to advance in knowledge & power worlds without end."[1] (Six months earlier, Jedediah M. Grant, Young's future second counselor, had complained: "I know brother Orson Pratt says we shall at some time come to a dead stand, but that time is a long way off ... I never want it to come, or to believe that it ever will come. ... I cannot see that we shall ever come to a dead stand. I

---

1. Qtd. in Kenney, *Wilford Woodruff's Journal*, 4:288.

have an idea that progression is eternal ... That which is limited is not Mormonism!")[2]

Young continued by further condemning Pratt's teaching that Adam had been literally created out of the dust of this earth, as well as his reluctance to accept that "Adam was our God or the Father of Jesus Christ." Young reiterated that Adam "came from another world & made this [one]. Brought Eve with him[,] partook of the fruits of the Earth[,] begat Children[,] & they were Earthly & had mortal bodies & if we were Faithful we should become Gods as [Adam] was." According to Apostle Wilford Woodruff, Young "told Brother Pratt to lay aside his Philosofical reasoning & get Revelation from God to Govern & Enlighten his mind more & it would be a great Blessing to him to lay aside his books & go into the canyons as some of the rest of us was doing & it would be better for him. He said [Pratt's] Phylosophy injured him in a measure."[3]

While Pratt was not the only one unwilling to accept certain of Brother Brigham's doctrinal speculations, his calling as an apostle placed him at the forefront of the dissent—especially when his disagreements became public. Less than three weeks after this confrontation, one lay Mormon observed: "There were some that did not believe the sayings of the Prophet Brigham. Even our beloved Brother Orson Pratt told me that he did not believe it. He said he could prove by the scriptures it was not correct. I felt sorry to hear Professor Orson Pratt say that. I fear lest he should apostatize."[4]

The next day Pratt addressed the general membership in the Tabernacle on Temple Square during the semi-annual general conference. Clearly alluding to his differences with Young, he said:

---

2. Sermon dated 12 Mar. 1854, in the *Deseret News*, 27 July 1854.

3. Qtd. in Kenney, *Wilford Woodruff's Journal*, 4:288. Young also chastised Pratt for having published the LDS temple marriage ceremony (see *The Seer* 1 [Feb. 1853], 31). It was later reprinted in the *Latter-day Saints' Millennial Star*, 2 Apr. 1853, 214-15. Pratt had wanted to assure non-Mormon readers that there was nothing unseemly in the rite.

4. Joseph Lee Robinson, Journal, 6 Oct. 1854, BYU Library.

[S]o far as I have ever preached abroad in the world, and published, one thing is certain, I have not published anything but what I verily believe to be true, however much I may have been mistaken[. A]nd I have generally endeavored to show the people, from the written word of God, as well as reason, wherein it was true. This has been my general course. I may have erred in some principles; I do not profess to be wise, or to have more understanding than many others. I am not called with the same calling as those who preside over all the Church. I may not have as great a degree of the spirit of revelation; but I have always tried, in my teachings, and in my proclamations, and publications, where I could not get light by the Spirit of the Lord (or did not get light; I will not say could not, for I believe it is the privilege of all Elders, authorities, and members of the Church of God to get light by the Spirit of the Lord), but where I did not get light by the Spirit of the Lord, I have generally been careful to back up all the doctrines and principles I set forth by reason, or by, Thus Saith the Lord, in some revelation either ancient or modern. Previous to declaring a doctrine, I have always inquired in my own mind, "Can this doctrine be proved by revelation given, or by reason, or can it not?" If I found it could be proved, I set forth the doctrine; but if I found there was no evidence to substantiate it, I laid it aside; in all this, however, I may have erred, for to err is human.[5]

The next day, 8 October, Young delivered his most explicit Adam-God statement to date. Elder Woodruff called it "the greatest sermon that ever was Deliver[e]d to the Latter Day Saints since they have been a People."[6] Young obviously intended his lengthy, in many ways extraordinary, speech to be a carefully reasoned response to the *Seer* series on the preexistence of humankind. It was probably also a response to Pratt's sermon the day before.

"So many among us are preaching, lecturing, contemplating

---

5. *Journal of Discourses*, 2:58-59.

6. Kenney, *Wilford Woodruff's Journal*, 4:290. Young's sermon must have been unusually powerful since ten years earlier Woodruff had recorded Joseph Smith's King Follett eulogy on the plurality of gods. I thank D. Michael Quinn for pointing this out.

upon, and conversing about things away beyond our reach," Young began. "[S]ometimes I wish to gratify the people by speaking upon these subjects; for I think upon them as well as you; I meditate upon the future and the past as well as you, and I now gratify myself by gratifying the people." "I believe in the eternities of worlds, saints, angels, kingdoms, and gods: In eternity without beginning." He continued more specifically:

> I believe the gods never had a beginning, neither the formation of matter, and it is without end; it will endure in one eternal round swimming in space, basking, living, and moving in the midst of eternity. All the creations are in the midst of eternity, and that is one eternity, so they move in one eternal round.
>
> Consequently, when you hear philosophers argue the point how the first god came, how intelligence came, how worlds came, and how angels came, they are talking about that which is beyond their conception; about that which never was, and never will be[,] worlds without end. It manifests their folly. It shows they know nothing of such matters; and if they do know some things they have a right to know, there are things they have no right to know; this applies to all classes of mankind.
>
> ... [T]here is an eternity of elements, and an eternity of space and there is no space without a kingdom; neither is there any kingdom without a space.

Refuting Pratt's appeal to the authority of the Bible and the revelations of Joseph Smith, Young quipped, "I have had so much to do, that I have not read the Bible for many years." Even so, he continued:

> I feel inclined here to make a little scripture. (Were I under the necessity of making scripture extensively[,] I should get Brother Heber C. Kimball to make it, and then I would quote it. I have seen him do this when any of the Elders have been pressed by their opponents, and were a little at a loss; he would make a scripture for them to suit the case, that never was in the Bible, though none the less true, and make their opponents swallow it as the words of an Apostle, or one of the

Prophets. The Elder would then say, "Please turn to that scripture, gentlemen and read it for yourselves." No they could not turn to it but they recollected it like the Devil for fear of being caught.) I will venture to make a little [scripture]. This God [the Father] is the God and Father of our Lord Jesus Christ precisely as He is our Father varying from mortality to immortality, from corruptible to incorruptible, and that is all the difference. He is the God and Father of our Lord Jesus Christ, both body and spirit; and He is the Father of our spirits, and the Father of our flesh in the beginning. ...

"Do you wish me to simplify it?" he offered. "Could you have a father without having a grandfather; or a grandfather without having a great grandfather? ..." The world and its inhabitants are part of an endless history and genealogy, he explained.

I believe we are all of one flesh, blood, and bones. We are made of the same matter, the same elements, we have sprung from one mother, Earth. Matter was brought together from the vast eternity of it that exists, and this terra firma upon which we stand was organized, then comes the world of mankind, the beasts, fishes, fowls, and every living thing to dwell upon the Earth after its kind; ...

There never has been a time when the creations of worlds commenced, they are from eternity to eternity in their creations and redemption. ...

"Do any of you know anything about the creation of this world?" he aimed a rhetorical volley again at Pratt and all but quoted the apostle: "Oh yes, we understand a good deal about it from the account given in the Bible," he said, gathering steam,

But let us turn our attention to the God with which we have to do. I tell you simply, He is our Father; the God and Father of our Lord Jesus Christ, and the Father of our spirits. Can that be possible? Yes, it is possible, He is the Father of all the spirits of the human family. ...

I tell you more, Adam is the Father of our spirits. He lived upon an earth; he did abide his creation, and did honor to his calling and Priesthood; and obeyed his Master or Lord, and probably many of his wives did the same, and they lived, and died upon an earth, and then were resurrected again to Immortality and Eternal Life. ...

I reckon that Father Adam was a resurrected being, with his wives and posterity, and in the Celestial Kingdom they were crowned with Glory[,] Immortality[,] and Eternal Lives, with Thrones, Principalities and Powers: and it was said to him[:] It is your right to organize the elements; and to your Creations and Posterity there shall be no end, but you shall add Kingdom to Kingdom, and Throne to Throne; and still behold the vast eternity of unorganized matter.

Adam then was a resurrected being; and I reckon, Our spirits and the spirits of all the human family were begotten by Adam, and born of Eve. ...

And I reckon that Adam came into the Garden of Eden, and did actually eat of the fruit that he himself planted; and I reckon there was a previous understanding, and the whole plan was previously calculated, before the Garden of Eden was made, that he would reduce his posterity to sin, misery, darkness, wickedness, wretchedness, and to the power of the Devil, that they might be prepared for an Exaltation, for without this they could not receive one. ...

"I will tell you," he stressed toward the conclusion, "when you see your Father in the Heavens, you will see Adam. When you see your Mother that bear[s] your spirit, you will see Mother Eve. And when you see yourselves there[,] you [will] have gained your Exaltation; you have honored your calling here on the Earth; your body has returned to its mother Earth; and somebody has broken the chains of death that bound you, and has given you a resurrection."[7] Aside from the clear explication of Young's views on God, the numerous and pointed references throughout his powerful sermon to Pratt's publications were unmistakable.

Seven days later Pratt faced the body of the Saints, and once more reluctantly admitted that if his teachings were erroneous—

---

7. Brigham Young, "I Propose to Speak upon a Subject That Does Not Immediately Concern Yours or My Welfare," 8 Oct. 1854, rpt. in *Essential Brigham Young*, 86-99.

although he was still unwilling to concede they were—he had nonetheless sincerely believed they were true. He could support them from the scriptures and had not learned of the president's views before publishing his own:

> I do not know that I have this day presented any views that are differ-
> ent from [President Young's]; if I have, when he corrects me, I will
> remain silent upon this subject, if I do not understand it as he does. ...
> In many of my remarks and teachings, I may have laid before you
> ideas, which, when you come to learn the President's mind upon
> them, may be declared erroneous and not sound doctrine. I have done
> the same things in many of my writings; but in all points of doctrine,
> relating to the plan of salvation, and the redemption of man, so far as I
> understood it, I have endeavored to write that which I[,] at the time,
> verily believed to be true.[8]

As he saw it, his mistake lay not in espousing error but in ex-pounding doctrine that contradicted the beliefs of the president. He clearly believed that Young was wrong, that his real sins were igno-rance of the president's views and poor timing. Still, Pratt must have known since at least the late 1840s that Young strongly disagreed with his beliefs regarding the absolute omniscience of God and the origin of Adam. Perhaps his passive-aggressive stance in mid-October 1854 was a not-so-subtle invitation to incite Young's equally public response. With their disagreements now known widely by members outside the church's top-level leadership, Pratt may have felt he stood a better chance of defending his position.

If he had hoped to elicit such a rejoinder from Young, the presi-dent obliged once again one month later on 19 November. Speak-ing publicly, Young testily announced:

> Br. Orson has been preparing to tell a great mystery to us. I have one
> request to make of him and the philosophers of the age, that's become

---

8. *Journal of Discourses*, 2:246-47.

Mormons ... Now I bring a comparison and tell you the philosophy of the day. You take a reservoir that will hold five thousand gallons, and you fill that with chaff, and put one kernel of wheat in that chaff and stir it up, and let them cry to you that there is a great treasure in that reservoir, and you may funnel over the chaff until you are blind to find that one grain. I say Br. Orson and to all the learned of the age, fetch it out like a Mormon, and not write a book of six hundred pages with that that ought to be told out in a few minutes. But to write books [is why they] write books[;] what for? To tell what they ought [to] tell in a minute. ...

"Philosophers sit down and tell us how [it is] that [the] Gods came into existance and how the first creation was made, and the planets," Young continued.

It proves to me they expose their poor ignorance before all intelligence and plant themselves in the pages of forgetfulness. There is no planet or kingdom that mortal man can decipher and find out without the revelation of the Almighty, but I am not an astronomer nor a philosopher, nor do I profess any learning. I have done only what the Lord taught me and what I got while I was in the wood rolling logs, and while I was in the wilderness. But there is knowledge and truth, and it is just as easy for the Lord to reveal to a person a mystery with regard to the planets' motion on their axis [so] that they can tell it to a congregation or to the world in one minute as to be six months about it—just exactly. I want something that will do us good.[9]

Three days earlier the *Deseret News* had announced the availability of Pratt's publication of Lucy Mack Smith's autobiography, *Biographical Sketches of Joseph Smith the Prophet, and His Progenitors for Many Generations, by Lucy Smith, Mother of the Prophet.*[10] During the closing months of 1852 while in Washington, D.C., Pratt had

9. Brigham Young, speech, 19 Nov. 1854, Brigham Young Papers; rpt. in *The Teachings of President Brigham Young, Vol. 3: 1852-1854*, comp. Fred C. Collier (Salt Lake City: Collier's Publishing Co., 1987), 413-14.

10. The book sold for $1.75.

learned of the manuscript, dictated by Joseph Smith's mother, chronicling her illustrious family. He had obtained the manuscript early the next year but realized that printing costs in the United States prohibited its publication. With Lucy's permission, he published it in England where he was vacationing that summer, released under church representative Samuel W. Richards's imprint. In his eagerness, Pratt had not sought Young's approval, nor had he corrected factual errors. He informed Young of his intentions as early as 31 December 1852, although he obviously thought that official permission was unnecessary.[11] Six weeks after the book's appearance in Utah in late 1854, Young wrote to Apostle Franklin D. Richards, editor of the *Latter-day Saints' Millennial Star* in England: "I take the opportunity of requesting you not to publish any more *Seers*, and I wish you to publish the enclosed article, entitled 'Publications,' in the editorial columns of the *Star.*

> There are many mistakes in the work entitled "Biographical Sketches of Joseph Smith the Prophet, and of his progenitors for many generations, by Lucy Smith, mother of the Prophet," and "published at Liverpool for Orson Pratt by S. W. Richards, 15 Wilton Street." I have had a written copy of those sketches in my possession for several years, and it contains much of the history of the Prophet Joseph. Should it ever be deemed best to publish these sketches, it will not be done until after they are carefully corrected. I take this seasonable opportunity to

---

11. "As I am publishing the plurality (of Gods) doctrine in the Seer," Pratt had written, "I shall probably defer publishing my pamphlet, entitled the 'Peopling of Worlds,' until spring, when I think I will step over to Liverpool and publish it, and also another work, which will be very interesting, namely, the narrative of Mother Smith, giving the genealogy of Joseph, back for seven generations, and a statement of many facts, visions, and incidents, connected with the finding & translating of the plates, the rise of the church &c. These items have never before been published, and I think that they will do much good both to the church & the world" (Orson Pratt to Brigham Young, 31 Dec. 1852, Young Papers). For a detailed chronology of the book's preparation and publication, see Lavina Fielding Anderson's introduction to her *Lucy's Book: A Critical Edition of Lucy Mack Smith's Family Memoir* (Salt Lake City: Signature Books, 2001).

inform the public mind, in order that readers may not be surprised or disappointed at finding discrepancies, and may know which is the most reliable, in case a corrected edition is ever published.

A monthly periodical called the "Seer," published by Elder Orson Pratt at Washington City, D.C., contains beautifully written articles; but notwithstanding the general beauty of the style, and the apparent candour and minuteness of the reasoning, the "Seer" has many items of erroneous doctrine. As it would be a lengthy and laborious operation to enter minutely into their dis[ap]proval, I prefer, for the present, to let the Saints have opportunity to exercise their faith and discernment in discriminating between the true and erroneous; and simply request them, while reading the "Seer," to ask themselves what spirit they are of, and whether the Holy Ghost bears testimony to the truth of all the doctrines therein advocated.[12]

Learning of Young's letter before it appeared in the *Millennial Star,* Pratt informed readers of the *Deseret News* on 21 March 1855 that Lucy's history did contain some inaccuracies; that Joseph Smith would not have been able to review it before his death, as Pratt had earlier assumed; and that all future editions "will be carefully revised and corrected." Pratt assumed that the problems were minor and would not detract from the book's value. "If the school of our Territory would introduce this work as a 'Reader,'" he wrote, "it would give the young and rising generation some knowledge of the facts and incidents connected with the opening of the grand dispensation of the last days." The other problem, that Pratt had not sought church sanction before publishing the book, loomed large in Young's mind. "[T]he brethren would have made it a matter of [Pratt's] fellowship," he later alleged, but he "did not have it in [my] heart to disfellowship but merely to correct men in their views."[13]

Throughout the intervening months, the discourses, both private and public, of Pratt and Young revealed that neither man had

---

12. Brigham Young to Franklin D. Richards, 31 Jan. 1854, in *Latter-day Saints' Millennial Star,* 12 May 1855, 297-98.

13. Qtd. in the President's Office Journal, 31 Jan. 1860, LDS church archives.

substantially altered his views. In mid–February 1855, Pratt broached for the first time from the pulpit his own ideas on divine particles and the attributes of godliness, a discussion he would develop further the following year in his expanded pamphlet on *The Holy Spirit*. "Those who have the most of the parts of God are the greatest, or next to God," he conjectured:

> and those who have the next greatest portions of the parts of God, are the next greatest, or nearest to the fulness of God; and so we might go on to trace the scale of intelligences from the highest to the lowest, tracing parts and portions of God so far as we are made acquainted with them. Hence we see that wherever a great amount of this intelligent Spirit exists, there is a great amount or proportion of God, which may grow and increase until there is a fulness of this Spirit, and then there is a fulness of God. ...

"This explains the mystery," he continued.

> If we should take a million of worlds like this and number their particles, we should find that there are more Gods than there are particles of matter in those worlds. But the attributes of Deity are one; and they constitute the one God that the Prophets speak of, and that the children of men in all worlds worship.
>
> One world has a personal God or Father, and the inhabitants thereof worship the at[t]ributes of that God, another world has another, and they worship His attributes, and besides Him there is no other; and when they worship Him they are at the same time worshipping the same attributes that dwell in all the personal Gods who fill immensity.

For Pratt, the logical conclusion of such reasoning was obvious. "We would just as soon worship that Holy Spirit or intelligence in Joseph Smith or in any person else, not the person, but the God that is in him, as to worship the same attributes somewhere else. And when we find the Father of Jesus Christ, we will worship Him, not the flesh and bones, but the attributes."[14]

---

14. *Journal of Discourses*, 2:342–43, 345, 346.

In Sunday morning services at the Tabernacle the next month, Pratt continued this line of thinking by commenting on the Mormon concept of opposition in all things with particular reference to Adam and Eve. He announced that "the plurality of Gods as written by [me] in the 'Seer' [was] for the benefit of the Elders who might be abroad at any [time] preaching to the world." During the afternoon session, Brigham, who had attended the morning service, arose and "spoke to the Meeting in a very interesting manner referring to several points touched upon in the morning by Bro. Pratt. [He] did not seem fully to fancy Orson's idea bout the 'Great Almighty God' referring so especially to his attributes" instead of to God himself.[15]

Six weeks later senior apostle Orson Hyde more pointedly attacked Pratt's views on divine omniscience and reliance on the scriptures for doctrinal authority, as recorded by Samuel W. Richards:

> He [Hyde] elucidated very clearly the fallacy of the doctrine advocated by some [Pratt], that we would obtain a fullness or in other words come to an end in Knowledge, and also the danger there was in clinging with too great tenacity to the early revelations given to the Church, even to the excluding or rejecting of any views that might seem in the least degree to conflict with them. If God should communicate to the poor degraded Lamanite [Native American, h]e would condescend to their capacity[. T]hey were not capable of receiving the same intelligence as we[,] before they have been properly instructed and prepared.

"His [Hyde's] discourse," Richards concluded, "appeared to be a studied one, and designed to refute certain principles put forth and believed in by Bro. O. Pratt. Prest. B. Young followed, ... [and] spoke upon the plan of creating and peopling Worlds as Adam our Father did this."[16]

---

15. Samuel W. Richards, Journal, 25 Mar. 1855, typescript, BYU Library.

16. Ibid., 2 May 1855. Hyde's comments may have been prompted by Pratt's criticisms three days earlier of Hyde's views on the baby resurrection. See ibid., 29 Apr. 1855.

Before week's end, during a prayer meeting of other general authorities, Young decided to outline once again his supra-scriptural belief:

> Adam & Eve had lived upon another Earth. Were immortal when they came here. Adam assisted in forming this Earth & agreed to fall when He came Here & He fell that man might be[.] & the opposite principle to good[,] the devel, the serpent, the Evil[,] was plased upon the Earth that man might know the good from the Evil[,] for without an Experience in these things[,] man Could not know the one from the other.
>
> As soon as the devil was on Earth He sowed the seeds of Death in evry thing. So as soon as they began to eat of the fruit of the Earth[,] they received into their system the seeds of mortality & of Death. So their children wer mortal & subject to death[,] sorrow[,] pain[,] & wo[e]. Then when they partook of life, Joy, ease, & Happiness[,] they would know how to prize it.
>
> Father Adam would never scease his labours to redeem his posterity & exhalt them to all the glory they were Capable of receiving. He [Young] did not doubt but that Father Adam knew in the beginning how many of his posterity would receive a Celestial glory & who they were & also a Terrestrial & a Telestial. Yet man had his agency to act[,] chuse[,] & refuse good or evil as seemed him good & he would be rewarded according to his works.

"Will Adam or any God continue to make worlds[,] people them[, and] taste of Death to redeem them?" Pratt asked as soon as Young had finished. Young answered, "I have no doubt but it is his privilege, but whether He will do it is a question in my mind." "How then can his seed increase to all Eternity?" Pratt pressed. "Through the increase of his posterity," Young replied.[17] To Pratt's mind, this confirmed that beings progress to a certain point, after which their offspring may progress but they do not. He sensed Young's contradiction of man's physical creation from the dust of

---

17. Qtd. in Kenney, *Wilford Woodruff's Journal*, 4:317.

the earth, man's subordinate position to deity, and the acquisition of all knowledge by those who attain ultimate exaltation. Ironically, the president's repeated espousal of Adam-God was prompted in large measure by Pratt's continued opposition to it.

Before the end of the year, Pratt took his eighth plural wife, Juliaet Ann Phelps, in Fillmore, Utah. Some nine months later, on 17 February 1856, during an evening meeting of the Quorum of the Twelve, Young turned to Pratt and asked if he believed that "intelligent beings would continue to learn to all Eternity." (Earlier that day, Young had told Mormon faithful: "We shall never cease to learn, unless we apostatize from the religion of Jesus Christ. Then we shall cease to increase, and will continue to decrease and decompose, until we return to our native element.")[18] With customary frankness, the fearless apostle responded that "[h]e believed the Gods had a knowledge at the present time of evry thing that ever did exhist to the endless ages of all Eternity. He believed it as much as any truth that he had ever learned in or out of this Church." Annoyed, Young retorted that "he had never learned that principle in the church[,] for it was not taught in the Church[,] for it was not true. It was fals doctrin[e.] For the God[s] & all intelligent Beings would never scease to learn except it was the Sons of perdition[;] they would continue to decrease untill they became dissolved back into their native Element & lost their Identity."[19]

The two men locked horns again three weeks later during a heated meeting of the Board of Regents of the University of Deseret. One observer recorded:

> A very serious conversation took place between Pres[iden]t B. Young and Orson Pratt upon doctrine. O. P. was directly opposed to the Pres[iden]t['s] views and freely expressed his entire disbelief in them after being told by the President that things were so and so *in the name of the Lord.* He [Pratt] was firm in the Position that the Pres[iden]t's

18. *Journal of Discourses,* 3:203.
19. Qtd. in Kenney, *Wilford Woodruff's Journal,* 4:401–402.

word in the name of the Lord, was not the word of the Lord to him. The Pres[iden]t did not believe that Orson would ever be *Adam*, to learn by experience the facts discussed, but every other person in the room would if they lived faithful.[20]

Apostle Woodruff was present during the altercation and added disapprovingly: "Elder Orson Pratt pursued a Course of Stubborness & unbelief in what President Young said that will destroy him if he does not repent & turn away from his evil way. For when any man crosses the track of a leader in Israel & tryes to lead the prophet[,] he is no longer lead by him but is in danger of falling."[21]

Young still recognized and continued to value Pratt's leadership abroad. It is doubtful that Pratt's numerous missionary assignments were motivated solely, or even primarily, by an unwillingness to tolerate him at home. Though the president no doubt appreciated that he did not have to personally manage the outspoken apostle, he probably would not have entrusted new converts to Pratt if he had doubted his ability to supervise them. As Young himself explained, "[I] did not ever remember having sent a man on a mission to punish him, but to do them good, and give them a chance to get the spirit of God."[22]

In late April 1856, Pratt again left for England, where he had several times earlier assisted in founding and organizing the church's European mission. A week prior to departure, he seemed willing to concede that, before succumbing to temptation in the Garden of Eden, Adam and Eve had possessed immortal bodies of flesh and

---

20. Samuel W. Richards, Journal, 11 Mar. 1856. The clash made a considerable impact on some regents. Discussion of the episode continued the next day. See ibid., 12 Mar. 1856.

21. Kenney, *Wilford Woodruff's Journal*, 4:407.

22. Qtd. in Minutes of the Salt Lake City School of the Prophets, 9 July 1870, LDS church archives. Ten years earlier, however, the president had quipped: "We have at times sent men on missions to get rid of them; but they have generally come back. Some think it is an imposition upon the world to send such men among them. But which is best—to keep them here to pollute others, or to send them where pollution is more prevalent?" (*Journal of Discourses*, 7:228-29).

bone. But he insisted that they would have been nonetheless ignorant of good and evil. While he felt that the Saints had become careless about studying the scriptures, he asked that they "pray for me that I may accomplish the mission that has been given to me ... acceptably to these my brethren that are presiding over me."[23] The following Sunday, Brigham Young explained that only the president of the church, or those acting with his permission, was authorized to teach the Saints: "Therefore when you hear Elders, High Priests, Seventies, or the Twelve ... say that God does not reveal through the President of the Church that which they know, and tell wonderful things, you may generally set it down as a God's truth that the revelation they have had, is from the devil, and not from God." He asserted that the scriptures erred in recounting the story of Adam and Eve—that, in fact, both had been married before coming to the garden and neither had been made from the dust of this earth "but were made as you and I are made, and no person was ever made upon any other principle."[24] That evening Pratt met with Young and other officials. Not surprisingly, the conversation turned to Pratt's and Young's discourses. Elder George A. Smith "spoke in plainness his feelings concerning some of the principles of Elder O Pratts wherein he differed from President Young concerning the creation of Adam out of the dust of the Earth & the final consumation of knowledge & many other things." Wilford Woodruff voiced his fear that "when [Pratt] comes to write[,] he will publish in opposition to President Youngs views." Pratt "promises he would not," Woodruff recorded.[25] (Everyone in attendance knew that earlier in the month, on 9 April, the *Deseret News* had published the portion of Joseph Smith's history dealing with Pratt's 1843 reinstatement, including reference to his having

---

23. See *Journal of Discourses*, 3:344-54.
24. See ibid., 316-27.
25. Qtd. in Kenney, *Wilford Woodruff's Journal*, 4:412-13.

been "cut off from the Quorum of the Twelve for neglect of duty.")

Pratt arrived in Liverpool in mid-June to begin his tenure as mission president.[26] American novelist and U.S. consul Nathaniel Hawthorne, residing in Liverpool, found the Mormon elder to be "a short, blackhaired, dark-complexioned man; a shrewd, intelligent, but unrefined countenance, expressively unprepossessing; and uncouth gait and deportment; the aspect of a person in uncomfortable circumstances, and decently behaved, but of a vulgar nature and destitute of early culture." "I think," Hawthorne carped, "I should have taken him for a shoemaker, accustomed to reflect in a rude, strong, evil-disposed way on matters of this world and the next ..."[27] At about the same time he met with the dour Hawthorne, Pratt became inflamed by the fires of the then-in-progress Mormon Reformation that had spread to England.[28] He published a small pamphlet on *The Holy Spirit*, rewritten in part from works he had first issued in 1850 and 1852.[29]

Despite reassurances to Young that he would avoid such topics, Pratt again outlined his concept of God and his divine attributes, appending an additional commentary on the nature of the Holy Spirit. In what would be the fullest expression yet of his controversial beliefs, Pratt conceived of this spirit "as a boundless ocean," possessing "in every part, however minute, a will, a self-moving power, knowledge, wisdom, love, goodness, holiness, justice, mercy, and every intellectual and moral attribute possessed by the Father and the

---

26. James Amasa Little, Journal, 14 June 1856, microfilm of typescript, BYU Library. Little served as second counselor to Pratt.

27. Qtd. in Richard Cracroft, "Liverpool, 1856: Nathaniel Hawthorne Meets Orson Pratt," *BYU Studies* 8 (Spring 1968): 271.

28. For references to the Mormon Reformation in England during Pratt's presidency, see James Amasa Little, Journal, 9 Oct. 1856, 4-5 Feb. 1857.

29. See the *Millennial Star,* 15 Oct. 1850, 305-309; 1 Nov. 1850, 325-28. Sales of Pratt's pamphlets were far from brisk, and he soon curtailed his publishing plans until the market improved. See Little, Journal, 8 Jan. 1857.

Son."[30] Through this omnipresent spirit, a fullness of godly attributes could be obtained. Pratt saw the spiritual tabernacles of the Father, Son, and Holy Ghost as the result of the varied combinations and unions of the particles of this indescribable spirit matter. Where Brigham Young envisioned the underlying principle of the cosmos to be priesthood power, Pratt saw it as being eternal intelligence. But even more distasteful to Young was the implicit possibility in Pratt's theory that the Holy Spirit existed for and enlightened to some extent Mormonism's lost souls, the Sons of Perdition, who had been condemned to suffer eternal death and ultimately dissolution into Outer Darkness. "The Holy Spirit[,] being omnipresent[,] is in every place at the same moment of time," Pratt noted the previous year. "If you go to the depths of hell, it is there, not suffering, but performing the works of His justice upon the ungodly. Go where you will, through endless space, and you will find the Spirit there, and consequently, when we speak of the omnipresence of God, we have reference to His Spirit, and not to His person."[31]

When Pratt's pamphlet reached Utah, Young's reaction was swift and unequivocal. His counselor Jedediah Grant condemned these theories as "lariatting" (lassoing) the gods—"My God is not lariatted out," he announced from the Tabernacle in late October 1856.[32] Young followed two months later in a private meeting in his office on 29 December. Apostle Woodruff reported that the president said, after criticizing others of the general authorities, "if he [Pratt] did not take a different course in his Phylosophy & order of reasening[,] he would not stay long in this Church."[33]

30. Pratt, *Series of Pamphlets,* 53.

31. *Journal of Discourses,* 2:344; see also 339. On Young's views, see Boyd Kirkland, "Eternal Progression and the Second Death in the Theology of Brigham Young," in Bergera, *Line upon Line,* 171-81.

32. Journal History of the Church, 26 Oct. 1856.

33. Qtd. in Kenney, *Wilford Woodruff's Journal,* 4:523.

Two months later, on 8 March 1857, the president openly de-
cried "our brother philosopher Orson Pratt" in a lengthy and
pointed public rebuttal:

> The Lord's giving does not diminish His foundation of spirit that
> our philosopher brother Orson Pratt speaks of, that he believes occu-
> pies universal space, or, in other words, that universal space is filled
> with, and [he further says] that every particle of it is a Holy Spirit, and
> that that spirit is all powerful and all wise, full of intelligence and pos-
> sessing all the attributes of all the Gods in eternity. I hardly dare say
> what I think and what I know, but that theory, though apparently very
> plausible and beautiful, is not true, for it is, or would be contradicted
> by the Prophets, by Jesus and the Apostles, and by all good men who
> understand the principles of eternity, both those who have lived and
> are now living on the earth. Brother [Orson] Hyde[34] was upon this
> same theory once, and in conversation with Joseph Smith advanced
> the idea that eternity or boundless space was filled with the Spirit of
> God, or the Holy Ghost. After portraying his views upon that theory
> very carefully and minutely, he asked brother Joseph what he thought
> of it? He [Joseph] replied that it appeared very beautiful, and that he

---

34. Three weeks earlier Young had condemned Hyde's other speculations, including the so-called "baby resurrection" and the "resurrection of other materials
than those composing the elements of this body, which will be raised also, [and]
Fatalism, that if a man is a drunkard, or a thief, liar, &c he will remain so." He
branded such views "erroneous" and "foolishness" (qtd. in the President's Office
Journal, 18 Feb. 1857, LDS church archives). Six days later, Young again dismissed
Hyde's views, showing

> him the danger of holding these ideas even if he do[es] not teach them. Would
> like them [Hyde] to preach these doctrines before a conference of Elders, and
> let him [Young] reply and correct them. Then showed in much plainness the
> doctrine of the ressurection of the elements of this body to unite with the
> spirit, that has honored and exalted it, as every element pertaining to the earth,
> however diffused in gass [sic], smoke[,] vapor &c[,] belongs to this earth & not
> to the moon [and] sun &c and will forever remain associated with this planet.
> So with the elements of a human body [that] are associated with the spirit, and
> ever will belong to one another (ibid., 24 Feb. 1857).

did not know of but one serious objection to it. Says brother Hyde, "What is that?" Joseph replied, "[I]t is not true."

"With all the knowledge and wisdom that are combined in the person of brother Orson Pratt," Young stressed,

> still he does not yet know enough to keep his foot out of it, but drowns himself in his own philosophy, every time he undertakes to treat upon principles that he does not understand. When he was about to leave here for his present mission, he made a solemn promise that he would not meddle with principles which he did not fully understand, but would confine himself to the first principles of the doctrine of salvation, such as were preached by brother Joseph Smith and the Apostles. But the first that we see in his writings, he is dabbling with things that he does not understand; his vain philosophy is no criterion or guide for the Saints in doctrine. According to his philosophy, the devils in hell are composed of and filled with the Holy Spirit, or Holy Ghost, and possess all the knowledge, wisdom, and power of the Gods. If he believes his own doctrine pertaining to the celestial and other kingdoms, viz., that the devils in hell possess the same power as the Gods, they being opposed to Jesus and his Father, the whole fabric must fall. When I read some of the writings of such philosophers, they make me think, "O dear, granny, what a long tail our puss has got!"[35]

As he met that evening for prayer, Young requested that Pratt's *Holy Spirit* be read aloud. According to Wilford Woodruff, President Young then "made the following remarks ... He said that Brother Pratt had got beyond the Stars. He had Carrelled [corralled] them & got beyond them."[36] Young's private remark was less biting than his dramatic public pronouncement which left no

---

35. *Journal of Discourses,* 4:266-67.

36. Kenney, *Wilford Woodruff's Journal,* 5:30. Before the close of that year, Young would be promised in a patriarchal blessing: "Your mind shall expand, the visions of the heavens shall be opened before you that you may comprehend the fulness of the truths of heaven" (John Young, Patriarchal Blessing to Brigham Young, 25 Dec. 1857, Young Papers).

doubt in anyone's mind that Pratt's teachings were dangerous and not to be relied on as statements of church doctrine. "Many" of his doctrinal claims "are incorrect," Young would publicly reiterate four months later.[37]

Pratt felt that these stinging denunciations were unjust and too vague, condemning virtually all of his writings. Most humiliating, however, was the *Deseret News*'s publication on 17 March 1858, two months after his arrival home, of Brigham Young's serialized auto-biography for August 1842 and January 1843 which once again dredged before the public the painful details of Pratt's "excommunication" and reinstatement.[38] In fact, one week later to the day, an obviously agitated Pratt brought complaint against Young before the First Presidency and Quorum of the Twelve, no doubt hoping that a majority of his colleagues would side with him in his theological pronouncements. Apostle Woodruff, who presented Pratt's concerns, explained that Pratt "did not believe in some of the teachings of President Young and thought President Young had reproved him unjustly. The subject was discussed at length by the Twelve and President Young. Much instruction was given. At the Close[,] Orson Pratt Confessed his faults and said that He would never teach those principles again or speak them to any person on the Earth. We all forgave him and voted to receive him into full fellowship."[39] What had begun as an official inquest initiated by Pratt resulted in near disfellowshipment for his unbridled, outspoken, and sometimes intemperate style.

For nearly two years thereafter, Pratt's public discourses were

---

37. Everett L. Cooley, ed., *Diary of Brigham Young* (Salt Lake City: University of Utah Library/Tanner Trust Fund, 1980), 8 July 1857.

38. The *Deseret News* was also serializing the "History of Joseph Smith." Less than four months later on 3 July 1858, it published the portion dealing with Pratt's 1843 reinstatement. For Pratt, the past was inescapable. One can barely imagine the LDS church today printing such material on the life of one of its sitting apostles.

39. Kenney, *Wilford Woodruff's Journal*, 5:179.

relatively free of doctrinal and philosophical speculations, though he and Young continued to disagree privately on other issues. For example, in February 1859, Young told the staff of the Historian's Office

> to take up that work [Pratt's edition of Lucy Mack Smith's history] & revise it & Correct it[,] that it belonged to the Historians to attend to it[,] that there was many fals statements made in it[,] and he wished them to be left out and all other statements which we did not know to be true, and give the reason why they are left out. ... That Book makes out William Smith [Joseph's younger brother,] according to Mother Smith's statement[,] to be full of the Holy Ghost & the power of God while at the same time I herd him say [traitorous things] in the presence of Heber C. Kimball while Joseph Smith was a prisoner in the hands of his enemies and I said that God would deliver him. William Smith said Dam him[,] Joseph Smith ought to have been hung up by the neck years ago and Dam him[,] he will get it now any how.[40]

Later that August the president and others reviewed a sermon Pratt had recently delivered on "Theocracy."[41] Given the practice of polygamy, Young may have worried that Pratt emphasized obedience to civil law: "Do we hold ourselves subject to the civil laws? Yes," Pratt had said. "God, notwithstanding he has given us Church laws, has not freed us from the authority of the civil law. We are subject to the ... laws of the United States as much as any Territory of the nation."[42] Yet Pratt wondered two months later if, in calling men to the apostleship, preference should be given to those who, like himself, "have been tried and proven in many responsible positions." In a slightly veiled reference to Pratt, Young answered coolly: "If a man was suggested to me of good natural judgment, possessing no higher qualifications than faithfulness and humility enough to seek to the Lord for all his knowledge and who would trust in him for

---

40. Qtd. in ibid., 287.
41. Historian's Office Journal, 21 Aug. 1859.
42. *Journal of Discourses*, 7:224.

his strength[,] I would prefer him in preference to the learned and talented."[43]

On a cold, foggy December Sunday less than eight weeks later, Pratt again broached his notion of God's attributes to members gathered in the Tabernacle for weekly religious services. According to Elder Woodruff, Pratt explained that "it was the atributes of God that He worshiped and not the person & that He worshiped those Atributes whether he found them in God, Jesus Christ, Adam, Moses, The Apostles[,] Joseph, Brigham, or in anybody Els[e]."[44] The published summary of Pratt's lengthy sermon[45] reported that he "preached on the necessity of the people understanding the character of the Being they worship." He "reasoned on the attributes of God and directed the attention of the congregation to Jesus Christ as an example for his people." He showed "that Jesus was made an example of humility, being born in a manger, cradled in poverty, and raised by parents of low degree; that in his birth he descended below all things, but in progress of time he advanced in knowledge, grew from grace to grace and from strength to strength, even till he exceeded Enoch in information and knowledge pertaining [to] eternal life." Pratt then "argued that we are in possession of the same powers of progress, but that these lie dormant, that they require to be exercised by the power and inspiration of the Holy Ghost." Finally, he "exhorted the Saints to be diligent in the discharge of all their duties, until, like Jesus, they attain to a fullness of the knowledge of God, and become able to see him face to face."[46]

---

43. Historian's Office Journal, 23 Oct. 1859. Orson may have been thinking of Parley P. Pratt Jr., who he hoped would fill the vacancy in the Twelve created by the murder of his father, Parley Sr., two years earlier. Young disagreed and eventually appointed George Q. Cannon to the position.

44. Qtd. in Kenney, *Wilford Woodruff's Journal*, 5:420.

45. Usually two speakers addressed the Saints on Sunday mornings in the Tabernacle, but according to the Journal History of the Church, 11 Dec. 1859, Pratt was the sole orator that day.

46. Journal History of the Church, 11 Dec. 1859, citing the *Deseret News*. I have searched available materials in the LDS church archives without finding the

He had previously discussed his views on the attributes of godliness, but he had never before applied them so unmistakably to the progression of Jesus from man to God. Inherent was the conclusion that it was not Jesus' divine birth that allowed him to attain godhood but rather because he had passed through a series of progressions, advancing in knowledge, until he achieved a fullness of perfection. Why Pratt publicly espoused a topic he knew would invite official reprimand may never be fully known. His sermon lessened the divinity of the Son and, by extension, the Father, and his idea that it is not God but his attributes that should be worshipped had been specifically refuted by Young. Perhaps Pratt felt justified, given the fact of Young's speculations about Adam. Maybe he deliberately attempted to initiate another last-ditch detailed discussion of his views. If so, his calculations proved successful, for they precipitated two specific, official, written statements of condemnation as well as his own repeated brush with excommunication.

complete text of Pratt's sermon. It may have echoed his published discourse of 18 February 1855 (see *Journal of Discourses,* 2:336-47).

SIX.

False Doctrine

*A*lmost immediately, Orson Pratt's December 1859 sermon infuriated church officials, who wanted to meet as a group to discuss the apostle's continued recalcitrance.[1] Pratt agreed to clear the air between Brigham Young and himself, and within less than two months, on Friday, 27 January 1860, Young called to order a high-level meeting in his office beginning at 6:00 p.m. The group included members of the First Presidency, Quorum of the Twelve, presidents of the Seventy, the presiding bishop, church secretaries, and lesser authorities—possibly as many as twenty-five men in all.

Following the opening hymn, "O Happy Souls Who Pray," and a prayer by Quorum of the Twelve president Orson Hyde, Young announced: "The object of the Meeting [is] to Convers[e] upon Doctrinal Points to see if we see alike & think alike. I Pray that we may have the spirit of God to rest upon us that our minds may be upon the subject & that we may speak by the Holy spirit."[2]

---

1. See President's Office Journal, 25 Jan. 1860.

2. All quotations, direct or paraphrased, are from "Minutes of a Meeting of the Presidency[,] Twelve[,] Presidents of Seventies[,] and Others assembled in

Young asked one of his secretaries, future apostle Albert Carrington, to read a copy of Pratt's discourse on the attributes of God that had been prepared for the church's *Deseret News* but had not yet been published.[3] Of those present, only Carrington, Pratt, and Young knew the author's identity, but the contents pointed unmistakably to Pratt.

Following the reading, senior elders Hyde and Taylor were called upon to respond. John Taylor confessed that he did not see things "in that light. He worshiped a personage and not the Atributes. He thought God was Located and [he] Could not worship the Atributes in any body."

After Hyde and Taylor, Young asked those who supported the speech's views to manifest it by saying "Yes." The room was silent. Young then announced: "Do I worship Atributes or the Dispencer of those atributes? I worship the Dispencer of those atributes and Not the Atributes."

"This is O Pratts Sermon prepared for the Press," he explained, then added:

President Youngs Council Room at 6 oclok," in Kenney, *Wilford Woodruff's Journal,* 5:420-30. Woodruff copied this entry from the original minutes of the meeting kept by George D. Watt (President's Office Journal, 27 Jan. 1860). It is not clear why Woodruff would transcribe such lengthy minutes into his journal, but the impact of the meeting is apparent. For the usually concise Woodruff, the extent of this entry is impressive: it covers some ten pages, easily one of the longest entries in his journals.

Of the evening's proceedings, Young's secretary summarized: "A council of the twelve was held to consider the doctrines that Orson Pratt had advanced in his last Sermon about worshipping attributes. The President and the twelve came to the conclusion that Orson Pratt was wrong on that point" (ibid.). The Journal History of the Church records simply: "At 6 p.m. the Presidency, the Twelve[,] and the presidents of the Seventies met in Council at President Young's office, where a sermon by Orson Pratt was read and rejected as false doctrine. Elder Pratt advocates the doctrine of worshipping an attribute instead of a God, the author and dispensor of those attributes. The night was spent in speaking on a [few] Doctrinal points until 12 o'clock."

3. Young did not personally hear Pratt deliver the sermon but had it read to him three days earlier. See President's Office Journal, 24 Jan. 1860.

I do not want to have it published if it is not right. Brother Orson Worships the Atributes of God but not God. I worship not the Atributes but that God who holds and dispenses [them]. If Eternity was full of atributes and No one to dispens them[,] they would not be worth a feather.

Suppose an Angel comes to us to Night with a message From God and he [God] tels the angel not to make himself known.[4] He Comes to us with a message and gives a New Law and a penalty for not obeying. You may ask[,] who are you? He may not tell you who he is[,] or he may say God sent me. You May say[,] whare is that God who sent you [or] I dont know or Care any thing about you or what you say. He might say to you[,] I am a god to you. Moses Said to Is-rael[,] I am a God to you. Joseph [Smith] said to us[,] I am a God to you. This was true[,] and upon the same principles I am a God to this people & so is any man who is appointed to lead Israel or the King-dom of God. If the people reject him[,] they reject the one who sent him. But we will let that drop, and turn to the other subject now.

"The other subject" he referred to was that of God's attributes. "Now suppose," he postulated,

we were all to receive a fullness of the Atributes of God and[,] accord-ing to Orson Pratts Theory[,] The Lord had a fulness and He Could Not advance[,] but we Could advance till we were Equal to him. Than if we worshiped the Atributes instead of God we would soon worship ourselves as soon as we had a fulness of those atributes. Then you Cannot worship any thing beyound yourself. You would then worship the atributes & not the dispenser of those atributes. This is fals doctrin.[5]

God did not say worship Moses because he was a God to the people. You may say to your wife or son do so & so. They will say[,] I will not[,] but I will go to a greater man. I will go to Brigham Young.

---

4. I have silently changed "Angels" to "angel" in this sentence. The original reads: "Suppose an Angels comes to us to Night with a message From God and he tels the angels not to make himself known."

5. Either Watt or Woodruff put quotation marks around the sentence "This is fals doctrin." I have silently deleted them.

You might say[,] I am your Counciller[,] Dictator[,] or your God. Either would be Correct. And they should obey your Just & righteous Command. Yet they should not worship you[,] for this would be sin.

"Orson Pratt has differed from me in many things," Young said, wondering out loud what should be done about Pratt's contrariness.

But this is a great principle & I do not wish to say [to Elder Pratt,] you shall do so and so. I do not know of a man who has a mathamatical turn of mind but what [he] goes to[o] Far. The trouble between Orson Pratt & me is I do not know Enough & he knows to[o] much. I do not know evry thing. Their is a mystery Concerning the God I worship[,] which mystery will be removed when I Come to a full knowledge of God.

One of the greatest things Joseph Smith ever did was to Familiarize Heaven & Earth and Cause them to shake hand[s] together and become Familiar Together. This was a great principle. It is simpl[e] yet true.[6] When I me[e]t the God I worship I expect to [meet a] personage with whom I have been acquainted upon the same principle that I would [if I were] to meet my Earthly Father after going upon a Journey & returning home.

Several apostles voiced their support of Young's remarks. Woodruff, in comments seconded by others, remarked:

It is our privelege so to live as to have the spirit of God to bear record of the Truth of any revelation that Comes from God through the mouth of his Prophet who leads his people and it has ever been a key with me that when The Prophet who leads presents a doctrin or principle or says thus saith the Lord[,] I make it a point to receive it even if it Comes in Contack with my tradition or views[,] being well satisfied that the Lord would reveal the truth unto his Prophet whom he has Called to lead his Church before he would unto me. And the word of the Lord through the prophet is the End of the Law unto me.

---

6. The original reads, "It is simply yet true."

As he finished, Woodruff recorded in his journal, Brigham's brother Joseph Young, who was one of the seven presidents of the Seventy, and Orson Hyde "both backed me up." Joseph Young said:

I do not believe in the doctrin o[f] worshiping the attributes and not the auther. I once loved a woman. She says to me[,] you shall have my respect & kind regards & she told me to go in peace. I told her it was not her good will that I wanted alone. I wanted her. So with my God. If he was to say to me[,] Joseph[,] here[,] take my attributes & go[,] I would say[,] No[,] father[,] it is not your attributes alone that I want[,] but I want you. When I read O Pratts views in the Seer I Could not swallow it. Joseph the Prophet said when you see your Father you will see him Just as he was in this life ownly he will be full of Strength Glory Immortality & Eternal Life.

Brigham turned to the group: "Now here is the Twelve," he motioned. Pratt was not the only apostle he had concerns about.

I wish to extend there Influence as Far as I Can but I Cannot do it while they teach Fals doctrine. One of the Causes of the declaration in England (as I understand the [number of] people [converting] are Clear down) is what Orson Pratt Preached in the Seer.[7] There is not a man in the Church that can preach better than Orson Pratt upon any subject which he understands. It is music to hear him. But the trouble

---

7. Young seems to blame Pratt, in part, for the church's recent poor showing in England. From 1850 to 1860, LDS membership in England decreased over 120 percent and would fall another 57 percent by 1870. Convert baptisms dropped more than 315 percent from 1850 to 1860 and another 143 percent by 1870. At the same time, excommunications jumped nearly 1,000 percent from 1849 to 1855. See V. Ben Bloxham, James R. Moss, and Larry C. Porter, eds., *Truth Will Prevail: The Rise of the Church of Jesus Christ of Latter-day Saints in the British Isles, 1837-1987* (Solihull, Eng.: Church of Jesus Christ of Latter-day Saints, 1987), 442; Richard L. Evans, *A Century of "Mormonism" in Great Britain* (Salt Lake City: Publishers Press, 1984 [1st ed., 1937]), 244; and William G. Hartley, "LDS Pastors and Pastorates, 1852-55," in *Mormonism in Early Victorian Britain,* ed. Richard L. Jensen and Malcolm R. Thorp (Salt Lake City: University of Utah Press, 1989), 210. A more reasonable explanation would be the church's public announcement of plural marriage in 1852.

is he will preach upon things he does not know any thing about and then he will preach fals doctrine & so will Elder Hyde. He preaches upon the resurrection & teaches things which are not true.

"I will tell you the God which you and I worship," he continued,

it is a Being that was on an Earth like this. He has been Cloathed in Mortality the same as we have been and he has had Devils to fight the same as we have had but I do not expect they were the same Devils that we have. That God says I am your God and there is none Els. Let us worship him and none Els. He is the God that we have. No matter what Gods Enoch saw when the heavens were opened unto him[, even] if the God he saw had been exalted millions of years before our God was. He also had to occupy an Earth like ourselves and we shall find it out at some period and this is all the mystery there is about it & if we are faithful we in our turn shall be Exalted and become Gods and there will be no mystery about it when we understand it.

As Young caught his breath, Orson Hyde quickly apologized for having taught any unauthorized doctrine. The suddenness of the criticism was not uncharacteristic, but Young's shift to Hyde had caught the quorum president off guard. "I am satisfied that I have used a good deal of Philosiphy which is not true," Hyde explained, "but that is all done away with, and I did not think I should meet with the Prejudices of Potawatamie[8] to night."

"If you bring Potawatamie with you," Young countered, "you [mus]t expect to meet it."

Hyde countered that he had not recently preached on the subject "as Brother Joseph Young reported he did. Brother Joseph was

---

8. Through the late 1840s, Pottawattamie referred to Indian lands on either side of the Missouri River, including Winter Quarters (Omaha, Nebraska, environs) and Kanesville (Council Bluffs, Pottawattamie County, Iowa), and it was here that church leaders debated whether to reconstitute the First Presidency in November–December 1847. It is unclear if Hyde and Young had specific doctrines in mind or if they were alluding to more generalized disagreements.

not Present," Hyde complained, "and he has been misinformed Concerning it."

Offering to clarify the issue for those who might be unaware of the "baby resurrection" controversy, Apostle Ezra T. Benson noted that Hyde "compaired the resurrection to taking a Journey around the world. We travel all day[,] stop at a station at night[,] lie down and sleep at night[,] arise in the morning[,] & Continue our Journey through another day & so on. So at the End of this life we sleep in the grave till the morning of the resurrection. We then arise and Continue our Journey" at the physical state and development we have attained to that point.

For himself, Benson added, redirecting the discussion back to Orson Pratt:

> I do not preach things which I do not know. I keep in shallow water. I wish to teach the people those things which they Can understand, and those things we Cannot understand[,] I do not trouble myself about. I know it is my duty to sustain the preside[n]t of this Church. If I do not respect the Preside[nt] of this church and believe his word and I set my self up against him[,] I am under Condemnation. I would as [soon] Cut off my right Hand. If he speaks to us[,] we must believe him and obey him. I mean to do it.

"President Young has put words in my mouth so that I Can Convey what I want," Erastus Snow agreed. "We are apt to say many things which we do not mean & we injure ourselves. I Cannot see things in the same light that Orson Pratt does[,] but when President Young has taught doctrin[e,] it has always tasted good to me. I do not wish to know more than God wishes me to."

Throughout the lengthy meeting, Pratt had remained subdued. The solitude of his position was heavy because he felt that his convictions were well founded. Finally he expressed his desire to speak:

> I have not spoaken but once in the Tabernacle since Conference. I then spoke upon the revelations in the Doctrins & Covenants con-

cerning the Father & son & their atributes. I spoke upon those attributes of the Father & son. I gave my views upon the attributes of God. I sincerely believed what I preached. How long I have believed this doctrin I do not know but it has been for years. I have published it in the seer. I spoke of a plurality of Gods. In order to worship this God[,] I said that I adored the atributes wherever I found them. I was honest in this matter. I would not worship a god or Tabernacle that did not possess Attributes. If I did[,] I should worship Idols. I have taught this doctrin.

Now the reson I worship the Father is because in him is Combined the attributes. If he had not those attributes[,] I would not worship him any more than I would this Chair. I Cannot see any difference between myself and President Young. If you had told me what you worshiped him for[,] you would have told me sumthing[,] but now I Can see no difference between us. I wish to Explain how Jesus Said I am in the Father & the Father in me. Now I do not suppose that the Father is in the Son & the Son in the Father in the Tabernacle, but in the spirit and Attributes, truth light power &c. We are told that the son represents the Father in Attributes &c.

I Called upon the Brethren to Come to this meeting to settel this[.] But I must have sumthing more than a declaration of President Young to Convince me. I must have evidence. I am willing to take President Young as a guide in most things but not in *all*. President Young does not profess to have revelations in all things. I am not to[o] loose in my agency. I have said many things which President Young says is Fals. I do not know how it is. I count President Young Equal to Joseph [Smith] and Joseph Equal to President Young. I find things in Josephs Revelations that govern me. I would as like believe Joseph as Brigham[.] When Joseph teach[e]s one thing & Brigham seems to teach another Contrary to Joseph (I say seems to) I believe them as Joseph has spoken them and as the Apostle speaks of them.

I do not know God[,] ownly by his Atributes[,] and that God who has the most Atributes I worship. I worship but one God, and God does not dwell in me[,] ownly by his Atributes. I have spoken plainly. I would rather not have spoken so plainly but I have No excuses to make. President Young said I ought to make a Confession But Orson Pratt is not a man to make a Confession of what I do not

Believe. I am not going to Crawl to Brigham Young and act the Hypocrite and Confess what I do not Believe. I will be a free man. President Young Condemns my doctrin to be fals. I do not believe them to be fals. I believe President Young to be sincere in sayin that my dotrin is fals.

I did not Believe the doctrin fals which I published in the Seer in England. It has been said we should let those things sleep. But you do not let them sleep. If I had thought while in England that President Young worshiped a God without attributes[,] I would not have written what I did.[9] But I do not believe it yet[.] I will not act the Hypocrite. It may cost me my fellowship But I will stick to it[. I]f I die tonight[,] I would say[,] O Lord God Almighty[,] I believe what I say.

The brethren were surprised by this dramatic declaration, and John Taylor interceded "at some length and tr[ying] to Convince Orson Pratt of his error."

Following him, Brigham Young turned to Pratt. Visibly upset by what he felt was intentional misrepresentation of his views, Young began: "Orson Pratt has started out upon false premises to argue upon. His foundation has been a fals one all the time and I will prove it false. You have been like a mad stoubern Mule," he thundered,

and have taken a fals position in order to accuse me. You have accused me of worshiping a stalk or Stone or a dead Body without life or attributes. You never herd such a doctrin taught by me or any leader of the Church. It is false as Hell and you will not hear the last of it soon. You know it is false. Do we worship those attributes? No[,] we worship God because he has all those Attributes and is the dispenser of them and because he is our Father & our God. Orson Pratt puts down a lie to argue upon. He has had fals ground all the time to night. There never was a time or Eternity but what a God did exist, and a God that had Children upon the same principle that Children are

_____

9. Woodruff noted parenthetically in his journal, "The above remark was an unkind Cut in Orson Pratt[;] he should not have said [it]."

now begotton. And I was begotton by the God I worship who reigns in the heavens and I shall also in my turn reign as a God & so will you.

Orson Hyde turned to Pratt and said, "My opinion is not worth as much to me as my fellowship in this Church."

Brigham was not yet finished. According to his understanding of the development of God, he continued, "Michael was a resurrected Being and he left Eloheem and Came to this Earth & with an im[mor]tal Body & continued so till he partook of Earthly food and begat Children who were mortal (Keep this to yourselves). The[n] they died."

Pratt, said Young, insists on "laying down [a] fals principle to work upon. That principle if Carried out would place us in a position that when a man got a fulness of the Attributes of God[,] they would have to worship themselves. But if we worship God[,] we worship him because he possesses all the Attributes and dispenses them to the Children of men. All these Attributes are the servants of God. They serve his purposes and are at his Command."

Young's counselor in the First Presidency, Heber C. Kimball, was also furious at Pratt's rebellion. He announced: "Brother Orson Pratt has withstood Joseph [Smith] and he has withstood Brother Brigham many times and he has done it to night and it made my Blood Chill. It is not for you to lead [the prophet] but to be led by him. You have not the power to dictate but to be dictated [to]."

Elder Woodruff faced Pratt and said solemnly:

I wish to ask you one or two questions. You see that the spirit and doctrin which you possess is entirely in a[n] oposition to the First Presidency[,] The Quorum of the Twelve, and all who are present this evening and it Chills the Blood in our veins to hear your words & feel your spirit. Should not this be an Evidence to you that you are wrong? What would become of the Quorum of the Twelve if we all felt as you do? We should all go to Hell in a pile to gether.

"You say you are honest in the Course you are pursueing," he pressed. "I wish to ask you if you was honest when you said that if you had known that President Young worshiped a God without life or Attributes that you would not have written what you did."

Confronted with this sarcasm, Pratt answered, "I will recall that."

"It was an insult to President Young and the Holy Priesthood which he holds," Woodruff emphasized, continuing:

> Evry man in this room who has a particle of the spirit of God knows that President Young is a Prophet of God and that God sustains him and He has the Holy Spirit and his doctrins are true, and that he is qualifyed to lead the people[,] and he has explained evry thing so plain this evening that a Child Can understand it and yet it is no evidence to you. Nothing Can make an impression upon you. No argument can reach your understanding.

"Now Brother Orson," his voice lowering,

> I have seen the day when you was in sorrow. It was when you was Cast out of your Quorum and out of the Church and that to[o] in Consequences of pursueing the Same Course you are this evening.[10] Then you Could both see[,] feel[,] & understand. Then argument Could reach you when you saw your glory and Crown departing from you. I beg of you to reflect and not let your will Carry you to[o] Far in these things.
>
> It would be better for us not to be able to Cast up a single sum in adition [mathematics] and be humble before the Lord than to have ever so much knowledge & permit that knowledge to lead us to destruction. There are but few men upon Earth upon whom God has bestowed such gifts, qualifications and reasoning powers as he has upon you, and he will hold you responsible for the use you make of them, and you should not make a wreck of your salvation for Contending for things which you do not understand. And I do feel at this

---

10. Woodruff refers to Pratt's difficulties in 1842 when, from Woodruff's point of view, Pratt resisted counsel.

advanced state of the Church and late day and with the information which you possess that neither you nor your Brethren ought to be troubled with Fals doctrin. Neither should you Cause your Brethren to listen to such a scene of things as we have herd to night or to insult the preside[n]t of this church as you have done.

He concluded with a prediction: "Although you are unbending in your will to night, the day is not far distant when you will be glad to bend to the preside[n]t of this Church and make reconciliation."

Others—Erastus Snow, Orson Hyde, Charles C. Rich, and Ezra T. Benson—added their own words of rebuke, Benson suggesting that "if Brother Pratt had the Confidence in Preside[n]t Young which he ought to have[,] he would Feel diferent. If he had the Confidence in his Brethren which he should have[,] I know He would feel different." According to the minutes, Pratt offered no further argument in his defense.

Before the close of the six-hour meeting, Young candidly remarked:

> I will tell you how I got along with Joseph [Smith]. I found out that God called Joseph to be a Prophet. I did not do it. I then said I will leave the Prophet in the hands of that God who called and ordained him to be a Prophet. He is not responsible to me and it is none of my business what He does. It is for me to follow & obey him.
>
> I once was ashamed of one thing which I did while in Missouri in Zions Camp. I got a revelation [t]hat God excepted [accepted] our offering. I had the same thing revealed to me twice & that we should not go into Jackson Co[unty]. I named this to some of the Brethren a day or two before Joseph got a Revelation upon the same subject. I felt ashamed that I named it first. I knew whare we were going and I now know that when we go to Jackson County we shall go from the west. And I will now tell you all and you right [write] it down that all my preaching by the Holy Ghost is revelation.
>
> I told Brother Joseph he had given us revelation enough to last us 20 years. When that time is out[,] I can give as good [a] revelation as their is in the Doctrins & Covenants.

Elder Taylor said in one of his sermons that if we walk in the light of the Lord we should have revelations all the time. It is the light that is within you. No man Can live his religion without living in Revelation[,] but [when Joseph was alive,] I would never tell a revelation to the Church untill Joseph told it first.

Joseph Once told me to go to his own house to attend a meeting with him. He said that He would not go without me. I went and Hiram [Smith, Joseph's brother,] Preached upon the Bible[,] Book of Mormon[,] & Covenants and said we must take them as our guide alone. He preached vary lengthy untill he nearly wearied the people out. When he Closed[,] Joseph told me to get up. I did so. I took the Books and piled them all up on top of Each other. I then said that I would not give the ashes of a rye straw for all those books for my salvation without the living oracles. I should follow and obey the living oracles for my salvation instead of anything Els. When I got through[,] Hyrum got up and made a Confession for not including the living Oracles.

"It may be thought strange by the Brethren," Young closed, "that I will still fellowship Elder Pratt after what He has said[,] but I shall do it. I am determined to whip Brother Pratt into it and make him work in the harness."

"If I gratifyed my feelings," Pratt rather meekly confessed, "I [would] rather go into the Canyon than to Preach. I have got to go to Tooele to get wood for my family."

"I will give you a mission in Tooele to preach & send word to the Bishop to get some man & draw up his wood [for you]," Young replied. "Brother Pratt has no business in the Canyon [chopping wood]. The Lord does not want him there." At this, Elder Franklin D. Richards delivered the closing prayer.

Early the next day, a subdued Pratt—"devastated," according to his biographer[11]—called at the president's office. He admitted that "he was excited, and for the future would omit such points of doc-

---

11. England, *Life and Thought*, 211.

trine in his discourses that related to the Plurality of Gods, &c. but would confine himself to the first principles of the Gospel." He asked if Young could find a vacancy for his twenty-two-year-old son, Orson Jr., as a clerk. Young replied that he would attempt to appoint Pratt's namesake as a teacher, as the president "meant to promote education as much as possible."

Young again remarked that "much false doctrine arose out of arguing upon false premises, such as supposing something that does not exist, as a God without his attributes, as they cannot exist apart." Pratt replied, as he had on past occasions, that "many of his doctrinal arguments had been advanced while he was in England in answer to the numerous enquiries that were made of him by reasoning men." Young was not unsympathetic and added: "[W]hen questions have been put to me, by opposers, who did not want to hear the simple Gospel message[, I] would not answer them." He asked Pratt "why he was not as careful to observe the revelations given to preach in plainness and simplicity as to so strenuously observe the doctrines in other revelations."[12] Existing records give no mention of Pratt's response.

Later that day Pratt attended his usual Saturday prayer meeting with other members of his quorum. Apostle Woodruff reported that Pratt did not dress in his temple clothing as was customary, perhaps out of contrition, "but said he wanted to be in the Society of the Twelve. He seemed much more soft in his spirit tha[n] he had been."[13]

Though Pratt no doubt anticipated and maybe encouraged, if not actually initiated, the tense, emotionally draining Friday evening meeting, he must have found it deeply humiliating to have stood alone among his brethren against his president. Intelligent, courageous, stubborn, but very much alone, he only now began to realize the gravity of his situation. He was not only out of harmony with

---

12. Qtd. in President's Office Journal, 28 Jan. 1860.
13. Kenney, *Wilford Woodruff's Journal,* 5:430.

Brigham but also with his quorum and church. Woodruff's calculated reminders of his disastrous difficulties with Joseph Smith
nearly twenty years earlier in Nauvoo over polygamy must have re-
verberated painfully in the apostle's mind. Having publicly voiced
his disagreements with Young, he now wondered if the time had
come for an equally public apology.

SEVEN

"Let Br. Pratt Do as He Will"

As leaders and faithful members met in chilly Sunday morning services in the Tabernacle two days after Friday's emotional confrontation, only one man at the 11:00 a.m. session, other than Orson Pratt himself, had been alerted to the momentous discourse to be delivered from the podium. Sometime earlier Pratt had discussed with fellow apostle Ezra T. Benson, who would share the program with him, the propriety of publicly commenting on the events of Friday evening.

Wilford Woodruff was one of the many Saints in attendance and recorded his relief at Pratt's surprising remarks:

> Orson Pratt was in the stand and Quite unexpected to his Brethren he arose before his Brethren and made a vary humble full confession Before the whole assembly for his oposition to President Young and his Brethren and He said he wished all the Church was present to hear it. He quoted Joseph Smiths revelation to prove that President Brigham Young was right and that all was under obligation to follow the Leader of the Church. I never herd Orson Pratt speak better or

153

more to the satisfaction of the People than on this occasion. He would not partake of the sacrament untill he had made a Confession. Then he partook of it.[1]

Equally positive was rank-and-file Mormon Charles Walker who similarly wrote:

Bro O Pratt spoke a little on the text, Except ye are one ye are not mine. Showed where in he had not been one with Bro Brigham in some of his writings in the Seer, and when Bro Brigham told him it was incorrect, he still held on to his own views and opinion. Made a Public Conffession and acknowledged he was in the wrong in not yeelding to Bro Brigham sooner than He did. ... Was glad to hear Bro O Pratt. Felt to bless him. Showed that we need not fear that Bro Brigham was wrong. If there was anything wrong[,] it was in us and not in Him [Young].[2]

Only slightly less ebullient was Henry Hobbs's summary:

Brother Pratt confessed that he had written in the Seer that [which] was conterary to the feelings of the president & yet he believed that he was rite & Brigham wrong & that he had also taught Some things of a philosophical nature that was not true & set up his standard against Brigham[. He] would not yeald his Judgement to that of the prophet & because he did not[,] his mind became Darkened & at times he felt to mourn. ... But Says Br. Pratt[,] Now I see my error[.] I will Labour to Back up our Prophet & those who surround him & the Lord being My helper I will show by my actions that I will do what I say[,] though Says he[,] I may not be able to carry out my ententions.[3]

For the emotionally drained Pratt, the speech was probably the most important of his life; certainly it was among the most wrench-

---

1. Kenney, *Wilford Woodruff's Journal*, 5:430.
2. A. Karl Larson and Katharine Miles Larson, eds., *Diary of Charles Lowell Walker*, 2 vols. (Logan: Utah State University Press, 1980), 1:106.
3. Henry Hobbs, Journal, 29 Jan. 1860, LDS church archives.

ing. Unfortunately, it would also soon prove to be an additional thorn among the seemingly irreconcilable differences between the outspoken apostle and his demanding church president.

Because of what it reveals of Pratt's state of mind, the burden of his guilt, his confused sincerity, as well as his tortured position on prophetic authority, obedience, and individual integrity, the entire text of his 29 January 1860 "confessional sermon" follows. Spelling errors have been corrected, and sections that were placed out of sequence in the galley sheets prepared by the *Deseret News* for publication on 22 February have been restored to their proper order. Words and sentences that were omitted from the officially approved text, subsequently printed in the *Deseret News* on 25 July, are italicized; additions appear in italicized brackets.[4]

Upon first reaching the dais, Pratt said: "I will read a passage of scripture to be found in Isaiah, lii, chap., 8 verse—'Thy watchman shall lift up the voice; with the voice together shall they sing: for they shall see eye to eye, when the Lord shall bring again Zion.'

"I will, this morning, take the words of the ancient Prophet as the foundation for a few remarks, applying them more directly to myself. And if they should be applicable to the congregation before me, I hope that they, together with myself, will be benefitted by the same.

"It is very evident from this passage of Holy Scripture that

---

4. The *Deseret News* galley sheets are in the Brigham Young Papers. Mention of Pratt's sermon first appeared in an abbreviated summary of the morning's program in the *Deseret News*, 1 Feb. 1860. The full sermon was scheduled to run on the first and second pages of the 22 February edition until Young ordered it removed. A portion still appeared (see n5). After the speech was corrected, it appeared in the *Deseret News* on 25 July, then in the *Latter-day Saints' Millennial Star*, 22 Sept. 1860. It was eventually reprinted in the *Journal of Discourses*, 7:371-76, and most recently in James R. Clark, ed., *Messages of the First Presidency of the Church of Jesus Christ of Latter-day Saints, 1833-1964* (Salt Lake City: Bookcraft, Inc., 1965), 2:214-23. Appended to it was a short statement carrying the signatures of the First Presidency detailing the specific points of Pratt's controversial theories under condemnation.

there is a period of time to come in the last days, in which all of the Elders of Israel and all the watchmen of Zion will understand alike, see alike, and have the same views in regard to doctrine and principles, and all division of sentiment will be entirely done away. Then that scripture will be fulfilled recorded in our Lord's prayer as he taught his disciples how to pray: 'Our Father who art in heaven, hallowed be thy name, thy kingdom come, thy will be done on earth as it is done in heaven.'

"When I reflect that in heaven there is a perfect union of spirit and feeling among the celestial throng; when I reflect that in that happy place there is no disunion one with another; no different views; but that all will have the same mind and feeling in regard to the things of God; and then reflect that the day is to come when the same order of things is to be established here upon the earth; and then look at the present condition of mankind, I am constrained to acknowledge that there must be a great revolution on the earth. Where are there two men abroad in the world that see eye to eye—that have the same view in regard to doctrine and principle—that are of the same mind? They can scarcely be found. I doubt whether they can be found in the world.

"How is it among us, the Latter Day Saints? One thing is true in regard to some few of them; shall I say few? No; I will say many of them; they do actually, in the great fundamental principles of the doctrine of Jesus Christ, see eye to eye. I cannot suppose that in our infancy and childhood we can attain to all this great perfection in a moment, and be brought to see and understand alike. But there is one great heavenly standard or principle to which we must all come. What is that heavenly standard or principle? It is the restoration of the Holy Priesthood, the living oracles of God to the earth; and that Priesthood, dictated, governed, and directed by the power of revelation, through the gift of the Holy Ghost, that is the standard to which all the Latter Day Saints and the kingdom of God must come, in order to fulfill the prophecy I have read in your hearing.

"It matters not how much information any man may have before he comes into this Church. It matters not how extensively he may be taught in the arts and sciences of the day, how extensively he may be taught in regard to various branches of learning; it matters not how much natural wisdom he may be qualified with; it matters not whether he has occupied a high station in the eyes of the world, or a low one; it matters not what his prior condition may have been, when he repents before God and enters into a covenant with the Father and the Son and with his brethren, and manifests before them and the whole world that he forsakes the world: that he is willing to forsake all things which are of the world that are inconsistent with the character of God, His attributes, His word, and His kingdom; that very moment he comes to that point, and goes forward in baptism, he becomes subject to a different power from what he had before been subject to. He becomes subject to a certain authority that is different; he becomes subject to an authority which has come from heaven; not an authority ordained of man; not an authority which has been originated by human wisdom, or by the learning of mankind; not by inspired or uninspired books; for books never yet bestowed authority, whether inspired or uninspired.

"The authority of Jesus Christ sent down from heaven, conferred upon man by His Holy Angels, or by those that may have previously received divine authority, is the true and only standard here upon the face of our earth; and to this standard all people, nations, and tongues must come, or be eventually taken from the earth; for this is the only authority which is everlasting and eternal; and which will endure in time and throughout all eternity.

"This brings to my mind a revelation which was given in a general conference of the 2d day of January 1831, the church then having been organized about nine months. All the Saints gathered together from various little branches that had been established, in the house of old Father Whitmer, whose sons became conspicuous in the last dispensation as being witnesses of the Book of Mormon —whose house also became conspicuous as the place where the

Prophet Joseph Smith received many revelations and communications from heaven. In one small room of a log-house, nearly all the Latter Day Saints east of Ohio were collected together. They desired the Prophet of the Lord to inquire of God and receive a revelation to guide and instruct the church that were then present. Br. Joseph seated himself at the table; br. Sidney Rigdon, who was at that time a member of the church, having just arrived from the West, where he embraced the Gospel through the administration of some of the elders, he was requested to act as scribe in writing the revelation from the mouth of the Prophet Joseph. I will read a portion of this revelation—'And again I say unto you, let every man esteem his brother as himself; for what man among you having twelve sons, and is no respecter of them, and they serve him obediently and he saith unto the one, be thou clothed in robes and sit thou here, and to the other, be thou clothed in rags and sit thou there, and looketh upon his sons and saith I am just. Behold, this I have given unto you as a parable, and it is even as I am: I say unto you, be one; and if ye are not one, ye are not mine.'

"This I consider is a very important item—'Behold, I say unto you—be one, and if ye are not one, ye are not mine.'

"This is very pointed, plain, and definite language, that no man can misunderstand. Upon what principle are we to be one? It is by hearkening in all things to that eternal and everlasting priesthood which has been conferred upon mortal man upon the earth. When I say that priesthood, I mean the individual who holds the keys thereof—[who] is the standard, the living oracle to the church. But, says one, suppose that we hearken to the word of God in the Old and New Testament; suppose that we hearken to the word of God in the Book of Doctrine and Covenants; suppose we hearken to the word of God in the Book of Mormon, and at the same time we feel disposed in our hearts to lay aside the living oracles, what then? I would answer, in the first place, that the premises are false. Why? Because the revelations of God command us plainly that we shall hearken to the living oracles. Hence, if we undertake to follow the written word, and at the same time, do not give heed to the living oracles of God, the written word will condemn us; it shows that we do not follow it according to our profession. This is what I wish to bring home to myself as an individual and, if the same thing will suit any other person in the congregation, I hold that he will take it home to himself. But, inquires one, how is it that you are going to apply this to yourself? I will tell you. But first let me quote from another revelation, contained in the Book of Doctrine and Covenants. Perhaps I had better read the passage which I wish now to bring to your understanding—'Behold there shall be a record kept among you, and in it thou shalt be called a Seer, a Translator, a Prophet, an Apostle of Jesus Christ, and Elder of the church through the will of God the Father, and the grace of our Lord Jesus Christ, being inspired of the Holy Ghost to lay the foundation thereof, and to build it up unto the most holy faith, which church was organized and established in the year of our Lord, eighteen hundred and thirty, and in the fourth month, and in the sixth day of the month, which is called April. Wherefore, meaning the church, thou shalt give heed unto His words and commandments which he shall give unto you as he receiveth them, walking in all holiness before me; for His word shall ye receive as if from mine own mouth, in all patience and faith.'

"Here then we perceive what is binding upon the church of the living God; what was binding upon them thirty years ago; and what has been binding upon them ever since, from the day that it was given, until the day the Prophet was martyred down until the year 1860 and until the present moment of time. All this time there have been a kingdom and church of the living God on the earth, and a man placed at the head of that church to govern, direct, counsel, preach, exhort, testify, and speak the truth to the people, and counsel them in the things pertaining to their duties, and pertaining to the kingdom of God.

"Now, then, let me get back again.

"The great subject before me this morning, is the words I have been repeating before you, and how they apply to myself. There have been a few things wherein I have been wrong; wherein I have disobeyed these instructions that are here laid down—wherein, no doubt, I have also brought at many times darkness upon my own mind. I want to make a confession today. I do not know that [B]rother Brigham or any of the rest of the Twelve who have come here this morning, except brother Benson, knew of my intentions. I did tell brother Benson I thought of making a confession this morning, but the others were not aware of this. There are a few things which have been a source of sorrow to myself, at different times, for many years.

"Perhaps you may be desirous to know what they are. I will tell you. There are some points of doctrine which I have unfortunately, *without knowing before-hand what the views of the First Presidency of this church of God were,* thrown out before the people.

"At the time I expressed these views, I did most sincerely believe that they were in accordance with the word of God. I did most sincerely suppose that I was justifying the truth. But I afterward learned *[from my brethren] the fact from the mouth of our Prophet Brigham, from the mouth of that person whom God has placed at the head of this church,* that some of the doctrines I had advanced in the 'Seer' at Washington were incorrect. Naturally being of a stubborn disposition *myself,* and having a kind of self-will about me; and moreover supposing really and sincerely that I did understand what true doctrine was in relation to these points, I did not feel to yield to his judgment, but believed he was in error. Now was this right? No, it was not. Why? Because *he [the Priesthood] is the highest [and only legitimate] authority [in the Church in these matters] there is here on the earth in this kingdom. He is the living oracle of God to the church—to all the quorums of the church—and to all individuals of quorums.*

"*It was my duty as a servant of God to have at once yielded my judgment to his judgment. But I did not do it. I did not readily yield. I believed at the time that he was as sincere in his views and thoughts as I was in mine;*

and thought that I had made up my mind upon the word of God in relation to the matter, and concluded that it was not my duty to yield my judgment to him.

"How is it about this? Have we not a right to make up our minds in relation to the things recorded in the word of God, and speak about them, whether the living oracles believe our views or not? We have not the right. Why? Because the mind of man is weak: and this man may make up his mind in this way, and another man may make up his mind in another way, and a third individual may have his views, and thus every man is left to his own authority, and is governed by his own judgment which he takes as his own standard.

"Do you not perceive that this would, in a short time, cause opposition, disunion, and division of sentiment throughout the whole church? That would never fulfill the words of my text—would never bring to pass the sayings of Isaiah, that their watchman should lift up their voices, etc.

"In this thing I have sinned, and for this, I am willing to make my confession to the Saints; I ought to have yielded *[to the views of my brethren]* my stubborn disposition to his will. I ought to have said as Jesus did to his Father on a certain occasion, 'Father, thy will be done.'

"I ought to have said to him that holds the keys, Br. Brigham, thy will be done in relation to this matter; thy judgement be correct; let that guide, and govern, and dictate my mind, and the minds of all the people of God. That was my duty; but I did not do it. The consequence has been, I have oftentimes felt to mourn, and have been sorrowful in my own mind in relation to this matter.

"If I had not sense in all things, I had sense enough to know that it was not my place to correct the public mind; it was the place of him who holds the keys; and it was my place to yield; and if I had published a doctrine that was incorrect, it is his place to pronounce it incorrect; for me to get

up and and declare it to be true from the *Word of God, in contradiction to his voice, would be sinning still more before God.*

"You have made this confession," says one, "and now we want to ask you a little question on the subject. What do you believe concerning those points now? *You may say it is incorrect for you to withstand the ideas of the President, who holds the keys of the kingdom; but what are your views, what do you know concerning these points of doctrine now?*

"I will answer in the words of Paul. 'I know nothing of myself; yet am I not hereby justified, but he that judgeth me is the Lord.' So far as revelation from the heavens is concerned, I have had none in relation to those points of doctrine.

"I will tell you what I have had revealed to me. I have had revealed to me that the Book of Mormon is from God; I have had revealed to me that the Book of Doctrine and Covenants is also from God; I have had revealed to me that this is the church and kingdom of God; I have had revealed to me that this is the last dispensation of the fullness of times; these things are matters of knowledge with me; I know them to be true, and I do know about many things in relation to God and to future events.

"But when I reflect upon the subject, I have very little knowledge concerning many things. *What do I know, for instance, about God's being infinite in knowledge? This is the point I had reference to in the Seer. I have said in the Seer that God comprehends all things past, present, and to come—that there is not a solitary thing that ever did exist, that now exists, or that ever will exist, but what he fully comprehends.*

"But when I come to ask the questions, how I know this? Have I had any revelation on the subject? I am constrained to acknowledge that I never had any revelation on this subject to myself. The vision of the heavens never has been opened to me to unfold this point of doctrine, and consequently I do not know this for myself. If there are any prophets who ever did know concerning it, they are the ones to testify of it and not me. Consequently I have no business to stand up and argue against a man that holds the keys of the

kingdom of God upon a point of doctrine of this nature. I have done it; I have set up my natural judgment on this point as a standard for my own mind.

"I have had many arguments with President Young upon this point; really supposing he was wrong, and that I was right; and that my understanding of the revelations upon this point were true. But when I come to reflect upon the subject, how do I know I understand this revelation correctly? Am I not liable to be mistaken in determining the meaning of this revelation? Are there not many things contained in the word of God we do not any of us understand?"

"What do I know, for instance, about much of what is revealed in the last book of the New Testament, called John's Revelations? What do I know about much written in the Book of Daniel? Some few things are quite plain; but what do I understand in relation to some few of the predictions in the 11th chap. of Daniel? I doubt whether there is a person, unless he has been favored with direct revelation from heaven, who knows but very little about John's Revelations.

"What do I know about many things in relation to the celestial kingdom? Has the celestial kingdom been opened to my mind? No. Have I gazed upon it in vision? No. Have I seen God sitting on his throne, surrounded by his holy angels? No. Have I knowledge of the laws, and order, and government, and rule which regulate that kingdom? No. *How then can I bear testimony that God knows all things past, present, and to come?* If the revelations seem to apparently convey this or that idea, still I may be entirely mistaken in regard to the meaning of those revelations.

"*We are told by the living oracle upon the earth that this is incorrect doctrine. We are told that every God will continue to progress in knowledge to all ages of eternity; and we are told this by the highest authority on the earth. Must not I yield? I will at least say, I will be silent upon the subject, until I learn the facts from the heavens, and am counted to bear testimony of the* [matter], *and then I can do it in truth.*

"There is one thing I will assure you of, God will never reveal anything to me, or to any other man which will come in contact with the views and revelations which he gives to the man who holds the keys. We never need expect such a thing.

"'But,' inquires one, 'have you not felt anxious that the church should follow your ideas as laid down in the Seer?' I have not; if I had, I should have preached them; I should have tried to reason with you to convince you of their apparent truth.

"I have always been anxious that the church should be governed by him who has the right to govern it—to receive revelations, and to give counsel for its guidance, through whom correct doctrine ought to come and be unfolded to the children men.

"*'But,' inquires one, 'Do you not believe that God will suffer a man, standing at our head, sometimes to be mistaken?' That is none of my business. If God suffers any man, standing at the head of this kingdom, to be mistaken, I am not to blame.*

"God placed Joseph Smith at the head of this church. God has likewise placed Brigham Young at the head of this church; and he has required you and me, male and female, to sustain those authorities thus placed over us in their position. He has never released you nor me from those obligations. We are commanded to give heed to their words in all things,[5] receive their words as from the mouth of God, in all patience and faith. When we do not do this, we get into darkness. *It matters not what they teach, what principles they advocate,* God has placed them here, and God requires you and me to continue in our faith and patience to receive *[the truth at their hands] their words and the doctrines which they advance.* I am going to do it. I

---

5. A portion of Pratt's confession was mistakenly pasted up on the second page of the 22 February 1860 issue of the *Deseret News* and printed before the oversight was detected. The editor explained obliquely to readers, "Through some inadvertency, part of a sermon that had not been intended [authorized] for publication in this number got inserted on the second page and that side of the paper was struck off before the mistake was discovered." This point marks the beginning of the accidental publication of Pratt's sermon.

am going to repent. I arose *on this stand* this morning to unburden my feelings in regard to these matters.

"What is repentance? Is it merely to say we will do thus and so, and then go and do directly the contrary? When I say, I am going to repent of these things, I mean that I am going from this time henceforth, through the grace of God assisting me, to try and show by my acts and by my words, that I will uphold and support those whom I do know God has placed over me to govern, direct and guide me in the things of this kingdom.

"I do not know that I shall be able to carry out those views; but these are my present determinations. I may have grace and strength to perform this; *and perhaps I may hereafter be overcome.* I feel exceedingly weak in regard to these matters.

"I know what I have got to conquer—I have to conquer *Orson Pratt,* my *[natural]* disposition, *judgment,* and feelings, and bring them to bow to the authority God has instituted. I see no other way. This is the only way for me, and the only way for you. I see no possibility for the words of my text to be fulfilled, and brought to pass in any other manner. You cannot devise or imagine any other way. The world have tried for six thousand years to become united, and they never have been, and never will be able to do it, if they should continue to remain as nations, kingdoms and peoples for six million years to come. They never can bring about this oneness of sentiment and feeling by each man's being his own standard. No; it never was ordained by the Almighty to be brought about in that way.

"The only way for us is to have a true standard which must be from heaven—a standard ordained of God, which we can follow with the upmost confidence—a standard we can have faith in—a standard to which all human wisdom and human judgment must give way. Such a standard only will be eternal, and will prevail when all other standards will fail.

"*There are some few other points; I have named one. I do not know that it is necessary for me to name all the various little items. There are some few points of philosophy wherein I really supposed I was right, and wherein*

I really supposed in my heart, in times past, that the man who holds the keys was wrong in his judgment. But all the arguments I have brought forth in relation to the one point mentioned are equally applicable to all other points of apparent differences of opinion.

"If the Prophet of the living God, who is my standard, lays down a principle, whether it be a principle of doctrine, or a principle in philosophy, or a principle in science, or a principle pertaining to anything whatever, it is not for you nor me to argue against it, and set up our standard, and our views, and our judgment in order to make a division in the church of the living God—even if the division goes no further than our own individual selves. We must bow, if we would bring about that oneness spoken of in the revelations of God. We must yield to these things; and it is my determination to do so.

"'But,' inquires one, 'suppose a Prophet of God should lay down a principle in philosophy which to all human appearance appears to be perfectly incorrect, what would you do then?' I would say I am weak—that my judgment is not to be set up against the judgment of the man placed at my head. If I Cannot fully understand his views, it is my duty at least to be silent in regard to my own.

"Do my ideas suit anybody else? It matters not whether they do or not; they suit me, and I am going to put the coat on. I am preaching to myself this morning. I did not come here to preach to the world, nor particularly to preach to the Saints, but I wanted to preach to myself, and see if I could not convert myself, and when I get converted myself, perhaps I may do some good in preaching to the Saints and to the world.

"I have not yet partaken of the sacrament this morning. I was determined to unbosom my feelings before I partook of these holy emblems, ordained of God for none to partake of only those whose hearts are honest and pure and upright before him. I recollected a certain scripture before I came here: 'Therefore, if thou bring thy gift to the altar, and there remember that thy brother hath aught against thee, leave there thy gift before the altar and go thy way; first be reconciled to thy brother; and then come and offer thy gift.'

"These words came forcibly to my mind before I came to this house; and inasmuch as there may have been any feelings in the hearts of the Latter Day Saints that are now before me, I desire to do all in my power to bring a complete reconciliation.

"I wish the whole Territory were here, and all the good people of England, and all the Saints that have ever seen any of my writings or read my views; I would say to them all—brethren, I make a confession; I have sinned; I have been so stubborn; I have not yielded as I ought; I have done wrong; and I will try to do so no more. And if the whole kingdom of God can be reconciled with me, I shall be very glad. At least I will do all I can to obtain their reconciliation.

"These are my feelings to br. Brigham. I will make a reconciliation to *him [the Presidency],* and the Twelve, and to *[the Church] all people,* so far as it is in my power, so far as I have *been stubborn and* not yielded to *[my brethren] the man God has ordained to lead me.* I consider these to be true principles, however imperfect I may have been; it has nothing to do with the principles; the principles are from heaven, *let br. Pratt do as he will:* Amen."

Relief no doubt engulfed the middle-aged general authority as he regained his seat. He had openly acknowledged his error in having publicly espoused beliefs and doctrines his president had declared to be false. On the other hand, what he had not done was recant the teachings themselves—declare them false and admit that he believed them to be incorrect. Still, he had reaffirmed his conviction in the necessity of aligning his thoughts and actions with those of God's appointed servant. He had expressed his commitment to refrain from further speculation, although he had also voiced concern at his ability to do so. Never before had such a high-level church official made such a complete public confession. His admission and repentance heartfelt, Orson must have settled back a little more comfortably into his chair.[6]

---

6. That evening Pratt joined Apostle Woodruff in addressing members of Salt Lake City's 14th Ward (Kenney, *Wilford Woodruff's Journal,* 5:430).

EIGHT.

Matters of the Gods

Two days following his public confession, Orson Pratt called at Brigham Young's office to make "a personal acknowledgement to the President" and admitted that "he had a self willed determination in him." Young consoled him by saying that "he had never differed with him only on points of doctrine, and he never had had any personal feelings, but he was anxious that correct doctrines should be taught for the benefit of the Church and the Nations of the Earth."

Young confessed that "in one thing he had felt vexed[,] that he [Pratt] did not consult them before he published the MS [manuscript] writing he got from Mother Smith about the life of the Prophet." According to Young's scribe, Pratt "admitted that he had done wrong and he now saw it but did not at the time of his purchasing and publishing it." Young said that "the brethren would have made it a matter of fellowship" but he personally did not "have it in his heart to disfellowship but merely to correct men in their views." The president remarked that Pratt "had been willing to go on a mission to any place at the drop of the Hat and observed[,] you might as well question my authority to send you on a mission as to dispute my views on doctrine." Pratt responded, albeit indirectly, that he "had never felt unwillingness in the discharge of his practical duties."[1]

Despite the president's congeniality, Pratt's Sunday confession actually exacerbated, rather than resolved, their differences. Young was upset by what he believed was Pratt's intentional misrepresentation of his teachings, that Pratt had said he worshipped a God who could not logically exist and who probably did not exist scripturally. Nor had Pratt admitted that he had taught false doctrine.

Before the close of the week, aided by secretary Albert Carrington and second counselor Daniel H. Wells, Young scrutinized extracts from Pratt's controversial *Seer* writings.[2] Saddened and increasingly angered, Young told Wells that Pratt went too far, that "there were many principles [in the *Seer*] that the world were unworthy to receive; for they would only trample on it." Young felt frustrated: "If [I] had ever erred it was in giving too much revelation; instead of not giving enough. The Lord designed keeping those in ignorance who would not seek unto him; and would impart Knowledge to those who Kept his commandments."[3]

Twelve days later, Elder Ezra T. Benson, at Young's request, visited the president to discuss "Orson Pratt's discourse, on the subject of attributes."[4] The following Tuesday, Young instructed the *Deseret News* not to run Pratt's January confession and instead to print "another sermon ... and give a reason for so doing."[5] Two weeks later,

---

1. Qtd. in the President's Office Journal, 31 Jan. 1860. The previous day Pratt had "waited upon the Pres[iden]t in relation to the appointment of his Son Orson as a [school] teacher" (ibid., 30 Jan. 1860). The official journal does not note if the two men discussed Pratt's confession. One week later Young met with Orson Jr. and asked him to teach the coming spring (ibid., 6 Feb. 1860).

2. Ibid., 4 Feb. 1860.

3. Ibid. Young publicly expressed virtually identical views less than five months later. See the *Deseret News*, 27 June 1860.

4. President's Office Journal, 16 Feb. 1860.

5. Ibid., 21 Feb. 1860.

on 4 March, Young, together with first counselor Heber C. Kimball and Apostles Wilford Woodruff, John Taylor, and Lorenzo
Snow, met with counselor Wells at his home where he was conva-
lescing from a recent attack of "inflamatory rheumatism." During
their visit Young again affirmed: "I did not say to [Pratt] that God
would increase to all Eternity. But I said that the moment that we
say that God knows all things[,] Comprehends all things[,] and has
a fulness of all that He ever will obtain[,] that moment Eternity
ceases. You put bounds to Eternity[,] space[,] & matter and you
make an end and stoping place to it. The people[,] or many[,] say
thay cannot understand these things. This is true. No man can understand the things of Eternity," he admitted. "And Brother Pratt
and all men should let the matter of the gods alone. I do not understand these things[,] Neither does any man in the flesh[,] and we
should let them alone. Some men profess infidelity but when they
go into Eternity[,] they will find [that] all they see in this life upon
the Earth is ownly a similitude of what thay will find in the next
world."[6]

The next day Young told attentive listeners in the Tabernacle,
without referring directly to Pratt:

> It has been stated that I teach the doctrine that the Gods continue to
> increase in all their attributes to all eternity. Have you ever heard me
> teach such a doctrine? I have taught doctrine; but have I called in
> question any of the Gods? It has been stated that God our Father
> comprehends eternity, from eternity to eternity, all there is, all there
> was, all there ever can be about eternity, in and through it. When a
> person undertakes to establish such a doctrine, what does he do? He
> gives bounds to that eternity which he at the same time admits to be
> boundless. Admit such doctrine, and eternity flees away like the
> shadow of morning; and that is as much as I ever teach about it. Do I
> say that heavenly beings improve? I am not yet there; I do not know.

Young's position was quietly shifting from certitude to qualified

---

6. Qtd in Kenney, *Wilford Woodruff's Journal*, 5:439.

ambiguity. In searching for a middle ground, he seemed to be saying that the gods could learn something new despite the fact that they already knew everything. In his quarrel with Pratt, his rhetoric would increasingly reflect this shift. Underscoring the point, he asked, "Understand eternity?"

> There is not and never was a man in finite flesh who understands it. ... This is a matter that wise men know nothing about. I do not know, though I know as much about it as any man in this house or in this generation. I can comprehend, by the words of eternal life, that there is an eternity before me. Has it bounds? Whether it has or not, neither we nor any other finite beings can comprehend it. I will leave this subject, because I am not capable of understanding it. You leave it, and do not contend about things that are beyond our reach—that are too great for you to know at present.[7]

Young had purposely delayed action on Pratt's discourse until Wednesday, 4 April, when a majority of apostles would be in Salt Lake City for the semi-annual general conference.[8] Besides permitting as many of the apostles as possible to be in attendance, Young hoped that the threat of public exposure at conference the next day would help elicit from Pratt the kind of apology he believed was overdue. Unlike January's meeting of the church's top authorities, April's meeting was attended by only a select few: Apostles Orson Hyde, John Taylor, Wilford Woodruff, Ezra T. Benson, and George A. Smith who had not been present at the 27 January meeting, and Presiding Bishop Edward Hunter. They were belatedly joined by

---

7. *Journal of Discourses*, 8:17-18.

8. The president met two days previously with Apostles George A. Smith and Ezra T. Benson and secretary Albert Carrington. From 7:00 p.m. to 9:00 p.m., the four men read through Pratt's confession, Young confiding that "he thought of presenting the principles involved to the conference, but he did not know but that it might hurt brother Pratt's feelings." The church officials concluded that "a council of the Twelve be called to meet on Wednesday evening to take this matter into consideration" (Historian's Office Journal, 2 Apr. 1860).

Apostles Erastus Snow and Charles C. Rich.[9] Also present were
church clerks George D. Watt, J. V. Long, Hiram B. Clawson, John

---

9. All quotations are from "Minutes of Meeting at Historian's Office, April 4,
1860, 7 p.m.," Brigham Young Papers. Most of the minutes were recorded by
Robert L. Campbell, with sections by Thomas Bullock. Unfortunately, the minutes are sketchy in places and Campbell's handwriting is sometimes difficult to
read. Every effort has been made to reproduce the comments exactly as they were
recorded and to attribute them to the correct speaker, but the possibility of textual
misreadings exists.

Brigham Young's secretary summarized the lengthy meeting as follows:

> In the evening President Young attended a meeting at the Historians Of-
> fice to consider the Doctrines of Orson Pratt as taught in the Seer and
> other[s] of his works. Bro. Orson Pratt, stated his views at the meeting and he
> [Pratt] could not see but what his doctrines were based upon the Revelations
> of Joseph [Smith].
>
> President Young, Bros Taylor, Woodruff, Geo. A. Smith, Erastus Snow,
> [and] Orson Hyde came to the conclusion that Br. Orson ought to retract the
> erroneous portions of his doctrine; and publish a sermon to that effect; this he
> might do with the assistance of the twelve[. I]f this was not complied with[,]
> the doctrines would be submitted to the general conference.
>
> President Young observed [that] the Confessional sermon of br Pratts
> merely stated [that] his views did not agree with mine and that he ought to
> yield his views to President Young. I want him[,] observed the President[,] to
> say that his views are contrary to truth and right[. H]is sermon represents me
> to the world as a tyrant trammelling them to believe as I do[,] right or wrong;
> it is my calling[,] observed the President[,] to see that right doctrines are
> taught.
>
> Bro O Hyde asked Br Orson if he believed Br Brigham was the man God
> had called to preside over the church and Kingdom of God. Br Pratt said he
> did[, and although he] believe[d] that the Prophets and leaders of every dis-
> pensation have been in error on different points[,] he did not question Br
> Brighams integrity[. B]ut he did question his judgment in arriving to correct
> conclusions in some matters of doctrine[. I]n regard to Br Brighams policy in
> government[,] he did not think it could be done better. Bro Pratt also ob-
> served [that] at time[s] he hardly felt he was competent to be an apostle and he
> left himself entirely in their hands[. B]ut he could not be hypocrite enough to
> retract his doctrines when he believed them, neither could he say he could re-
> ceive doctrines that he could not believe; and if he was disfellowshipped[,] he
> could not help it. (President's Office Journal, 4 Apr. 1860.)

The Historian's Office Journal was more detailed:

Prest. Young set forth the object of the Council, as follows.

Bro. Orson[,] your late sermon came near [to] being published in the Deseret News, before I had an opportunity of reading it. I am not satisfied with it as a confession [because] it does not present me in a true light[. I]t makes me appear to be a tyrant, and [gives the impression that] because I am the President of the church[,] every man's will and judgement must bend to mine.

I want to get an understanding of your views, and see [to] it [that] we see things aright; perhaps if I could see it as you do, it would be all that I could ask, but if not, we want to have the matter talked over, and laid before the Conference in a manner that will injure Bro. Orson's influence as little as possible and so that we can show that we see eye to eye. I have delayed this matter, because of the absence of some of the brethren, but I presume brother Pratt has no objection to our taking this course and having it all laid before the Conference satisfactorily.

T[homas] B[ullock] read O. Pratt's sermon delivered in the Tabernacle, Feb. 22 [29 January].

Pres[iden]t Young asked the Twelve if they were satisfied with that sermon as a confession, considering what Bro. Pratt has put forth to the people in England and in Washington. And said he did not want to do any thing but what would be for the best and promotion of the public good.

O. Hyde made a few remarks.

Erastus Snow made remarks.

Pres[iden]t Young said he thought the matter could be got along with very easily[. H]e would suggest that Bro Orson Pratt and the Twelve get together and write out a sermon that would set forth Bro. Pratt's true position, and brother Pratt could read [it] in the Tabernacle and then have it published to the world.

Bro. Young asked brother Pratt to speak his mind on the subject.

Brother Pratt said he thought that Pres[iden]t Young was perfectly satisfied with the confession, as he was informed by bro. Watt when he handed him the sermon to revise, that the President had read it and approved of it, and wished to have it ready for the paper that week; and he was quite astonished when bro. Young made the remarks he did on the stand a short time afterwards.

And as for publishing to the world that the doctrines he had preached and published, on certain points, were false, he could not do it, because if he did[,] he would prove himself a hypocrite and that the revelations of Joseph Smith were false and that Pres[iden]t Young had preached false doctrine[. A]s upon the revelations of Joseph Smith and the sermons of Brigham Young[,] he had formed the belief that he had promulgated [based] on those points of doctrine [as revealed by Joseph Smith and preached by Brigham Young]. While bro. Pratt was sanguine that the points of doctrine which he had set forth [were in harmony with Joseph's revelations and Brigham's sermons,] the rest of the

T. Caine, Amos M. Musser, Thomas Bullock, Robert L. Campbell, R. Bently, and George Sims.[10]

As the men began taking their seats, Brigham turned to Orson and asked, "Has Bro Benson spoken to you about that for which we have met to night?"

"No!" the apostle responded.

"Well it is this[,] bro. Orson," Young returned, echoing an earlier scene:

> Your late sermon had like to get into the paper. I want to get an understanding of your views; and see if we see things aright[. P]erhaps if I could see it as you[,] Orson[,] does[,] perhaps its all that I could ask, but if not[,] we want to have the matter talked over and ~~that~~ laid before the Conference in a manner that we all see eye to eye[.] I have delayed this, because of the absence of some of the brethren, but I presume[,] bro. Pratt[,] you have no objections to our taking this course and having it all laid before the Conference satisfactorily.

The president asked one of his clerks, Thomas Bullock, to read aloud Pratt's confession from the *Deseret News* galleys. As Bullock

---

> Twelve were equally sanguine that those revelations and sermons from which he quoted would not back him up.
> After much counsel and good advice from Pres[iden]t Young & the Twelve to O. Pratt[,] the council adjourned until tomorrow at 10 a.m.

Wilford Woodruff wrote in his diary:

> I attended a Council of the Presidency and Twelve at the Historians Office in the evening upon the subject of the sermon of Orson Pratt. The sermon was read & the time was occupied till half past 11 oclok in discussing the subject. ... President Young made many remarks Concerning Doctrinal points & the Situation of Orson Pratt who seemed vary dark in his mind upon many points of Doctrin[e]. President Young wished the matter to be settelled before the Quorum of the Twelve and not go before the Conference. After spending several hours in investigating the subject[,] it was decided for the Twelve to meet in the morning in prayer & Fasting and settle the business among ourselves. (Kenney, *Wilford Woodruff's Journal*, 5:445.)

10. Historian's Office Journal, 4 Apr. 1860.

finished, Young faced the members of the Twelve present. "Are the 12 satisfied with this read[ing] & what Bro. Pratt has put forth to the people?" he queried. "I do not want to do anything but what will be for the best & promote the public good."

Quorum president Orson Hyde answered first, saying he "thought when the prophet pronounced upon favorite doctrines, it was for us to repudiate ours, and sustain his. As to wh[e]ther we should sustain the prophet in evry scienctifical subject contrary to our own judgement, it might not be policy to say that[,] for as invoking a principle of absolutism which would not look well."

Erastus Snow, who had missed the bulk of Young's opening comments as well as the Pratt confession itself, followed suit. "One impression made upon my spirit," he offered, "as Bro. B. wishes to hear us":

> While I feel as though I could readily appreciate bro Pratts position before his God & the people, & his wish to gain his true position before God and the people, I am of [the] opinion that if Bro P. had consilled [reconciled] the workings of [the] Sp[irit] of G[o]d in him a little more & first made himself one in Spirit before with Bro. Brigham[,] he would have been able with less words to accomplish more, without cutting with his sword [in] back handed licks. The ~~confession~~ speech itself is in back handed licks & they operate back on bro B. & [are] uncalled for in on[e] or 2 instances & [otherwise] uncalled for. [I] dont know whether my views are correct or not[,] but [I] understand that we should look at [our] fa[ther] in H[eaven] & his Prophets in Earth as kind fathers, not as tyrants & oppressors, but dealing out things lovely. As far as we should look upon Bro Brig[ham,] the discourse sets forth [this idea] correctly. We submit to [the] Prophet & to God, not merly because [they are] our superiors, & [are] before us & bear the keys, but because they bear those keys in truth & righteousness, & that because they are true.

"The sole cause I wish to make," he concluded, "is [that we should] not hold our F[ather] in h[eaven] nor J[esus] C[hrist] nor

J[oseph Smith] nor Bro Brigham, as rulling with a strong hand, [as a] dictator, nor to control our conscience, but ..."

"Bro Erastus," Young interrupted, perhaps fearing a drawn-out sermon, "a few words[;] be short[, or] the evening will be spent." Snow quickly finished.

Young then arose. "The sermon is splendid," he began with a rehearsed criticism, "but [there is] no confession of his errors, but [only] a confession to me. As though a confession was to be made to me or I will take off Orson's or John [the Baptist]'s head." Gesturing to the galleys, he said that he was especially offended by Pratt's promise to be silent in the future if his private views differed from his own.

"I wish to connect this with items preached by Orson in the *Seer*," he continued, "as to matter getting together & then [becoming] organized & [that it] framed [itself into] a deity & he [Pratt] has said that God know[s] all things from all eternity. Did you ever hear me say that the Gods will learn from all eternity to all eternity[?]" he asked the men around him.

> Have any of you heard me argue such a doctrine[?] I have no recollection of ~~anything~~ [such] saying. This does not come to me as right. It points to me as a tyrant[, a] dispot[, a] ruler pinching[11] [off the] spirit. Orson wants a revelation to know that I am wrong—No matter whether the men are right or wrong who head the church. This is not the retraction that the statements made by Orson demands. I have said to Orson we could not understand the first deity while here in the flesh[. T]here are things we do no[t] know about [it] ...

Orson interrupted to explain what he had meant. "What will the result be[?]" Young forged ahead.

> I have these books [before me.][12] [M]y children unborn are to read them[, and] they are held [by the Saints to be] as sacred as the bible[.

---

11. The original word seems to be "prinching."
12. By "these books," Young probably means Pratt's publications.

W]hat I want to learn to night is what items [to pass on to my children][13]—I'm willing to go into the endowment house & dress [in temple clothing][14] before any Quorum or [dress] as we are now & [stand] before [the whole membership at General] Conference & lay down item upon item. & let them decide. You make attributes [a] Deity[. You might] as well say [there is] no deity now, or [say] that we have to be dispersed to receive those attributes & go back to atoms, before we get an exaltation. When he [Pratt] lectured several years ago, I asked him, where [is] empty space[, for] when the wicked call for rocks to fall[,] I could tell them where to go [to hide]—for there[,] God could not act[,] for [there would be] nothing to act upon. That I dont care anything about, & to put that forth to the people; it should be covered up, & let the doc[trine] & cov[enants] & bible not stand[. O]ne man said [to] me that he had persued those items which Orson has preached & which you have tried to lightly efface.

"It's a confused mess," Young cut the anecdote short, his voice softening to a low growl, "& I want to wipe it carefully out & hurt nobody." He paused momentarily, perhaps shifting his weight.

"Bro Orson [admits he is] stubborn," he said. But "what should [he] be stubborn about[? I]f [it is] about dollars [and] cents [or our] farms, these [are] things [to be] stubborn about[. B]ut what shall we be stubborn about [when it comes to] the things of God[? N]o-[thing. N]othing, but [that we] promote the truth. If some~~thing~~ persons there [in the Tabernacle] would have jumped on Bro. Orson," Young quipped, "[he would] have done it.

"What did I write," the president demanded, "that such things should not be received[?] Bro. Orson's honest integrity I know," he allowed. "I dont doubt them [motives], I never did it. When ~~in England~~ going to England first, he said [he was] incapable of taking

---

13. He is probably alluding to the possibility of censorship.

14. The Quorum of the Twelve and First Presidency, and sometimes others, occasionally met together, dressed in the clothing of the temple, for a special prayer circle and sacrament service.

hold of a paper [and writing, that] he could not tread on new doctrine, when [before long,] he had gone a head of all that [the] seers
& prophets have written & delineated upon—[He] has not got
good judgement.

"I'm either [in favor] of giving [an airing in general confer-
ence] to have the quarrelle there or having it [done now,] going
through [it] in a parental spirit," he said.

> I want to save bro Orson[.] I feel calm as like an old shoe. If his con-
> fession had been right[,] I would have bound up my particle so that it
> would [not] have hurt his influence.[15] Maybe[,] tho[,] he don't think I
> have revel[ations]—if I dont[,] I dont magnify my calling. There are
> hundreds of these I could write. As fast as dog[s] trot. When I write &
> send forth my Revelations[, they] are then [as] are the Rev[elations]
> of etern[ity]. I never look at my sermons, I don't cross my tracks. ...[16]

Facing quorum president Orson Hyde, Young stressed, "I
know his [Pratt's] integrity[.] I love him, [and] I mean to hang on to
him[.] I want a confession that I can send to the whole of the people that will cover all the church & preserve bro Orson a whole
Apostle, before the whole church, then we want bro Orson[,] that
can save him.

"I want such a thing published all over the world," Young ordered. "When he has written on baptism & the first prin[ciples, he
teaches true doctrine,] but when [he has] written on God &c [it is
a] chimera of the brain[, a] philosopher['s doctrine, and we] dont
want that. Thus saith the Lord[.][17] [G]o do that[, and] they dont

---

15. There are nine illegible lines here.
16. The rest of the line is illegible.
17. Young's invocation of "Thus saith the Lord" is one of only a handful of instances when he felt compelled to do so (see his criticism of those who insist that a
prophet say "Thus saith the Lord" in *Journal of Discourses*, 8:138). Unlike his prede-
cessor, Young believed it was unnecessary to invoke God's name to support his
teachings since he believed that "when I have spoken by the power of God and
the Holy Ghost, it is truth, it is scripture" (qtd. in the *Deseret News*, 6 June 1877).

have to ask [if] any [teaching is a] hypothesis [and he] dont have to stop philosophizing.

"Now you understand what I want," Young insisted. "[I]f Bro Orson thinks [about it and writes his sermon] & take[s it to] the 12, to fix the items[,] then get the thing right & read it to the people & say that [it is an update of his] last [sermon, and he should say] I could not speak it [extemporaneously as well as] I have written it."

Seconding Young's comments, John Taylor said that he "finds it easier to get out of the path than to get into it. I heard Bro. Orson & thought in somethings he meant right. It is important for the 12 to teach correct doctrine & it is for Prest. Y to see that we get [it] right."

"It's not the matter [of what] Bro. Orson has at heart[,] its the manner," Young clarified.

"I said to a man," offered Hyde, "[W]hat would you give to know the truth[?] I would not yield to the truth. I told him the truth trammeled [and was] no good. [Now] I feel as though the truth would make us free."

"[Where there is a] difference in opinion & judgement," Young concluded, "their [the apostles'] judgement should be left at rest until the truth forms that judgement. [A]ny judgement [should] not [be] framed out [until it can] be framed by the prin[ciples] of eternal truth. Bro. Orson Pratt, should say I have no judgement upon the matter, or should have had none. Bro O. Pratt," Young asked, turning to Pratt, "what do you think about it?"

Pratt could see but one response. "I have no doubt but what the first Presidency & Twelve could get up a thing that would suit them," he confessed.

> I have tried very hard to bring my feelings & judgement [in line] with Bro. Y[oung']s & that for several years. [But] its my duty to get my judgement. I find that when a man's wound up, he may have strong faith in regards to views what he considered to be true & Revelation.

There are certain points taught by Bro. Y. as being true, that there does seem to be disputed between those & the Revel[ations] & when I reflect that there is item upon item, doctrine upon doctrine [upon which he and Young disagree], I would be a hypocrite if I came out & said that these views on which I have strong faith [are wrong; I] would be acting too much a hypocrite. If [only] I could get rev[elations] of those things which have lingered upon my mind & which I have believed it to be true. The Bre[thren] are at liberty to publish anything that they see proper or [to address this] at Conference.

"I would like to ennumerate items [upon which we disagree]," Pratt continued. "Firstly, [President Young] preached & publish[ed], that Adam is the fa[ther] of our spirits, & father of [the holy] Spirit & father of our bodies.[18] [But] when I read the Rev[elations] given to Joseph [Smith,] I read directly the opposite. [There] the Lord spake to Adam. [Also,] that men [will] eventually become Adams."[19]

"Your statements to night," Young retorted—

you come out to night & place them as charges, & have as many against me as I have [against] you. One thing I have thought that I might still have omited[:] It was Joseph's doctrine that Adam was God[20] & when in Luke Johnson's,[21] at O. Hyde's,[22] the power came

---

18. Pratt is referring to Young's Adam-God teaching.

19. Three lines in the original minutes were left blank at this point, probably for the scribe to record other areas of disagreement (Young's belief in a progressing God, for instance), which he neglected to do.

20. This is the earliest known attribution of Adam-God to Joseph Smith. For other occasions, see Kenney, *Wilford Woodruff's Journal*, 6:381; Journal History of the Church, 14 May 1876. (Young also alluded to the impact of Smith's teachings on his own views in a sermon on 8 June 1873, reported in the *Deseret News*.) The issue of what Joseph said on the topic and what he meant by it will be further discussed the next day (see chap. 9).

21. While residing at the home of Luke Johnson's father, John, in the early 1830s, Joseph Smith received a series of impressive revelations, including his vision of the three degrees of heavenly glory (Doctrine and Covenants 76), and also revised large portions of the Bible. Luke was ordained an apostle in 1835, excommunicated in 1837, rebaptized in 1846, and died in Salt Lake City in 1861.

At the same time, Brigham Young may not have had Luke Johnson in mind

upon us, a shock that alarmed the neighborhood[.][23] God comes to earth & eats & partakes of fruit. Joseph could not reveal [all of] what was revealed to him, & if Joseph had it revealed [to him by God], he was not told to reveal it [to others].[24]

---

but rather Benjamin F. Johnson, who was living in Ramus, Illinois, when church leaders met on 2-3 April 1843 to discuss the book of Revelation, the book of Daniel, and other mysteries. Orson Hyde stated at the time that "[i]t is our privilege to have the Father and Son dwelling in our hearts," to which Smith replied: "The Father has a body of flesh and bones as tangible as man's." When general conference convened later that week, Orson Pratt spoke on "Father Adam," the "Ancient of Days," while others addressed topics from the book of Revelation (see Faulring, *American Prophet's Record*, 338-60). Benjamin later intimated that he had heard Smith teach Adam-God (see Johnson to Gibbs, qtd. in David John Buerger, "The Adam-God Doctrine," *Dialogue* 15 [Spring 1982]: 25).

22. This would presumably mean Orson Hyde's cabin in Kanesville, Iowa, where the apostles met to decide whether to organize a First Presidency. The scribe probably omitted text between "in Luke Johnson's" and "at O. Hyde's"; otherwise it is unclear what relationship might be implied and if Young spoke generally about the power of revelation or specifically about Adam-God and if he was claiming that it had been preached on one or both occasions.

23. Apparently, the "shock that alarmed the neighborhood" occurred at Orson Hyde's cabin and attended the decision to appoint a First Presidency in December 1847 (see chap. 3). Six months later in October 1860, Hyde would report this event, which he dated to February 1848: "The voice of God came from on high, and spake to the Council. ... 'Let my servant Brigham step forth and receive the full power of the presiding Priesthood in my Church and kingdom' That was the voice of the Almighty unto us ... I do not know that this testimony has often, if ever, been given to the masses of the people before ... We said nothing about the matter in those times, but kept it still. [After seating myself in the stand, I was reminded of one circumstance that occurred, which I omitted in my discourse. Men, women, and children came running together where we were, and asked us what was the matter. They said that their houses shook, and the ground trembled, and they did not know but that there was an earthquake. We told them that there was nothing the matter—not to be alarmed; the Lord was only whispering to us a little, and that he was probably not very far off. We felt no shaking of the earth or of the house, but were filled with the exceeding power and goodness of God]" (*Journal of Discourses* 8:234; brackets in original).

24. It is difficult to track the logic of Young's comments in this fragmented quotation. For instance, does Young assign the statement "God comes to earth & eats & partakes of fruit" to Joseph Smith or is this Young's interpretation of something Smith said? It offers an interesting possibility, assuming that Smith said what

"The Spirit is sent [into the body] when the mother feels [the dust of the] earth [forming a child.] God put it [fruit] into his mouth, & when God, wanted to translate [himself,] he had the power," Young explained.[25]

"[There is] not a contradictory thing in what I have said. Bro. Pratt had the Spirit of God like us all in Pottawatomie & believed when the Revel[ation] was given to us. Could a being in a telestial or terrestrial kingdom keep a celestial law, is it reasonable to expect such a thing?

"I knew in Nauvoo that there would be a first Presidency," Young said, alluding to his prophetic foresight. "[B]ro. Woodruff [was] the first that I named it to, Geo A. perhaps next. If I have named anything that the people were not worthy of [receiving], I have prayed that it might be forgotten. I have prayed fervently when Orson published the [marriage] sealing ordinance [in the *Seer*] that it might be forgotten.

"Orson," Young charged, "it is for you to call the 12 together & do as I have suggested or do as you please. [Otherwise] it will be brought before [the] conference and you will be voted [down] as a false teacher, & your false doctrines discarded. I love your integrity, but your ignorance is as great as any philosopher[']s ought to be."

In the face of Young's ultimatum, Pratt's was deliberate: "I am willing [that] you should publish what you have a mind to. I cannot retract from what I have said. I sometimes feel unworthy of the apostleship which I hold."

---

is cited, about how Young may have interpreted a statement about Adam and Eve being God's literal children to mean that Adam is God (see also the next paragraph). Equally confusing is the ongoing puzzle (see nn21-23) about what occurred at "Luke Johnson's," or perhaps at Benjamin Johnson's, and the connection to "O. Hyde's."

25. Presumably the missing words convey this idea, which Young expressed elsewhere. Without insertions, the sentence reads: "The Spirit is sent when the mother feels earth, God put it into his mouth, & when God, wanted to translate he had the power."

A flurry of comments erupted. "These are temptations of Satan," Elder Snow warned.

"Bro. Pratt," Elder Hyde pleaded, "take the Council of bro Brigham[. H]e is doing the best he could for you."

"There is no missionary who understands the spirit of his calling, who will communicate a new doctrine," Young said.

"It is a trick of the Devil," George A. Smith added, "to ruin a man, when it is suggested to him that those who are trying to put him right, are trying to put him down."

"It is my duty to see that correct doctrine is taught," Young repeated, "& to guard the church from error[. I]t is my calling."

"I am willing," Pratt said again, that "the 12 should publish all they consider necessary for the salvation of the church."

This was enough for George A. Smith who, growing furious at Pratt's defiance, moved that his speculations be publicly condemned the next day. Interestingly, a majority of the apostles wanted to continue deliberating—"to have it laid before the 12 & not go before the conference."

A less heated Young agreed and "wished the Twelve to take hold & pray with Bro. Orson & have a good flow of the spirit. It will go off smoothly," he promised.

"Bro. Pratt counts too little on his standing, & [prizes his] calling too little," Young added, "or he would not let his private judgement, stand between him & his salvation, or he would yield. [B]ut I attribute it to his ignorance."

Young then called the nearly five-hour meeting to a close and offered the benediction. According to the minutes, he "prayed for Orson Pratt, & prayed [with] feelings." Following the prayer, Orson Hyde announced that the Twelve would meet the next morning for a pre-conference fast meeting.

While offering no new insights into the fundamental areas of dispute between Young and Pratt, the 4 April gathering served to alienate Pratt further, not only from Young but also from his increasingly leery colleagues in the quorum. Clearly, Young believed his duty lay in preventing the kind of freedom of thought that Pratt demanded. Young could hardly disagree with the apostle's insistence on revelation as the ultimate arbiter of truth.[26] Yet Pratt's tenacious belief that only personal revelation could provide the impetus to proclaim publicly his error was met with frustration. It was Young's privilege to receive revelation for the church, but Young was not the revelator Joseph Smith had been, nor did he feel the freedom that Smith had claimed. Ironically, in retrospect, Young's may have been the more speculative teachings, even though his loyalty was also to what he remembered—or believed he remembered—Joseph Smith had taught. If he expanded on Joseph's theology, it was only to explain more fully what the latter had not been able to complete. This was Pratt's intent as well. Ultimately, Pratt believed that revelation trumped reason. On the other hand, Young did not necessarily agree that divine intervention was an indispensable ingredient in the formulation of doctrine.[27]

In his 29 January discourse, Pratt had referred to Young as God's appointed representative on earth. But as Young sensed, Pratt had also implied that the church president did not always represent the unified views of the entire membership or even the governing councils. Though no doubt sincere in his declaration of personal subjection, Pratt had exaggerated the extent to which this was binding upon members—at least as far as Young was concerned. In the same breath, Pratt contradictorily implied that he would continue thinking as he saw fit, while feebly attributing this to personal weakness. Insisting that church leaders were not infallible, Pratt made the mistake of citing the most extreme possibilities to illustrate his point.

---

26. Young felt that revelation could be incomplete: "I do not even believe that there is a single revelation, among the many God has given to the Church, that is perfect in its fulness" (*Journal of Discourses*, 2:314).

27. "It is only where experience fails," Young once explained, "that revelation is needed" (*Journal of Discourses*, 2:32).

Not surprisingly, Young felt that this was a threat to his presidency and an insult to him as an individual. Compromise was impossible at this juncture. For the sake of church harmony and his own self-esteem, Young saw no other alternative but to insist that Pratt recant, preferably before the Twelve, and that he publicly announce his error. Otherwise, the dangerous apostle would be presented to conference as a false teacher and condemned as such.

The seasoned, intellectually gifted Pratt had successfully withstood a seemingly endless barrage of attacks on his religion during his earlier missions to Great Britain and the eastern seaboard of the United States. In fact, suggested Craig James Hazen, "the system of thought that Pratt developed was, in his mind, infallible."[28] Pratt's knowledge of the scriptures, keen mind, and logical reasoning had served him well, and in good conscience he could not abandon them now even if they pitted him against the man whom he sustained as God's mouthpiece. For Pratt, freedom of thought—freedom to do what he believed was right and in keeping with God's will as he understood it—had greater value than church fellowship. He idolized the martyred Joseph Smith, a devotion for which he had paid heavily in Nauvoo, and he could not admit to himself or to anyone else that any revelation, written or oral, received by Smith and interpreted by Pratt might be outmoded or, worse, false. His ties to the founding prophet were strong and complex, and he saw himself, much like Brigham Young saw himself, as merely bolstering original tenets rather than expounding new doctrine.

When Young announced specific doctrines that Pratt could not agree with, or that seemed to contradict Joseph Smith's earlier teachings, the apostle initially kept silent, anticipating that supporting revelations would explain the contradictions. No such revelations were advanced, and Pratt was to perceive that his own views were as valid as Young's or those of any other member of the

---

28. Hazen, *Village Enlightenment,* 62.

Twelve. His paramount allegiance was to truth, and he believed
that Joseph Smith had revealed it. Young's unwillingness or inability to resolve the controversy by divine fiat merely convinced Pratt
of the soundness of his dissent. In honesty to his beliefs and conscience, he could not admit error where he saw none, even if it
meant severance from the church he was devoted to.

As Pratt himself later testified:

> If I were to deny the gifts of the Gospel, or any of the revelations that
> God has given—that are published in the Book of Doctrine and Covenants—if I were to do such a thing, could I look upon my Father's
> face without blushing? [C]ould I think upon anything that was pure
> and holy, without being, in my own [mind], in perfect torment? If I
> were to be so ungrateful as to deny anything that God has given me, I
> should be unworthy of the kingdom of God. I do most sincerely and
> humbly hope and trust that the Lord will not call me and try me in
> this respect, for I know the weakness of man; I know that man has
> been weak in all ages, and I do not wish to be thus tried[.] I do not
> covet this trial, I do not pray for it[. B]ut if ever I should be brought to
> this condition, with my present feelings, with the feelings I have had
> for a great many years, I would say: "Come martyrdom, come burnings at the stake, come any calamity and affliction of the body, that
> may be devised by wicked and ungodly men—let me choose that,
> and have eternal life beyond the grave; but let me not deny the work
> of God."[29]

29. *Journal of Discourses,* 21:173. On such occasions Pratt "asked his family, as
they engaged in their secret and family prayers, to petition God to open Brigham
Young's mind that he might understand his [Pratt's] ambitions" (Lyon, "Orson
Pratt—Early Mormon Leader," 86-87).

NINE.

Apparent Contradictions

When quorum members met the next day, Thursday, 5 April 1860, Brigham Young was conspicuous by his absence. He hoped that Pratt's peers would resolve the seemingly interminable controversy without his having to interpose his will further, which he also probably sensed was proving ineffective.

As Elders Orson Hyde, Orson Pratt, John Taylor, Wilford Woodruff, George A. Smith, Charles C. Rich, and Franklin D. Richards and secretary Thomas Bullock reached their seats in the prayer room of the Church Historian's Office shortly before 10:00 a.m., Pratt commented, "I have come here by bro. Taylor's request, and if there are any objections I will withdraw."[1]

---

1. All quotations are from "Great Salt Lake City, Council of the Twelve in Historian's upper room, April 5, 1860, 10 a.m.," Thomas Bullock, scribe, Brigham Young Papers. According to Woodruff's diary: "The Quorum of the Twelve met this morning in the prayer room[. W]e talked the matter over concerning Brother Pratt[,] dressed [in temple clothing,] & prayed[, and then] read over his sermon and Corrected it[,] and the Twelve voted to receive the Confession o[f] Orson Pratt" (Kenney, *Wilford Woodruff's Journal*, 5:446). The Historian's Office Journal, 5

"We want you here," quorum president Hyde replied. "We dont want you to withdraw[. W]e have been together so long in Mormonism, that we are spoiled for any thing else[. I]t is too late to talk of casting out, or separating."

Recalling his experience in Carthage Jail when Joseph and Hyrum Smith were shot and killed in late June 1844, John Taylor said, "I have three shots in my leg, I know how a wounded bird feels. I felt a fluttering and fell in an instant[.] I have a piece out of my thigh as large as my hand, [and] it left a big scar.

"About Bro. Pratt," Taylor continued:

> I dont feel like giving him up, for we have gone too far[. H]e feels too stiff now[;] It would be better for him to give way a little[. A]ll our acts and particularly our writings ought to be true[; otherwise,] it is an infringement of the rights of the others[. W]e ought to be governed by the Spirit of revelation and truth[. A]ny subject that is debateable, when I am abroad, I try to avoid. I would not introduce a question that could put me in a rough place [because] I feel to keep as far from a precipice, as I can.

As he finished, Apostles Ezra T. Benson and Erastus Snow entered the room. Now a majority of the quorum was present. Hyde rose from his seat and announced: "As we are now all together, we will open with prayer; then converse aw[h]ile, then clothe & pray."[2] At Hyde's request, Apostle Richards offered the opening prayer.

Following the prayer, Hyde began a carefully rehearsed approach:

> I do not feel competent to take up the points of difficulty in doctrine

---

April 1860, reported: "The following of the Twelve met in council in the prayer room of the Historian's Building: Orson Hyde, Orson Pratt, Wilford Woodruff, G. A. Smith, John Taylor, Erastus Snow, ~~Lorenzo Snow~~, C. C. Rich, E. T. Benson, [and] F. D. Richards. Tho. Bullock was called upon to act as clerk. See T. B.'s minutes."

2. By clothing and praying, Hyde means that they would discuss thoroughly the subject of Pratt's disagreements with Young, then dress in sacred temple clothing and offer a ritualized group prayer for guidance.

between Bro. Pratt, & bro. Young. [W]hen we have the spirit of an office and calling, and are in subjection one to another, in this is safety,
and as the Savior says[,] unless you become as a little child, you can
not enter into the kingdom of God[. O]ur character and tenacity to
sustain ourselves, has led higher beings than we are, to rebel against
God[.] Lucifer did not acquicise [acquiesce] with the presiding
power[. T]here was a split, and we all know the consequence.

"To acknowledge that this is the Kingdom of God, and that
there is a presiding power, and to admit that he can advance incorrect doctrine, is to lay the ax at the root of the tree," Hyde explained.

Will He [God] suffer His mouthpiece to go into error? No. He would
remove him, and place another there. [B]ro. Brigham may err in the
price of a horse, or a House and lot, [but] in the revelations from God,
where is the man that has given thus said the Lord when it was not so?
I cannot find one instance. David was led by his lust, but the Lord will
not suffer Brigham to introduce incorrect doctrine, and he escape[.
B]ut He has honored him. Then who are we to condemn another
man's servant? [I]f we have the spirit of submission, if we have the
Spirit of God, it will not be so. [W]e have seen too much, and felt too
much to oppose the ruling power.

"What Joseph Smith said," he reminded his colleagues, "was
applicable then[. I]f we can not go nearer the truth, then go home,
and keep you[r] children where they are, that they may not grow
any further. We ought to be wedded to the truth—to the Priesthood—and to the authority of God[.] The presiding power in
Heaven rebukes Angels, and what is the result, then[,] if the presiding power cannot rebuke us, who are we? [B]ro Brigham is responsible for the doctrine taught in this Church," he addressed his remark to Pratt,

and if he did not watch us, and reprove us when wrong, he would not
do his duty[. A]nd again if any of the Twelve was abroad, and an Elder
was propogating a false doctrine, we dealt with that man[. T]hen why

should we not be dealt with in the same manner? [S]hall he [Young] mourn, and we not respond? It is a duty we owe to ourselves; he is the presiding authority of God on the Earth. [So] then[,] he is legitimate, and every thing opposed to him, is not legitimate.

"Bro. Pratt said he was discouraged and felt reckless," he concluded, "[but] he ought not to be so! God is a jealous God, and His servants are jealous with a godly jealousy, that the stream may roll on in purity. I have been chastised and knocked about, but I respect the authority of the kingdom, and go ahead."

Elder Woodruff spoke next. "The remarks of bro. Hyde are dictated by the spirit of wisdom, and the spirit of the Lord," he said.

> Our position is very responsible, and we could not aspire to any thing greater[. H]aving received the Apostleship, we should try to honor it; when bro. Pratt made his confession, it made me rejoice, because I thought it was the first time that he felt to fall into the Channel[.] I would not do any thing to lose my Apostleship, I would rather lose my hand, or my life[.] I think bro. Pratt has gone too far in advancing the doctrine of the Godhead[. T]hey [the doctrines] come in contact with the presidency of the Church. [B]ro. Hyde has been mauled & hammered, but he has yielded, and we have either to say that we are the leaders of the church, or to yield to the leader[. I]t is natural [that] the Lord will reveal His doctrine to his mouthpiece; for the interest of our wives and children, we should submit. I feel to thank the Lord for giving us as good a leader as bro. Brigham. [N]o man had a right to call in question what Joseph [Smith] did. He was led by the spirit of God. [B]ro. Brigham is careful, cautious, and wise, and is a Father[. H]is feeling is to save the people[. E]very thing is Godlike and is filled with wisdom. I want to see bro. Pratt saved, to be one with the Presidency and his brethren.

Woodruff summed up his feelings more pointedly: "If bro. Pratt has taught a false doctrine, it is no worse for him, than me, or bro. Hyde, and [he] should retract[. W]hen a man takes a stubborn course, all Israel feels it; I desire that he may right that matter up. The moment we launch out into the unrevealed doctrine, we are liable to get into error[. B]ro. Pratt ought to make the thing right with Pres. Young."

"Who is our Heavenly Father[?]" Orson Hyde said, referring to Pratt's disagreement with Young over the Adam-God doctrine. "I would as soon it was Father Adam, or any other good and lawful being. I shall see him some time, if I do right. What do I know about Adam, in the Councils of the Great God before he came here, or His privileges[?] I dont know."

"I have confidence that bro. Pratt is just as anxious, as we are to make the plaster as big as the wound," Erastus Snow followed:

It can be done and not to violate his conscience[. T]he Majority of the Church feels that some of his writings are open to serious objections; it is common for all writers to revise their writings, and qualify many portions, [and] it is always ennobling to such men[. B]ro. Brigham wants bro Pratt to qualify it, with credit to themselves[.] I have read some sweeping declarations in his [Pratt's] writings, and thought some of them were dipping into too deep water. He can qualify those words, so as to wipe them out. [I]f bro Pratt had not set his stakes so strong, he would not have had this now. It is given to the presiding officer to discern all things, and tell a man whether he is on the track or not. [W]hen bro. Pratt feels a reluctance to credit bro. Brigham, he takes a course opposed to the truth[. I]f bro. Pratt had continued to rejoice in the revelations given to bro. Brigham, at bro. Hyde's, he would not have been in this situation now.[3] [W]e should resist every temptation, and pray over it, until we overcome.

"It has been a sorrow to me," said Charles Rich,

that there has [been] any difficulty arisen between bro. Brigham and bro. Pratt, [and] I feel very anxious on this subject[. I]t is simply for bro. Pratt to remove the objectionable items[. T]he brethren rejoiced

---

3. Snow refers to the meeting of the apostles at Hyde's cabin when a new First Presidency was formed in late 1847. The proceedings had begun to assume their own mythology, including the assertion that God spoke directly to the Twelve (*Journal of Discourses*, 8:234; see also chap. 8, n23).

at his confession, and it was an increase to his influence[. I]t is not right for a member to have doctrines opposed to his quorum, or the Presidency[. H]e can cure the evil that is wanted to be cured. I would not want to yield the good that I can do, for any light thing[.] I would be glad to see bro. Pratt make it right.

Reading one of Joseph Smith's published revelations (Doctrine and Covenants 26:2) urging that "all things shall be done by common consent," Elder Hyde reminded the quorum that "for one member to advocate new doctrine without common consent is beyond our pale or jurisdiction."

With all eyes now on him, Pratt, although anxious and uncertain, began to feel his way through a response. "I do not see how I can mend the matter, one way or the other," he offered.

> I think the brethren are laboring under a wrong impression. [I]n all of my writings on doctrine, I have tried to confine myself within revelation[.] I do not remember one item that I consider new[. M]any of the exceptions [to President Young's teachings] that I made last night are not in [my] writing[s.] On my subject of pre-existence, I have quoted largely from Genesis and the Book of Abraham[.] I have given it [as it appears in scripture], [about] how Adam was placed here, and quoted it[. I]t was not the subject under consideration, [but I mentioned that] Adam and Eve came here and took bodies of flesh and bones[. T]he doctrine was in the Church when I came into it, and I have always rejoiced in it[. I]n regard to Adam being our Father and our God, I have not published it[;] altho I frankly say, I have no confidence in it, altho advanced by bro. Kimball in the stand, and afterwards approved by bro. Brigham.[4]

"In regard to the infinite knowledge of God," he pressed on,

> it was not a new doctrine, but I quoted largely from revelation[. T]here is no doctrine so absurd as to think that God will eternally

---

4. Pratt's comment supports T. B. H. Stenhouse, whose claim was that Heber C. Kimball's speculations triggered Young's teachings on Adam-God. See T. B. H. Stenhouse, *Rocky Mountain Saints* (New York: D. Appleton and Co., 1873), 561n.

progress in knowledge[.] In regard to empty space, I considered it a philosophical idea, and my opinion is the same as when I published it. I have never intended to advance new ideas, but to keep within revelation. It is said [that] the revelations given to Joseph Smith, answered [questions that were posed] then, and if Joseph would translate now, it would be so very different.[5] [I]f that was so, I should never know when I was right, [and] in fourteen years hence, all the revelations of Brigham may be done away[;] but I do not admit it. The Lord deals with us on consistent principles[. T]here may be apparent contradictions, but to suppose that the meaning would be different, I do not believe. One [revelation] says Adam was formed out of the Earth, and the Lord put in his spirit; and another that he came with his body, flesh and bones[. T]hus there are two contrary revelations[. I]n the garden[,] it is said, that a voice said to Adam, in the meridian of time, I will send my own begotten son Jesus Christ[. T]hen how can that man [God] and Adam both be the Father of Jesus Christ?

"For me to publish to the world that the writings that I have sent to the world, backed up by Joseph's revelations[,] are untrue," he lamented, would mean that

all these revelations will be overturned[. A]s Joseph's [revelations] now are, they are written plain. I was willing [that] all these things should slumber. I made a confession as far as my conscience would allow me, to be justified, [but] I could not state it from knowledge[.] I supposed it was all right, until I heard bro. Brigham's declarations from the stand; *that* threw a damper on my mind[.] I will leave the event in the hands of my brethren[. I]n relation to the doctrine, it is already corrected by bro. Brigham[. B]ro. Hyde advanced [suggested] the same doctrine to Joseph, and he [Hyde] says that Joseph said it was not correct.

---

5. Two years later Young would state publicly: "I will even venture to say that if the book of Mormon were now to be re-written, in many instances it would materially differ from the present translation" (*Journal of Discourses*, 9:311).

"That was so," agreed Hyde.[6]

"I really believed in regard to the omnipresence of the Spirit," the forty-eight-year-old Pratt pleaded; "I did really believe that Bro. Brigham had preached the same doctrine[.] I have not tried to introduce new doctrines into the Church[. B]ro Young's sermon was published by me as soon as I received it, without comments, *and I do not intend [that] it shall come from me, while I believe in Joseph Smith's revelations*—but I do believe that bro. Brigham errs in judgment" (emphasis in original).

"When there is a want of union," Hyde interjected,

> it requires us to speak plain[. B]ro Pratt does not claim any vision or revelation, but keeps within the scope of Joseph's revelations. The Universalists have their belief, The Presbyterians do the same, [and] they consider they believe that [they] are in the pale of revealed religion[. A]ll the Sects do the same, yet how widely they differ. [T]hen here comes a man (B. Y.) who says he has a revelation, but it means the sects [are wrong], it is Antagonistic. I see no necessity of rejecting Joseph's revelations, or going to War with the living ones, that is nearest to us[. B]ro. Pratt is like the Jews, who garnish the sepulchres of the dead, but reject those that were the nearest to them[.] I do not see any contradiction or opposition between B. Young & J. Smith.

"B. Young must have feelings towards me," Pratt suggested. "I wish the brethren would point out to me where my pamphlet on 'the Holy Spirit' is wrong."

"When bro. Brigham tells me a thing, I receive it as revelation," countered Taylor. "Some things may be apparently contradictory, but are not really contradictory."

Pratt stressed that "it was the Father of Jesus Christ that was talking to Adam in the garden—B. Young says that Adam was the Father of Jesus, both of his Spirit and Body, in his teachings from

---

6. Like Young, Hyde must have thought that what Joseph Smith said implied that Adam was God, or Hyde would not have asked the question.

the stand, [while B]ro. Richards published in the Pearl of Great Price, that another person would come in the meridian of time, which was Jesus Christ."

"David in spirit called Jesus Christ, Lord, how then is he [h]is Son?" offered Orson Hyde. "It would seem a contradiction[.] I went to Joseph and told him my ideas of the Omnipresence of the Spirit, [and] he said it was very pretty, and it was got up very nice, and is a beautiful doctrine, but it only lacks one thing[.] I enquired what is it[, and] bro. Joseph, he replied that *it is not true*" (emphasis in original).

"If Christ is the first fruits of them that slept," Taylor added, "there must be some discrepency, he must have resumed his position, having a legitimate claim to a possession some where else, [and] he ought not to be debarred from his rights[. T]he power of God was sufficient to resuscitate Jesus immediately and also the body of Adam." Taylor then commented briefly on the density of air and water, but cautioned, "I dont profess to speak philosophically."

Perhaps anticipating a drawn-out exchange, Hyde announced, following Taylor's remarks:

> We have come here to arrange that discourse, to the sanction of bro. Young, that it may go forth under the sanction of bro. Pratt[. I]s he willing to put that discourse in a shape to recall or qualify certain points of doctrine, not [as an] extorted [confession], but in an easy way to shew reflection, and that truth had led him to make this confession[? A]nd to leave Bro. Young out as a dictator, and [not in a way except] what would be satisfactory to Bro. Young[?] I am pleased with the leniency extended by bro. Young to bro. Pratt, it is more than he has extended to me, or others.

Despite the attempt to wrap things up quickly, Pratt remained uncompromising. "I have heard brother Brigham say," Pratt said, "that Adam is the Father of our Spirits, and he came here with his resurrected body, to fall for his own children; and I said to him, it leads to an endless number of falls, which leads to sorrow and death;

that is revolting to my feelings, even if it were not sustained by revelation."

"Is there any revelation saying that the Body of Adam should return to the dust of *this* Earth?" Erastus Snow asked (emphasis in original).

"If you bring Adam as a Spirit," Pratt countered, "and put him into the tabernacle [of flesh], [this] runs easy with me; another item, I heard brother Young say [was] that Jesus had a body, flesh and Bones, before he came, [before] he was born of the Virgin Mary[. I]t was so contrary to every revelation given."

As Pratt paused, Hyde turned to George A. Smith, silent until now. "Brother Geo. A. Smith[,] just tell us what will be satisfactory to the Church?"

The ailing George A. Smith was Young's closest friend and confidante among the apostles. In his view, the answer was simple: "For him to acknowledge Brigham Young as the President of the Church, in the exercise of his calling[. B]ut he [Pratt] only acknowledges him as a poor drivelling fool, [and says] he preaches doctrine opposed to Joseph, and all other revelations." He could not have been more emphatic. "If Brigham Young is the President of the Church, he is an inspired man. If we have not an inspired man, then Orson Pratt is right."

Hyde agreed. "The world does not know that bro. Pratt acknowledges bro. Young as an inspired man."

"The only thing," Smith said, "is for bro. Pratt to get a revelation that bro. B. Young is a Prophet of God."

"I dont think that any light can come to Bro. Pratt, while he resists it," echoed Erastus Snow.

"I did make a confession with my heart," Pratt pleaded. "I am only an individual, [and] I can not possibly yield to say I have published false doctrine[.] I did say it was only my belief, and not revelation[.] I thought I could go on with the Twelve, and preach and exhort, [but] I leave it entirely in the hands of the Church[.] I am willing to take out the article, but [I am] not willing to say I have taught false doctrine," he declared. "I have been in the Church many years, and have learned that so long as we want to keep things smooth, we can do so[. A]ny modification you feel to make in that sermon, will be right, even to cutting it down one half."

"I feel you will yet acknowledge that you have taught false doctrine," Hyde predicted. "I dont think you will receive a revelation, only thro brother Brigham, and you will yet confess that you have stubbornly resisted the Council[.] I tell you, you will not get a revelation from God on the subject."

"Paul say[s he saw] things in the third heaven that he could not reveal to the world," explained Woodruff.

[O]ur [temple] endowments cannot be revealed to the world[.] Joseph Smith & B. Young are inspired men[,] but [they] can not reveal them [the endowments]. [A]s our leaders are inspired to talk, they are inspired oracles, and we should be as limber as a dish cloth[.] I have wondered why the Lord could not have cooked up something easier than to see the human family going to hell, or send his Son to be crucified, [but] I would follow the leader and do the best I could.

"We will dress and pray," Hyde announced, "then have that sermon [read], and read [it] over item by item, and see what [changes] will agree with bro. Pratts conscience."

"I dont like any patching," rejoined John Taylor, "but [will] follow the dictates of our Presidency[.] I dont believe in having things thrown on bro. Brigham[. I]f that mouthpiece has not power to dictate, I would throw all Mormonism away[. A]ll that can be asked is to carry out the doctrine in his sermon."

"I have always felt [that] if I can be convinced," Orson responded, "nothing would give me greater pleasure than to make the confession."

Woodruff then placed Pratt's 29 January sermon with quorum secretary Thomas Bullock. Soon, vested in their temple robes, all unitedly formed a close circle. Elder Rich offered a prayer, after which Apostle Benson, in the center, led the sacred ritual.

"Our Father and our God," Benson intoned solemnly,

in the name of the Lord Jesus Christ, and by the authority of the Holy Priesthood[,] we come before thee, having offered up the holy and sacred signs of the Holy Priesthood, to ask thee for such things as we need, and to pardon and forgive all of our sins, and to send thy Holy Spirit to come and enlighten our minds that they may be clear on the subjects to come before us.

We now feel our weakness and pray thee to remove the cloud of darkness, let the destroyer have no power over us[. M]ay the council of thy servants be clear and comprehensive, and we pray thee to pour out thy spirit upon us as a Quorum to discharge our duties.

Help us by the light of thy glorious countenance, to rest upon thy servant Orson Pratt, and we pray thee that double of thy spirit may rest upon him. [L]et his mind be clear, and divest him of selfishness and hardness of heart, and may he be filled with the Holy Ghost that he may subject himself to his brethren[. C]omfort his heart, & rend the vail of unbelief, cause the scales of blindness to fall from his eyes, that he may see, and his ears to hear the whisperings of the Holy Spirit, soften his heart as a little child to the will of his brethren, and [may he] reconcile himself to the will of our God[. H]elp him, raise him up, to magnify his apostleship, that he may do good among his brethren[. W]e dedicate him unto thee, and we pray thee that his way may be opened up, and may he be blessed with great faith and power of God, and be a blessing to his family, that he may be relieved in temporal things necessary to make him comfortable, and [that he may] acknowledge the hand of God in all things[. M]ay he rise up and rebuke the destroyer, and be removed from oppression and darkness of mind[. W]e ask the Father in the name of Jesus Christ to remove the darkness in our midst, that the spirit of revelation may be open to us. [A]ccept of us, our prayers, our dedication, as thy children, servants and Apostles.

We ask thee to bless bro. [Orson] Hyde as President of this quorum, may he have wisdom to preside as a man of God, filled with the Holy Ghost, that he may have eyes to see and understand thy spirit and be guided aright in all things, bless us as a quorum, may our faith increase, and the power of God be manifested from time to time.

We pray thee to bless bro. George A. [Smith], who has been a long time afflicted[. D]o thou strengthen him up and [that] his ancle [may be] healed by the power of God. [A]nd may he be healed of all of his infirmities.

We pray thee in behalf of brother Brigham Young, who we acknowledge as our leader: Prophet, Seer, and Revelator. [D]o thou speak unto him by visions and dreams, and let him be clothed in revelations continually, and stand as a Prophet over thy people, and do thou keep and preserve him for ever.

And do thou also bless thy servants Heber [C. Kimball] and Daniel [H. Wells], may they stand by him in prosperity and adversity; bless them with health, heal them of their infirmities, [and] may they live long even as long as life is sweet[. C]omfort and bless them, and may they be a blessing to thy Saints scattered abroad in these vallies.

Bless the officers in thy Church and Kingdom, who are placed to preside over and to counsel thy people[. B]less their fields, flocks, herd[s], cattle and soil[;] bless them in sowing seed in the Earth, that it may bring forth to sustain man and beast, that they may be made glad. [B]less thy Saints scattered abroad, [and] gather Israel; even thy scattered people who are crying for deliverance[;] bless thy Saints who are preaching the gospel, enable them to do good, magnify their calling, do a good work and return in peace and safety

Bless bro. Hooper,[7] [and] may the power of God be on him, & enable him to magnify his calling, fill his office as Delegate to Washington for thy people and accomplish all that is necessary[. G]ive him power over the members of Congress, the President and the Cabinet. Do thou soften the nations of the Earth to bring all things about, even those things that are not fulfilled.

We dedicate ourselves unto thee, with our Wives and Children, flocks and herds, fields and grain[. D]o thou temper the elements for our good that we may be prospered in all things and do good to thy people[. M]ake thy people happy and glorious and cause thy holy spirit to shine forth in our hearts continually. even so. Amen.

---

7. William H. Hooper was the church's representative and lobbyist in Washington, D.C.

Following Benson's emotional petition, Orson Hyde invited secretary Bullock to read Pratt's lengthy 29 January discourse. For the next two to three hours, corrections were suggested by various quorum members, discussed, and when acceptable to Pratt, recorded by Bullock.

The bulk of the revisions omitted Pratt's opinions and personal judgments regarding Brigham Young. A few clarifying comments were incorporated. Significantly, nothing in the way of an admission that Pratt had advanced false doctrine was added. When finished, approximately 25 percent of the controversial sermon had been excised with the apostle's tacit approval. John Taylor moved that the quorum officially accept the new confession, and the motion was seconded and carried unanimously.

At their showing, a clearly exhausted Pratt commented weakly: "Brethren[,] I must say I am very thankful for the many items that are struck out, if this will suit the Presidency[.] I pray that from henceforth, I may be one with you, and preach with you."

Before adjourning at 5:30 p.m., members agreed to meet with Brigham Young that evening at eight o'clock. Elder Hyde then offered the benediction.

Earlier in the day, President Young had alluded to his on-going difficulties with Pratt in a public discourse on the importance of obedience to authority. "We have very scanty ideas concerning the great plan call[ed] the plan of salvation," he told listeners in the Tabernacle, "the system of doctrine, ideas, and practices that pertain to all the intelligence that exists in eternity." He continued:

> Very small, minute, and abstract ideas and principles are given to the children of men in relation to it, because they can bear but little—a little here and a little there, as it is written by the Prophet [Joseph Smith], "line upon line, and precept upon precept." If you can receive one line to-day, it may prepare you to receive another to-morrow pertaining to the things of God. I am very happy and rejoice much, because I believe that I am now looking upon men and women who are steadily increasing in knowledge, firm in their integrity, truthful,

and lovers of virtue in their hearts; though some, as has been observed, give way to temptation, are overcome by the enemy, and are
led away. This we expect. As many as will be faithful to their calling,
and manifest their faith by their good works, will find that they belong to the elect; and every one that forsakes his covenants and his
God, and turns away from the holy commandments delivered to
him, will find that he belongs to that class who are reprobates. God
has given us ability to do good or evil. According to certain principles
inherent in the organization of the people, they can believe the truth,
or disbelieve it and believe a lie. They can falsify, or cling to the truth.
They can continue to do good, or forsake it and commence to do
evil. Every man is capable of doing either good or evil: he has his own
choice, and will be judged by his works.[8]

Young had anticipated the course and result of the quorum's
actions, and that evening, with members of the Twelve seated
around him in the Historian's Office, the president's enthusiasm was
evident. Pratt handed him the corrected copy of his discourse,
which Young accepted, adding that "he should attach a few remarks
to it" before it appeared in print.

Obviously concerned about the possible direction Young's use
of the sermon might take, Pratt wondered if the "subject was to be
dropped; or was it to be resurrected again."

Young replied that "he never wanted the subject, to be mouthed
again, and wished those in the room, not to mention it. This day
[evening] I have seen the best spirit manifested," he said. "I have
heard 15 or 16 men all running in the same stream. I was delighted.
Tomorrow the Church will be 30 years old, about the age that Jesus
was when he commenced his mission.

"We are improving, and I just know it," Young continued.
"[M]y path is like the noon day sun, and I could cry hallelujah! hallelujah! Praise to God who has been merciful to us and conferred
on us His Holy Spirit. A private member in this church is brighter

---

8. *Journal of Discourses,* 8:32.

than the power of Kings and Princes of the World, to secure an eternal existence; the wicked have to be blotted out of existence for ever[, no longer to be] written in the Lamb's book of life.

"Bro. Orson Pratt," he announced, "I want you to do just as you have done in your Apostleship, but when you want to teach new doctrine, write your ideas, and submit them to me, and if they are correct, I will tell you. There is no man's sermons that I like to read [more], when you understand your subject, but than yours— but you are not perfect[. N]either am I," he concluded.[9]

To the general conference the following day, Young said, "How many Gods there are, and how many places there are in their kingdoms, is not for me to say. But," he proceeded:

> I can say this, which is a source of much comfort, consolation, and gratification to[o]: Behold the goodness, the long-suffering, the kindness, and the strong parental feeling of our Father and God in preparing the way and providing the means to save the children of men— not alone the Latter-day Saints—not those alone who have the privilege of the first principles of the celestial law, but to save all.[10]

In presenting the names of the general authorities of the church, including Pratt's, the president stressed:

> I have not inquired whether there are any cases of difficulty between brethren or differences in doctrine that should be presented before the Conference. I have heard of none; consequently I have not given an opportunity to present any. I do not expect there is any such business requiring our attention.
>
> We will first present the authorities of the Church; and I sincerely request the members to act freely and independently in voting—also in speaking, if it be necessary. There has been no instance in this Church of a person's being in the least curtailed in the privilege

---

9. Pratt's and Young's comments are combined from three sources: the President's Office Journal, 5 Apr. 1860; "Minutes in office, of Pres. Young, April 5[, 18]60," Brigham Young Papers; and the Historian's Office Journal, 5 Apr. 1860.

10. *Journal of Discourses,* 8:34.

of speaking his honest sentiments. It cannot be shown in the history of this people that a man has ever been injured, either in person, property, or character, for openly expressing, in the proper time and place, his objections to any man holding authority in this Church, or for assigning his reasons for such objections.[11]

After conference, true to his word, Young reviewed Pratt's revised confessional, examined the apostle's disputed writings, and saw to the composition of several brief "Instructions to the Saints" in mid-July. He was aided by counselors Heber C. Kimball and Daniel H. Wells and by his personal secretary Albert Carrington.[12] The statement, under the signatures of the First Presidency, was appended to the revised text of Pratt's confession, now titled simply "Remarks." Both articles appeared in the *Deseret News* on Wednesday, 27 July 1860, five months after Pratt had delivered the controversial sermon.

The final draft[13] of the First Presidency statement read:

> Elder Pratt sustains an unimpeachable character, so far as strict morality, tried integrity, industry, energy, zeal, faithfulness to his religion, and honesty in all business transactions are concerned; but it will be readily perceived, from his "Remarks," that he does not claim exemption from liability to err in judgment in relation to "some points of doctrine." Br. Pratt's preachings and teachings upon the first principles of the Gospel are excellent.
>
> With regard to the quotations and comments in *The Seer* as to Adam's having been formed "out of the ground," and "from the dust

---

11. Ibid., 7:227.

12. President's Office Journal, 10 Apr., 14 July 1860. Ironically, Pratt had just delivered a 4th of July sermon in which he denounced the federal government. His speech had to be toned down before it appeared in print. See ibid., 6 July 1860; *Journal of Discourses*, 8:111-13.

13. What follows is a transcription of the second draft from the Brigham Young Papers. The earlier version in the Young Papers differs only slightly. Besides appearing in the *Deseret News*, the statement was included in Clark, *Messages of the First Presidency*, 2:214-23.

of the ground," &c., it is deemed wise to let that subject remain without further explanation at present, for it is written that we are to receive "line upon line," according to our faith and capacities, and the circumstances attending our progress.

In *The Seer,* pages 24 and 25, par. 22, br Pratt states: "All these Gods are equal in power, in glory, in dominion, and in the possession of all things; each possesses a fulness of truth, of knowledge, of wisdom, of light, of intelligence; each governs himself in all things by his own attributes, and is filled with love, goodness, mercy, and justice towards all. The fulness of all these attributes is what constituted God." "It is truth, light, and love, that we worship and adore; these are the same in all worlds; and as these constituted God, He is the same in all worlds." "Wherever you find a fulness of wisdom, knowledge, truth, goodness, love, and such like qualities, there you find God in all his glory, power, and majesty. Therefore, if you worship these adorable perfections, you worship God."[14]

Seer, page 117, par. 95: "[T]hen there will be no Being or Beings in existence that will know one particle more than what we know; then our knowledge, and wisdom, and power will be infinite; and cannot, from thenceforth, be increased or expanded in the least degree;" Same page, par. 96: "[B]ut when they" (the Saints) "become one with the Father and Son, and receive a fulness of their glory, that will be the end of all progression in knowledge, because there will be nothing more to be learned. The Father and the Son do not progress in knowledge and wisdom, because they already know all things past, present, and to come." Par. 97: "[T]here are none among them (the Gods) that are in advance of the others in knowledge; though some may have been Gods [for] as many millions of years, as there are particles of dust in all the universe, yet there is not one truth that such are in possession of but what every other God knows." "None of these Gods are progressing in knowledge: neither can they progress in the acquirement of any truth."

In his treatise entitled "Great First Cause," page 16, par. 17, br Pratt states: "All the organizations of worlds, of minerals, of vegetables,

---

14. Actually, these quotations appear only on p. 24 of *The Seer.*

of animals, of men, of angels, of spirits, and of the spiritual personages of the Father, of the Son, and of the Holy Ghost, must, if organized at all, have been the result of the self combinations and unions of the pre-existent, intelligent, powerful, and eternal particles of substance. These eternal Forces and Powers are the Great First Causes of all things and events that have had a beginning."

The foregoing quoted ideas, and similar ones omitted to be quoted, with the comments thereon, as advanced by br. Pratt in an article, in the *Seer,* entitled[15] "Pre-existence of men," and in his treatise entitled "Great First Cause," are plausibly presented. But to the whole subject we will answer in the words of the Apostle Joseph Smith, on a similar occasion. One of the Elders of Israel[16] had written a long revelation which he deemed to be very important, and requested br. Joseph to hear him read it. The Prophet commended its style in glowing terms, remarked that the ideas were ingeniously advanced, &c., &c., and that he had but one objection to it. "What is that?" inquired the writer, greatly elated that his production was considered so near perfect. The Prophet Joseph replied, "It is not true."

Thus, where Pratt had been unwilling to admit to teaching false doctrine, insisting that he be told specifically where he had erred, Young and his counselors offered this detailed condemnation of his perceived theological excesses. Of the four excerpts from the *Seer,* three referred to the omniscience of God; the fourth dealt with God's omniscience and the attendant attributes of godliness. The quotation from the small tract Pratt published in England nine

---

15. Initially, reference was made here to Pratt's pamphlet, *The Absurdities of Immaterialism,* but this was stricken from the First Presidency's first and second drafts before publication. Young would similarly conclude, recounting his experience hearing the sermon of an unidentified American philosopher: "After laboring long on the subject, he straightened himself up—he was a fine looking man—and said he, 'My brethren and sisters, I must come to the conclusion that the soul of man is an immaterial substance.' Said I, 'Bah!' There was no more sense in his discourse than in the bleating of a sheep or the grunting of a pig" (*Journal of Discourses,* 14:198).

16. This was Orson Hyde.

years earlier, *Great First Cause, Or the Self-Moving Forces of the Universe*, defined the attributes of godliness as particles which, when combined, created God. Significantly, the First Presidency did not refer to Pratt's *Holy Spirit* tract which contained other ideas Young would not have sanctioned.[17] Within less than five years, this pamphlet would also be officially condemned.

"This should be a lasting lesson to the Elders of Israel not to undertake to teach doctrine they do not understand," Young, Kimball, and Wells closed. "If the Saints can preserve themselves in a present salvation day by day, which is easy to be taught and comprehended, it will be well with them hereafter."

That fall, Pratt received a call to serve a mission to the eastern United States where he was to help the financially destitute converts gather to the West.[18] Ironically, Pratt himself was in serious financial straits at the time[19]—a poverty that Young believed was Pratt's punishment for having "forced" British Saints to purchase his publications. Young worried that Pratt would produce additional pamphlets and that immigrating Saints would feel obligated to buy them. "The Book debt was the worst trouble the Saints had to Contend with for 6 years," he informed Pratt on 9 September. "Orson Pratt has done more to make that debt than any other man. So many Books are forced upon the people and they are forced to take them or they will not be fellowshipped. Now stop publishing & getting your portraits taken & fill[ing] the kingdom with them & mak[ing] the people pay for them. This keeps the people poor and keeps them from Emigrating." Pratt replied that "he had used his

---

17. "We cannot believe for a moment that God is destitute of body, parts, passions or attributes," Young would later say. "Attributes can be made manifest only through an organized personage. All attributes are couched in and are the results of organized existence" (*Journal of Discourses*, 10:192).

18. See President's Office Journal, 14 Apr. 1860.

19. Earlier that year Young told local church leaders that Pratt was "poor." The next year Pratt's assessed valuation was $2,575, while Young's was $52,250 and his two counselors an average of $11,750 each. See President's Office Journal, 14 Apr. 1860; Assessment Records, Salt Lake County Assessor's Office.

own means and not any of the means of the Church. He had got it all [done] by [the sale of] his publications." "It all come out of the poor Saints," Young retorted, "[j]ust as much as tho he [Pratt] had begged it."[20]

In his last public sermon prior to leaving the valley two weeks later on 26 September, Pratt bore a surprisingly honest, heartfelt testimony, the memory of recent events no doubt still vivid in his mind. "Have I this hope [of eternal life]?" he asked.

I have to some degree, and I would to God that I had it to a greater degree. Promises have been showered upon my head; blessings have been pronounced upon me by the Priesthood at different times; other blessings have been sealed upon me through the holy ordinances of the Gospel, by the proper authority; but I contemplate that these are conditional. There is a small degree of trembling and fear that, after all, I may prove unfaithful, and that I may not be able to endure unto the end.[21]

"I can say amen to what brother Pratt has just said," Young followed at the same Sunday meeting:

I think I can with propriety say to him and a great many of the Elders of Israel that they may dismiss those little doubts that brother Pratt has spoken of in regard to proving faithful. You who are in the Church and have been a long time faithful, the Lord will never suffer [you] to so fall away that you cannot be saved. I hardly know of a man who has been in the Church fifteen, twenty, or twenty-five years and longer,

---

20. Qtd. in Kenney, *Wilford Woodruff's Journal*, 5:496. Pratt was not oblivious to the financial possibilities in publishing books. "Your writings are highly esteemed in England," he wrote earlier to his brother, Parley. "You no doubt obtain a handsome profit on each successive edition: if you do not, you may depend that it is worth looking after, and would be a benefit to you in your deep poverty. The office in Liverpool brings in many thousand dollars clear profit annually which is a great benefit to the church. Should they be indebted to you for any profits arising from the sale of [your publications], they would no doubt cheerfully pay you" (Orson Pratt to Parley P. Pratt, 12 Sept. 1853, Orson Pratt Papers).

21. *Journal of Discourses*, 8:311.

but what had better be thankful that that time is past, and not wish to live it over again, for fear he would not do as well. True, some of the brethren have taken mis-steps—have dealt amiss in some instances, and have not done so well as they could, had they lived so as to have known more; but I am satisfied with them, if they will continue to learn and improve upon their gifts and become perfect.[22]

Passing though Salt Lake City in early September (and, in fact, present for the above remarks), British adventurer Richard Burton offered an educated, if irreverent, outsider's view of Pratt's and Young's recent difficulties. "There had been a little 'miff' between Mr. President and the 'Gauge of Philosophy,' Mr. O. Pratt," he wrote.

> The latter gentleman, who is also an apostle, is a highly though probably a self-educated man ... [t]he Usman of the New Faith, writer, preacher, theologian, missionary, astronomer, philosopher, and mathematician—especially in the higher branches[. H]e has thrust thought into a faith of ceremony which is supposed to dispense with the trouble of thinking, and has intruded human learning into a scheme whose essence is the utter abrogation of learning; of relying, in fact, rather [than] upon books and mortal paper[, on] the royal road to all knowledge, inspiration from on high[. H]is tendencies to let loose these pernicious doctrines often bring him into trouble and place him below his position.[23]

One week later, and only three days before his departure, Pratt gathered with other general authorities and departing missionaries in the Historian's Office. Pratt and missionary companion Erastus

---

22. Ibid., 167.

23. Richard Burton, *The City of the Saints and across the Rocky Mountains to California* (New York: Harper & Brothers Publishers, 1862), 353. "He is a free noble minded man," wrote Apostle Woodruff after meeting Burton. "He has traveled so extensively that he has Cast of[f] that Cloak of prejudice and Superstition which most men have against all who do not embrace their own political & religious faith. He will tell the truth about all men & things as far as he Can obtain it" (Kenney, *Wilford Woodruff's Journal*, 5:492).

Snow were customarily blessed by their brethren for their new assignment. Then, separating themselves from the rank-and-file, the leading councils retired to the adjoining prayer room where, as Wilford Woodruff wrote, "we had a vary interesting meeting."

Heber C. Kimball, one of several brethren who thought that Pratt's revised confession had not adequately addressed the issue of his erroneous doctrines and stubborn insistence on unsound notions, asked that Pratt again "make satisfaction to Preside[n]t Young" before leaving the city. Young answered that "he did not wish him to make any acknowledgements to him."

Pratt, Young remarked, "was strangely Constituted. He had acquired a good deal of knowledge upon many things but in other things He was one of the most ignorant men he ever saw in his life. He was full of integrity & would lie down & have his head Cut off for me or his religi[o]n if necessary[24] but he will never see his Error untill he goes into the spirit world. [T]hen he will say[,] Brother Brigham[,] how foolish I was.

"Now Brother Pratt thinks that he and all the gods will be learning for many millions of years," he continued,

> but by & by [the gods] will know all things & all will know it alike & that will be the End of their Exhaltations & knowledge. He Cannot see the folly of forming this opinion here in the flesh & in his ignorance. But a thousand years hence he will see the folly of it. I will hold on to Brother Pratt & all these my Brethren of the Twelve notwithstanding all their sins, folly, & weaknesses untill I me[e]t with them in my Fathers kingdom to part no more because they love God and are full of integrity.

Pratt replied defensively, "I do not believe as Brother Brigham & Brother Kimball do in some points of doctrine & they do not wish me to acknowl[edge] to a thing that I do not believe."

---

24. Kimball remembered this comment as: "[I]f Bro Orson was chopped up in[to] inch[-long] pieces[,] each piece would cry out [that] Mormonism was true" (President's Office Journal, 1 Oct. 1860).

"No," Young replied, "you Cannot See the truth in this matter until you get into the spirit world."[25]

Why was the subject of Pratt's doctrines raised once again, considering Young's 5 April admonition that he wanted the topic dropped? Kimball was not present at the April meeting and may have been unaware of Young's request. Yet, given Young's and Kimball's close friendship,[26] he must have known of the overall ebbs and flows of the dispute. Perhaps because of his strict deference to the president, he found Pratt's disobedience more troubling than did others in the hierarchy. In early 1843, Kimball had criticized Pratt after Joseph Smith had determined that the matter of Pratt's disloyalty should be closed. Eight days following the farewell in the Historian's Office, Kimball told the church president's clerks that "there were men that were trying to ride down Br O. Pratt; but it would not do[.] Br. Pratt, was a man of unusual firmness."[27] Kimball helped to keep alive both the controversy and Pratt's fears that the matter he wanted forgotten would not die.

---

25. Qtd. in Kenney, *Wilford Woodruff's Journal,* 5:506-507.

26. See Stanley B. Kimball, "Brigham and Heber," *BYU Studies* 18 (Spring 1978): 396-409.

27. Qtd. in President's Office Journal, 1 Oct. 1860.

TEN.

While Wickedness Stalks Unrebuked

*O*rson Pratt returned from his eastern states mission in early September 1861, a year after his departure. One month later to the day, 6 October, Brigham Young asked him to help oversee one of the church's recent moves toward economic self-sufficiency: the Utah Cotton Mission headquartered 325 miles south in St. George.[1] Pratt and members of his first family would join some 300 other Saints in the southern Utah settlement before the year's end. For the next two and a half years, Orson would perform a variety of public service and church callings, whether south in Utah's Dixie or as a member of the territorial legislature in Great Salt Lake City.

During this time, Young began to soften somewhat his criticisms of Elder Pratt. On 18 March 1862, Apostle John Taylor and others called on the president at his office to speculate about the future of the Civil War. As an aside, Young "remarked there were

---

1. For an overview of this Mormon enterprise, see Leonard J. Arrington, *Great Basin Kingdom* (Lincoln: University of Nebraska Press, 1958), 216-23.

213

some things that Elder Orson Pratt did not believe in," mentioning "that on one occasion Br. Orson wanted to prove that the moving forces were caused by the law of repulsion and not attraction." Young commented that since "an opposition in all things existed, [then] necessarily there must be attraction as well as repulsion." Yet "Br. Orson," the president concluded, "was a righteous man."[2]

In early 1864, Pratt unexpectedly requested a change in church assignment. Young obliged that April by calling him to Austria and Britain. Although Pratt would be denied entry into Austria, he would fill most of his three-year assignment to Great Britain.[3] In anticipation of his new appointment, he took on a considerably less important role in the affairs of the church in southern Utah as Elder Erastus Snow, who had earlier accompanied Pratt to the east coast and later acted as his subordinate in the small desert village, was appointed successor to the senior apostle.

While Pratt was abroad, an incident in St. George would exert a profound impact on his future public conduct and personal views. Some months prior to his departure, his sensitive and musically inclined twenty-six-year-old namesake politely declined an offer from Brigham Young to serve a church mission. "During your recent visit to St. George," Orson Jr. wrote to the church president in mid-1863,

> I informed you of the change that had taken place in my religious views, thinking that, in such a case, you would not insist on my undertaking the mission assigned me. You received me kindly and gave me what I have no doubt you considered good fatherly advice. I was much affected during the interview and hastily made a promise which, subsequent reflection convinces me it is not my duty to per-

---

2. Qtd. in Historian's Office Journal, 18 Mar. 1862.

3. Only months before Pratt arrived in England, the *Latter-day Saints' Millennial Star*, 5, 12 Mar. 1864, reprinted portions of Brigham Young's "History" from the *Deseret News* dealing with Pratt's 1842 "excommunication" and 1843 reinstatement.

form. ... Should any thing hereafter occur to convince me that my present decision is unwise I shall be ready to revoke it.[4]

Less than a year later, with Orson Sr. now abroad, Elder Snow instructed the young skeptic to resign from his position on the Southern Utah Mission High Council, an ecclesiastical body that governed the Cotton Mission and colony. Snow reportedly offered "some feeling remarks" at first but then decided he "could not conscientiously, and in justice to the cause we are engaged in," allow Orson Jr. to continue, "doubting as he does the divinity of the calling of the Prophet Joseph Smith and the consequent building up of the Church."[5] The young man was told to renounce any claim he held as a high priest in the church's Melchizedek priesthood.

Thoughtful, well-read, and widely traveled, Orson Pratt Jr. demanded as much reason from religion as his father had. "Every friend of human freedom and progression should steadily discountenance and oppose every attempt to deprive man of his mental independence," he wrote during this time. "The time will come when reason will predominate instead of superstition, and universal philanthropy instead of narrow-minded selfishness." "Faith is often regarded as something unconnected with reason," he later added.

This is a sad error and as such, is calculated to lead to much mischief. He who looks upon faith as beyond, and superior to, reason, is very likely to neglect the proper cultivation of the latter and consequently, to become the victim of blind credulity. Every species of imposition finds in him a firm, unwavering supporter. ... Why and wherefore seldom occur to him. ...

Let us then examine and canvas freely, with an earnest desire for the truth. Let no preconceived notion founded in prejudice bar the

---

4. Orson Pratt Jr. to Brigham Young, 13 June 1863, Orson Pratt Collection.

5. Qtd. in Andrew Karl Larson, *Erastus Snow: The Life of a Missionary and Pioneer for the Early Mormon Church* (Salt Lake City: University of Utah Press, 1971), 367. Pratt says that Snow "desired" his resignation, whereas Snow seems to suggest that he merely acquiesced to Pratt's request.

way if we are able to remove them. Let us tear aside the vail of hypocritical sanctity, behind which, the seemingly pious conceal their moral deformity, at the same time that we respect the humble and sincere inquirer, although doctrines may not be consistent with our own views.[6]

Orson Jr. refused at first to resign from the high council because he was concerned about the possible backlash for his father.[7] In fact, when Young learned of Orson Jr.'s apostasy, he immediately blamed his father, commenting privately that "O[rson] Prat Senior was at heart an infidel."[8] St. George leaders prevailed in having young Pratt dismissed from his quorum. Four months later, on 15 September, the St. George high council met and, under pressure from Apostle Snow, formally voted that Orson Pratt Jr. be excommunicated from the church for "unbelief." Fearing the repercussions to his family when it became known that the oldest son of one of Mormonism's leading apostles had been expelled from his church, Orson Jr. publicly addressed the southern Saints before the official announcement of his excommunication was made on Sunday, 17 September 1864.

While it is not known to what extent Orson Sr. learned the specifics of his son's public comments (below), the apostle's later discourses exhibited a pronounced—though not complete—absence of earlier doctrinal speculations or insistence on reason. This is not to suggest that the series of emotional meetings during the first four months of 1860 failed to exercise a significant dampening effect on him. But the stark realization that his first-born could not embrace the religion for which the apostle himself had sacrificed so

---

6. Qtd. in ibid., 368.

7. Pratt's remarks were recorded verbatim by James G. Bleak in "Annals of the Southern Utah Mission," 172-75, typescript, BYU Library; Larson, *Erastus Snow,* 368-70.

8. Qtd. in Lorenzo Brown, Diary, 12 Sept. 1864, BYU Library. Brown, with others, was accompanying Young and his party on a tour of southern Utah settlements.

much could have caused him to question as never before his own actions and attitudes. Perhaps in Orson Sr.'s mind, the personal revelation he had demanded during his early confrontations with Brigham Young had been visited upon his own son.

"Brothers and sisters," Orson Pratt Jr. began,

> for I suppose I may still continue to call you so, as we are all the children of One Father[. N]otwithstanding [the] action [that] may be taken to-day which will sever me from the Church, I still continue to look upon those before me as my brethern and sisters, as I also do every child of God.
>
> Brother McArthur visited me this morning and told me my presence was needed here, as action would be taken upon my case. I thought I would not attend any more meetings here, as Brother Snow had desired me to resign my position in the High Council. And they wanted me to resign my calling as a High Priest, although on second thought I refused to do so. Not that I am anxious to retain my position, for I have never asked for an office, but I did not know what would be thought at Head Quarters when they came to hear of my resigning my various positions[. B]ut they dropped me from the Quorum.
>
> In Salt Lake City I was made a High Councilor, although I was then an Unbeliever, as now, and continued in the position till I came down here. In regard to my faith, I wish to say that I have long since seen differently to this people, and although I am not in the habit of saying anything in self justification, yet ever since I have been in this Church I have led a godly and upright life; at the same time, I resolved I would accept nothing that my conscience would not receive. I was, at eight years old, baptized into the Church, and I was brought up in the Church. Well, if I had been asked at that time what I was baptized for, I should have said, for the remission of my sins, for I had learned it all, parrot-like, and I had confidence in Mormonism, as I had been brought up in it.
>
> When my father was called on a mission to England I accompanied him and went about distributing tracts, not because I knew anything of what I was doing, but because I liked to see the old women, when they slammed the door, or threw the tracts into the streets in

their anger[. A]nd [I did it] because my father thought I might take a part in it if I chose.

I came out again to the Valleys with my father, and we were required to be baptized again. I complied, for all this time I was a believer in Mormonism. But sometime afterwards, there was much said about receiving a testimony; that unless one had the testimony that Mormonism is true, there was something deficient. I asked myself the question, if I had it, but was sensible I had not. Yet I saw young men who come from England, and who had not been raised in the Church, stand up in the Ward Meetings, and say they had this testimony. I could not account for it.

During a conference held in the City, I, with some other young men was called upon to speak, and bore testimony to the work, and I set forth the ground for my belief. Afterwards the President stood up, and no doubt without any reference to what I had said, as I presume, he had almost forgotten it, said that this, that[,] and the other stood for nothing unless we had a knowledge for ourselves. Well, I thought I would know something about the matter, and set to reading the works published in favor of the work, and I came to the conclusions I hold at the present day.

Well, it is strange, how the people will form such difference of opinions from the same testimony. It reminds me of a case that was tried in one of the courts in England—where evidence was to be received concerning the existence of a certain monument in London, and the testimony varied even as to the color, etc. etc. etc., by persons who were constantly passing by it, so much that had the natural course been carried out, the testimony would have been entirely rejected.

"Well I have come to the conclusion," young Orson now announced,

that, Joseph Smith was not specially sent by the Lord to establish this work, and I cannot help it, for I could not believe otherwise, even if I knew that I was to be punished for not doing so; and I must say so, though I knew that I was to suffer for it the next moment.

When I was brought up before the High Council they said that I bore a good character, and that they had nothing against me, only I did not believe in some of the principles, for let me here say, that there are some of the principles of Mormonism that I believe to be good, though there are others that I cannot believe in. Now let me mention that, let a man be guilty of ever so heinous a crime, if he can stand up and say that he believes the same as you do, you will hold to him and keep him in fellowship,[9] and I admit that it makes me feel somewhat strange that, when I find that, Because I don't believe the same as you, although nothing can be said against my moral character, yet I must be dropped off. This is the way I feel. I see many friends around me in this congregation who don't believe as I do, yet I can respect them for all that, for I don't care what they believe. And I claim the same privilege for myself. I am confident of one thing, that, while conscience does not upbraid me, and I do not sin against my Heavenly Father, none, by their actions can shut me out of the light of His presence.

Before leaving the podium, Orson Jr. touched briefly upon a subject several others no doubt wished he had not. "I wish to speak a few words in regard to another matter," he continued:

I was called down here and came with my father—I would like the people to understand this matter [that] I am about to refer to. We settled at Grafton.[10] My father had not been down here long, when he found that there was a secret influence working against him. I did not feel it, but I wish to say, that if it had not been for this influence, he would have been in your midst this day. The person would not come out like a man against him, but would keep himself in the dark and work against him like a snake in the grass.

---

9. Pratt may have had the perpetrators of the Mountain Meadows massacre in mind. Only seven years earlier, a group of local firebrands had ambushed and killed an emigrant party on its way to California, and some of the participants were probably present for Pratt's comments. For more information, see Will Bagley, *Blood of the Prophets: Brigham Young and the Massacre at Mountain Meadows* (Norman: University of Oklahoma Press, 2002).

10. About thirty miles northeast of St. George.

Well, father bore up against it as long as he could without coming to an open rupture, and then sought for another mission.

"When he went away," Pratt continued, "the same influences were working against me, and he would even meet my wife in the dark and try to make her divide against me by saying to her that 'Your husband is not in the right way, he is in the dark', but he was not successful." His audience now rapt, Pratt announced, "I will tell you [who] it was. The individual is Erastus Snow."[11]

The disclosure must have had a dramatic effect on the audience. However, it is not known if Snow was, in fact, guilty of this "secret influence" he was accused of, although Snow's biographer noted that "the rumor persisted that the two apostles did not see eye to eye."[12] At least as late as March 1860, Snow felt some admiration for Pratt since he named his newborn son Orson Pratt Snow. But several years earlier, Snow had publicly outlined his views on dissent within families—a position which no doubt dictated his response to the dangers he believed young Orson Jr. posed to the fledgling community. "If a man of God lives his religion," he told members gathered in Salt Lake City for general conference in late 1857, but has a rebellious wife or child—"a turbulent, disobedient spirit in his family"—this bad element should be

> separated from his family, upon the same principle that turbulent persons that repent not are severed from this church by the vote of this people; and when that turbulent person is severed, he will dry up and wither, and will be gathered and burned with the ungodly. ...
>
> Every man in Israel is responsible in a certain degree for the conduct of his wives and children. He has covenanted that he will assume that responsibility; that is, he will assume the responsibility of the sins

---

11. Snow's biographer feels the criticism was unjustified. Snow, not Orson Sr., "was the driving and guiding force of the mission" because, unlike Pratt, he was practical and had good sense (Larson, *Erastus Snow*, 370). At the same time, Orson Jr.'s allegations should not be ignored; see England, *Life and Thought*, 221.

12. Larson, *Erastus Snow*, 370.

of his wives, if he fails to discharge his duties towards them in teaching and leading them in ways of life and salvation. ...

Sometimes we may err by being remiss in duty—too lenient in our families, and some of us may be under condemnation by being too careless about transgressors in our families; for if we hold fellowship with transgressors and spirits that are in rebellion against God and that will not repent and humble themselves—if we close our ears to it and go to sleep while wickedness is stalking unrebuked through our habitations, we become partakers in that transgression, and the consequences thereof will stick to us. ...

If any man have members in his family whom he cannot control by the principles of the Gospel, far better were it for him, if they want to go to the States or to any other country, to give them a good outfit and send them off, get them out of the way, and let them go their own way; far better this than to harbour them where they were like a viper in his bosom corrupting and corroding in the midst of his family.[13]

Whatever Snow's opinion of Orson Pratt Sr., it would not have produced the same remorse and guilt for the aging overseas apostle as did the disaffection and excommunication of his son. Orson Sr.'s intellectual bent and emphasis on reasoning had found a willing disciple in his son, whose youthful desire had been to discover for himself the truthfulness of the church he had been raised in. What seemed to be a foregone conclusion in Orson Sr.'s mind was for Orson Jr. less certain. In consequence of his father's influence and in honesty to himself, his ideals, and his upbringing, Orson Jr. was not able to accept the basic foundation of his father's religion. With disarming irony, the young man's declaration of freedom echoed a similar proclamation made by his father four and a half years earlier. Yet while Orson Sr. retained his devotion to the church, Orson Jr. could not.[14]

Following the excommunication, Sarah Pratt moved her small

---

13. *Journal of Discourses*, 5:288-90.

14. Orson Pratt Jr. would become one of early Utah's distinguished musicians. He died in Ogden, Utah, in 1903.

family back to Salt Lake City accompanied by Orson Jr. and his wife. Orson Sr. did not return from England until late 1867, and Sarah, like Orson Sr.'s other wives, was left in the interim to fend for herself. While her son made no mention of polygamy in his *cri de coeur*, the doctrine lay clearly at the center of his parents' now moribund relationship. As Sarah's biographer has observed:

> [Orson Pratt] had not seen [his wife Sarah] since late 1862; and for too many years, she had coped with the deaths of her children and poverty alone. From 1839 to 1868, Orson had been away on church assignments at least eleven years—41 percent of the time. Home from England, fifty-seven-year-old Orson courted sixteen-year-old Margaret Graham, who would become his tenth wife on 28 December 1868. At fifty-one, Sarah could no longer bear children and bitterly resented his relationships with women younger than their daughter Celestial.[15]

"Here was my husband," Sarah later told a newspaper reporter, "gray headed, taking to his bed young girls in mockery of marriage. Of course there could be no joy for him in such an intercourse except the indulgence of his fanaticism and of something else, perhaps, which I hesitate to mention."[16] "I don't wish to wrongfully accuse [him]," she said,

> although we have been hopelessly separated for ten years. I believed, when he decided to enter upon the practice of polygamy, that he did so not from any violence of individual passion, but from sheer fanaticism. He told me that he believed it was his duty to take other women besides myself to wife, and at first he said that this would make no difference in his affection for me, which would continue pure and single as it had ever been. But think of the horror of such an announcement. He took wife after wife until they numbered five, and for a long time they were kept away from me and I was spared from intercourse with them. By and by he told me that he intended to put these five women

---

15. Van Wagoner, "Sarah M. Pratt," 92.
16. Qtd. in "The Utah Theocracy," *New York Herald*, 18 May 1877.

on an exact equality with me; that he could spend a week with one, a week with another, and so on, and that I should have the sixth week! Then patience forsook me. I told him plainly that I wouldn't endure it. I said, "If you take five weeks with your other women you can take the sixth with them also." Orson responded, "If you don't choose to live with me I don't know that I'm obliged to support you. You may have my permission to go to hell. Stick to it or to starvation."[17]

By 1868, the couple had formally separated. Late the next year, Sarah was struggling to make a living. (Orson married his last plural wife, Margaret Graham, on 28 December 1868.) "I am out of wood," Sarah wrote to Brigham Young in September 1869. "I have applied to the Bishop several times with no success. Orson [Jr.] has furnished one load but it is so expensive to buy [and since] he cannot get for himself and me too this winter, will it not be possible for some wood to be raised from the missionary fund[?] I have a stove for coal or wood, either will do. I need it immediately. Your Sister in the gospel."[18] Following a protracted legal dispute with Young over ownership of the house Sarah occupied—a case she first won and then lost[19]—she was excommunicated for "apostasy" on 4 October 1874. The next day her son Arthur, age twenty-one and a U.S. marshal, was also expelled for "apostasy." Less than three months later, Sarah publicly affirmed that she "was formerly a member ... I have not been a believer in the Mormon doctrines for thirty years, and am now considered an apostate, I believe."[20] In fact, she later confessed that since the mid-1850s she had tried

> to rear my children so that they should never espouse the Mormon faith, and, at the same time, to conceal from my neighbors and from

---

17. Ibid.

18. Sarah M. Pratt to Brigham Young, 19 Sept. 1869, Brigham Young Papers. For years, Orson and his wives had relied on Young's largesse to help them survive difficult periods. See, e.g., President's Office Journal, 14 Apr. 1860, 22 Apr. 1961.

19. See Journal History of the Church, 26 Nov. 1875, 8 July 1876.

20. Qtd. in Journal History of the Church, 22 Jan. 1875.

the Church authorities the fact that I was thus rearing them. Fortunately my husband was almost constantly absent on foreign missions ... Many a night, when my children were young and also when they had grown up so as to be companions to me, I have ... locked the door, pulled down the windows curtains, put out all but one candle on the table ... and talked to them in whispers for fear that what I said would be overhead.[21]

"I will tell you why [I am not a Mormon]," Arthur concurred. "I am the son of my father's first wife, and had a mother who taught me the evils of the system [i.e., polygamy]."[22] In the 1880s, Arthur, son of Mormonism's most zealous advocate of plural marriage, would stand at the forefront of the federal prosecution of Mormon polygamists.[23]

Yet some four years after her excommunication, Sarah, now sixty-one, seems to have mellowed in her feelings towards her ex-husband and even asked that he stay in touch while he was in the East. A letter from him dated 18 September 1878 was probably not what Sarah had hoped for. Instead of a friendly communication, Orson reminded her of her failure over the years to perform her "conjugal duties" and took the opportunity to justify himself for having "done my duty" (although not financially) to his other wives despite his "trials" (i.e., Sarah) which were "hard to endure" and his "circumstances" (i.e., poverty). The letter was nevertheless an overture, however clumsy, and survives as the last known correspondence between the two:

> Dear Wife: As you requested me to write to you, I do so, addressing you, as formerly, under the affectionate title of *wife*. You once

---

21. Qtd. in "Orson Pratt's Harem," *New York Herald,* 18 May 1877, 2.

22. Qtd. in *Anti-Polygamy Standard* 11 (Feb. 1882): 81.

23. Arthur became warden of the Utah Territorial Prison in 1888, served as Salt Lake City Chief of Police from 1894 to 1897, and again as warden of the Utah State Prison from 1904 to 1917. He died in Salt Lake City in 1919. See Richard S. and Mary Van Wagoner, "Arthur Pratt, Utah Lawman," *Utah Historical Quarterly* 55 (Winter 1987): 22-35.

permitted me to use this title, with the utmost confidence. You once were one with me in the new and everlasting covenant. You once, professedly, believed in the sealing ordinances, according to the revelation on Marriage for eternity. You, at several times, did put the hands of others into my hand, and did give them to me as *wives*, immediately before the marriage ceremony was pronounced. Those women I took with all confidence, and with your consent. After several years had elapsed, I proposed to you, to commence living upon principles of greater equality in regard to my attentions: this proposition you positively rejected; and you further said, that if I introduced this equality, you would never live with me again, in time, nor in eternity. This was a hard and grevious trial to me: but believing it my proposition to be, not only right, but a duty, I firmly concluded to follow my convictions, though it should be at the sacrifice of life itself. I have done so, with all the faith and sincerity that I ever had in receiving any religious principle. You, doubtless, looked upon the trial as one too great for you to endure, and accordingly separated yourself from me, as far as some of the conjugal duties of a wife were concerned. My trials, though hard to endure, have been somewhat lightened, by the constant knowledge that I have done my duty to other branches of my family, and have thus fulfil[l]ed the obligations, entered into with them, under the law of the marriage covenant for eternity, which I esteem as equally sacred with all other divine laws and covenants. Under the laws of man, you could, at any time have easily obtained a divorce from me, and could have been free to marry another; but you have not sought this, but have preferred to remain still *my wife*; and as such, I have felt it a duty to still render what little aid I could to you, consistent with circumstances. How long I shall live to contribute my mite to you, is unknown to me. If I should pass away before you, I trust that your children and grandchildren will do all they can for you. ... (Emphasis in original.)[24]

Sarah had not abandoned her hatred of polygamy and proclaimed in 1884, three years after Orson's death:

---

24. Orson Pratt to Sarah M. Pratt, 18 Sept. 1878, Orson Pratt Collection.

Polygamy is the direst curse with which a people or a nation could be afflicted. ... It completely demoralizes good men, and makes bad men correspondingly worse. As for the women—well, God help them! First wives it renders desperate, or else heartbroken, mean-spirited creatures; and it almost unsexes some of the other women, but not all of them, for plural wives have their sorrows too. An elder once said to me, "Sister Sarah, you are a regular Satan." I answered him, "There are only two classes of Mormon women, devils and fools."[25]

Sarah lived another four years, finally succumbing to heart failure on Christmas Day 1888 at age seventy-one. Laron Pratt, her only child who had remained faithful to Mormonism, alleged that as she lay dying she said, "If Mormonism is not true then there is no truth on earth."[26] Even so, her funeral was conducted in her son Arthur's residence and performed by a Protestant clergyman. She was interred in the Salt Lake City Cemetery where, her biographer notes, "Sarah gained what she had been denied in life: no other wife rests beside Orson."[27]

---

25. Qtd. in Jennie Anderson Froiseth, ed., *The Women of Mormonism* (Detroit: C. G. G. Paine, 1884), 38-40. For the experience of another of Orson's plural wives, see Mrs. T. B. H. [Fanny] Stenhouse, *Tell It All: The Tyranny of Mormonism, or an Englishwoman in Utah* (Hartford, 1874), 324ff. The wife is Eliza Crooks, whom Pratt married in Liverpool, England, on 24 July 1857.

26. Qtd. in Lyon, "Orson Pratt—Early Mormon Leader," 155.

27. Van Wagoner, "Sarah M. Pratt," 97.

ELEVEN

The Interests of Posterity

During the years preceding the arrival of the transcontinental railroad in 1869, Brigham Young, with other church leaders and members of his entourage, traveled periodically throughout the region on tours of the church's settlements.[1] Young's efforts to keep abreast of the temporal and spiritual developments in the colonies, as well as to minimize his own austerity, were for the most part successful. As one of Young's articulate outside observers wrote of her trip with the Mormon president:

> When we reached the end of a day's journey ... the leading "brothers and sisters" of the settlement would come in to pay their respects. ... They talked to Brigham Young about every conceivable matter, from the fluxing of an ore to the advantages of a Navajo bit, and expected him to remember every child in every cotter's family. And he really seemed to do so, and to be at home, and be rightfully deemed infallible on every subject. I think he must make fewer mistakes than most popes, from his being in such constant intercourse with his people. I

---

1. For more on these trips, see Gordon Irving, "Encouraging the Saints: Brigham Young's Annual Tours of the Mormon Settlements," *Utah Historical Quarterly* 45 (Summer 1977): 233-51.

noticed that he never seemed uninterested, but gave an unforced attention to the person addressing him, which suggested a mind free from care. I used to fancy that he wasted a great deal of power in this way; but I soon saw that he was accumulating it.[2]

It was during such a tour of northern Utah's Cache Valley in early May 1865 that Young, together with Elders John Taylor, Wilford Woodruff, George A. Smith, Franklin D. Richards, and George Q. Cannon, learned that Orson Pratt's theories had not been abandoned by the people nor had his edition of Lucy Mack Smith's history of Joseph Smith. Indeed, the Smith biography enjoyed a prominent place in the homes of leaders and members alike. It had even been adopted in some settlements as a territorial school "Reader."[3] Pratt's popularity seemed unquenchable.

Addressing "the largest [congregation] ever convened in Cache Valley," Young identified Lucy Smith's history and Pratt by name and then continued:

We have advertized to have them [Smith's book] gathered up and destroyed, so that there might not be any copies of ["the book" added interlinearly] among the people. ... The inquiry arises at once, "why do you want to destroy these books?" It is because the book is a tissue of falsehoods. There are witnesses here present, in this room, who know that there are false statements in it ... So far as I am acquainted with the statements in the book, they are palpably false, and I [do not] wish such a book to be lying on our shelves to be taken up in after years and read by our children as true history. ... When I find brethren of the Twelve and Bishops and men in authority in the Kingdom of

---

2. Elizabeth Wood Kane, *Twelve Mormon Homes Visited in Succession on a Journey through Utah to Arizona,* ed. Everett L. Cooley (Salt Lake City: University of Utah Library, 1974), 101.

3. The Historian's Office Journal notes that the president's party left on Wednesday, 3 May 1865, and returned a week later on Thursday, 11 May, at 4:30 p.m. For Lucy Mack Smith's history being used as a reader, see the Gottfredson Family History, typescript, 7, Utah State Historical Society. The fullest treatment of these events is found in Anderson's introduction to *Lucy's Book.*

God hugging such a book to their breasts, and keeping it in their houses, after what has been said and printed concerning it before, I must speak plainly ["on the matter" added interlinearly].

I require the Twelve, the High Priests, the Seventies, the Bishops, and every one in the Church, male and female, if they have such a book, to ~~burn it up~~ destroy it. If they do not, the responsibility of the evil results that may accrue from keeping it will rest upon them & upon me. ... Orson Pratt obtained this Manuscript, and through his greed for money, published it in England. ... Brother Pratt had it printed, and published it without saying a word ["to the First Presidency or the Twelve" added interlinearly] of what he was doing. ... This (is) the way the book came into being. It was smuggled, juggled and gambled into existence as a book, and ["all for selfish gain" added interlinearly].

Anyone who owned the history was "transmitting lies to posterity" and therefore, the president predicted, "the curse of God will rest on every one who keeps these books in their houses." He regretted that Pratt had not been "brought before the High Council and disfellowshipped, but we bore, and bore, and continued to forebear." "I will not bear such things any longer," he concluded. "My words have been unheeded and my counsel disregarded in this matter and I will not endure it."[4] In his anger, Young overstated Pratt's motives and misstated the process by which Pratt had acquired the manuscript. He also evidentially forgot that Pratt had, in fact, notified him before publishing.[5] The president would perpetuate these errors in his future pronouncements on Lucy Smith's biography.

Just over a month later on a warm June afternoon, Young called

---

4. Brigham Young, "Remarks," 6 May 1865, recorded by E. O. Sloan, Brigham Young Papers.

5. While Pratt did not seek approval, he did advise Young in late December 1852 of his intention to publish the manuscript. "I think I will ... publish ... another work," he wrote, "which will be very interesting, namely, the narrative of Mother Smith, giving the genealogy of Joseph, back for seven generations, and a statement of many facts, visions, dreams, and incidents, connected with the finding & translating of the plates, and I think that they will do much good both to the

his first counselor, Heber C. Kimball, and Elders Woodruff, Richards, and Cannon (who had all accompanied the president to Cache Valley) to the Historian's Office in Salt Lake City. Earlier Young had mentioned his growing concern about Pratt to Cannon, whom he now called upon to read aloud from Pratt's 1851 English pamphlet, *Great First Cause*.

The men adjourned for one hour, then reassembled at 4:00 p.m., joined by Elder George A. Smith, official Church Historian. The first sections of Pratt's 1850 *Holy Spirit* pamphlet, which had been reprinted in 1852, were read and discussed, after which Young asked those present "what should be done with these works written by Orson Pratt."[6] After some debate, Young emphasizing the errors of Pratt's logic as well as the implicit challenge to the president's authority, a vote was taken and Pratt's writings were once again "rejected as fals doctrin."[7] The six men decided that more than a public censure was required because their earlier statement had not produced the intended results. This time Pratt would be notified

---

church & the world" (Pratt to Young, 31 Dec. 1852, Brigham Young Papers). Since Young possessed a copy of the manuscript, he could have read the biography in advance. Mormon historian Howard Searle concluded charitably:

> The authoritarian manner in which the history was suppressed has appeared somewhat incongruous to the attitudes and practices of many later leaders of the Church and must be understood in light of some of the emotional issues surrounding the publication and content of the book. ...
>
> The Church leaders wanted to protect readers from the misconceptions and errors they perceived in the book. ... Whether such paternalism was based on a distrust of the future Saints to judge the truth for themselves or the belief that those closer to the events could make this judgement better and easier, it was, nonetheless, felt to be necessary and appropriate. To those familiar with modern historical methods, there are obviously less drastic means than those adopted by the Presidency for correcting and preserving a historical narrative for posterity, but these methods were not known, understood, or practiced by the Church Historians or the Church authorities in the mid-nineteenth century. (Searle, "Early Mormon Historiography," 402-403.)

6. Qtd. in the Historian's Office Journal, 13 June 1865.
7. Kenney, *Wilford Woodruff's Journal*, 6:228.

that if he did not comply, he would "lose his priesthood." That he was in Europe and could not immediately respond no doubt facilitated the mens' resolve to issue the condemnation.

Five days later, Young addressed church members and, in the course of his remarks on the personality and attributes of God, lambasted the views of "a certain celebrated philosopher. We believe in a Deity who is incorporated—who is a Being of tabernacle, through which the great attributes of His nature are made manifest," he said. By contrast:

> It is supposed by a certain celebrated philosopher that the most minute particles of matter which float in space, in the waters, or that exist in the solid earth, particles which defy the most powerful glasses to reveal them to the vision of finite man, possess a portion of divinity, a portion of infinite power, knowledge, goodness and truth, and that these qualities are God, and should be worshipped wherever found. I am an infidel to this doctrine. I know the God in whom I believe, and am willing to acknowledge Him before all men. We have persons in this church who have preached and published doctrines on the subject of the Deity which are not true. Elder Orson Pratt has written extensively on the doctrines of this church, and upon this particular doctrine. When he writes and speaks upon subjects with which he is acquainted and understands, he is a very sound reasoner; but when he has written upon matters of which he knows nothing—his own philosophy, which I call vain philosophy—he is wild, uncertain, and contradictory.

"In all my public administration as a minister of truth," the president vowed, without acknowledging his own controversial Adam-God teachings, "I have never yet been under the necessity of preaching, believing or practising doctrines that are not fully and clearly set forth in the Old and New Testaments, Book of Doctrine and Covenants, and Book of Mormon."[8]

Over the next two days, Elders Smith, Richards, and Cannon met to prepare "an article on Orson Pratt's writings and in relation

---

8. *Journal of Discourses*, 11:121. "Were I under the necessity of making scrip-

to a work entitled Jos. Smith the Prophet, etc."[9] The following Saturday, Young and Apostles Smith, Hyde, Taylor, and Woodruff left for central Utah. While in Nephi, they held two private meetings "in relation to the writings of Elder Orson Pratt."[10]

Apparently no public reference was made to Pratt again until two months later on Wednesday, 23 August, when Young personally oversaw publication of two separate, though overlapping, official declarations: the earlier 1860 proclamation and a more recent one carrying the signatures of the First Presidency, except Daniel H. Wells who, like Pratt, was out of the country, and all of the Twelve except Pratt. The two statements appeared together on the first and second pages of the day's *Deseret News*. Sections authored by the Smith-Richards-Cannon committee dealing with the Lucy Mack Smith history prefaced the 1860 announcement. The longer denunciation of Pratt's *Holy Spirit* treatise, which had also come under scrutiny, completed the joint declaration.

The lengthy statement constituted an unusually comprehensive, unequivocal, official denunciation. For Young, it represented what he hoped would be the final resolution of some twelve years of conflict with his fellow apostle. There can be little question that Young considered the initial 1860 statement sufficient at the time—or had hoped that it would be. Only in the intervening years had he come to realize that it would not lay to rest the inexplicable popularity of Pratt's doctrinal theories. Ironically Young himself had contributed to Pratt's stature: he had assigned him to postitions of leadership over the eastern states and foreign missions and had allowed his writings to be published under the church's imprimatur.

"HEARKEN, O YE LATTER-DAY SAINTS, AND ALL YE INHAB-

---

ture extensively," Young had quipped eleven years earlier, "I should get Brother Heber C. Kimball to make it, and then I would quote it" (qtd. in Brigham Young, "I Propose to Speak upon a Subject That Does Not Immediately Concern Yours or My Welfare," in *Essential Brigham Young*, 86-99).

9. Historian's Office Journal, 19, 20 June 1865.

10. Ibid., 24 June 1865.

ITANTS OF THE EARTH WHO WISH TO BE SAINTS, TO WHOM THIS WRITING SHALL COME," the authoritative wording to the epistle began.[11]

Happening lately, while on a preaching trip to Cache Valley, to pick up a book which was lying on a table in the house where we were stopping,[12] we were surprised to find that it was the book bearing the title, on the outside, of "Joseph Smith, the Prophet," and on the title page, "Biographical Sketches of Joseph Smith, the Prophet, and his progenitors for many generations, by Lucy Smith, mother of the Prophet, published for Orson Pratt by S. W. Richards, Liverpool," etc. Our surprise at finding a copy of this work may be accounted for by the fact of our having advertised some time ago that the book was incorrect, and that it should be gathered up and destroyed, so that no copies should be left; and, from this, we had supposed that not a single copy could be found in any of the houses of the Saints.

We now wish to publish our views and feelings respecting this book, so that they may be known to all the Saints in all the world. In Great Britain diligence has been used in collecting and in disposing of this work, and we wish that same diligence continued there and also exercised here, at home, until not a copy is left.

The inquiry may arise in the minds of some persons "why do you want to destroy this book?" Because we are acquainted with individual circumstances alluded to in it, and know many of the statements to be false. We could go through the book and point out many false statements which it contains; but we do not feel to do so. It is sufficient to say that it is utterly unreliable as a history, as it contains many falsehoods and mistakes. We do not wish such a book to be lying on our shelves to be taken up in after years and read by our children as true history, and we, therefore, expect the High Priests, the Seventies, the Elders, the Bishops, and every one in the Church, male and female, if they have a such a book, to dispose of it so that it will never be

---

11. *Deseret News,* 23 Aug. 1865, 372-73. The statement also appeared in the *Latter-day Saints' Millennial Star,* 21 Oct. 1865, 657-63, and in Clark, *Messages of the First Presidency,* 2:229-40. As will become apparent, Young's comments in Cache Valley served as a first draft for this statement.

12. This was the residence of Ezra T. Benson, stake president and apostle.

read by any person again. If they do not, the responsibility of the evil results that may accrue from keeping it will rest upon them and not upon us.

Without entering into all the details of the writing of this book and its production in print, we may say that at the time it was written, which was after the death of the Prophet Joseph, mother Smith was seventy years old, and very forgetful. Her mind had suffered many severe shocks, through losing a beloved husband and four sons of exceeding promise, to whom she was fondly attached, three of whom had but recently fallen victims to mobocratic violence, and she could, therefore, scarcely recall anything correctly that had transpired. She employed as amanuensis a lady by the name of Coray.[13]

Those who have read the history of William Smith,[14] and who knew him, know the statements made in that book respecting him, when he came out of Missouri, to be utterly false. Instead of being the faithful man of God, and the Saint which he is there represented to have been, he was a wicked man, and he publicly expressed the hope that his brother Joseph would never get out of the hands of his enemies alive; and he further said that had he had the disposing of him, he would have hung him years before.

When the book was written mother Smith sent it to us to examine. In company with some others, who were acquainted with the circumstances alluded to in the book, we read the manuscript and we soon saw that it was incorrect. We paid the amanuensis who wrote the book for mother Smith for a copy of the work, and that copy is now in the Historian's Office, and has been in our possession ever since we left Nauvoo. But the original manuscript was purloined, we suppose, from mother Smith, and went into the hands of apostates, and was purchased of them by Orson Pratt. He had the work published in England. We do not know that Samuel W. Richards, who printed the work, knew anything about the manner in which it was

---

13. Martha Jane Coray acted as Lucy Smith's scribe. For more on Coray, see Anderson, *Lucy's Book,* 77-94.

14. William was Joseph's mercurial younger brother. For more on him, see Irene M. Bates, "William Smith, 1811-93: Problematic Patriarch," *Dialogue* 16 (Summer 1983): 11-23.

written or how br. Pratt obtained it. He printed it, we suppose, as he
would any other book. But brother Pratt had it printed, and published
it, without saying a word to the First Presidency or the Twelve about
what he was doing. This is the way the book came into being. It was
smuggled, juggled and foisted into existence as a book.

The preface of this book was written by brother Orson Pratt. In
that he stated that the book was "mostly written previous to the
death of the Prophet, and under his personal inspection," which statement is false, and which brother Pratt afterwards corrected in the
DESERET NEWS, March 21st, 1855, ...

Many of the Saints may not know that the book is inaccurate but
those who have been instructed respecting its charac[t]er and will still
keep it on their tables and have it in their houses as a valid and authentic history for their children to read, need rebuke. It is transmitting lies to posterity to take such a course, and we know that the curse
of God will rest upon every one, after he comes to the knowledge of
what is here said, who keeps these books for his children to learn and
believe in lies.

We wish those who have these books to either hand them to
their Bishops for them to be conveyed to the President's or Historian's Office, or send them themselves, that they may be disposed of;
and they will please write their names in the books, with the name of
the place where they reside, and if they wish to hand them over without pay in return, state so; and if they wish to get pay for them, state
whether they desire it applied on tithing or wish the value returned
in other books.

When we commenced this article we did not think of extending
our comments beyond the work already alluded to. We consider it
our duty, however, and advisable for us to incorporate with this,
which we have already written, our views upon other doctrines
which have been extensively published and widely received as the
standard and authoritative doctrines of the church, but which are unsound. The views we allude to, and which we deem objectionable,
have been published by Elder Orson Pratt. We have expressed our
disapproval of some of these doctrines through the columns of the
Millennial Star, published in England, and the DESERET NEWS of this
city; there are others, however, of a kindred character, which have not
been alluded to in public print, that also require comment, in order

that a correct understanding may be had by the Saints respecting them. We do not wish incorrect and unsound doctrines to be handed down to posterity under the sanction of great names, to be received and valued by future generations as authentic and reliable, creating labor and difficulties for our successors to perform and contend with, which we ought not to transmit to them. The interests of posterity are, to a certain extent, in our hands. Errors in history and in doctrine, if left uncorrected by us who are conversant with the events, and who are in a position to judge of the truth or falsity of the doctrines, would go to our children as though we had sanctioned and endorsed them. Such a construction could very easily be put upon our silence respecting them, and would tend to perplex and mislead posterity and make the labor of correction an exceedingly difficult one for them. We know what sanctity there is always attached to the writings of men who have passed away, especially to the writings of apostles when none of their contemporaries are left, and we, therefore, feel the necessity of being watchful upon these points. Personal feelings and friendships and associations ought to sink into comparative insignificance and have no weight in view of consequences so momentous to the people and kingdom of God as these.

Moses wrote the history of creation, and we believe that he had the inspiration of the Almighty resting upon him. The prophets who wrote after him were likewise endowed with the Spirit of revelation. The Apostles of Jesus Christ, the Savior of the world, the personal witnesses of his ministry, revealed many great and glorious truths to the people. The Prophet Joseph, in our own day, was chosen of God, and ordained as a Seer and Revelator, and was made the means of bringing much knowledge to light respecting God and the things of God. But none of these prophets and apostles—no, not even the Son of God himself—has ever been able, to our knowledge, to inform the world respecting the "Great First Cause" and to explain how the first organized Being was originated. They never were able to reveal to man that every part of the Holy Spirit, however minute and infinitesimal, possessed "every intellectual or moral attribute possessed by the Father and the Son;" or that "the spiritual personages of the Father and the Son and the Holy Ghost, if organized at all, must have been the result of the self-combinations and unions of the pre-existent, intelligent, powerful and eternal particles of matter." The reader may inquire "why they could not reveal this?" It was because there was no such fact in existence. They were evidently content with the knowledge that from all eternity there had existed organized beings, in an organized form, possessing superior and controlling power to govern what Brother Pratt calls the "self-moving, all-wise and all-powerful particles of matter," and that it was neither rational nor consistent with the revelations of God and with reason and philosophy to believe that these latter Forces and Powers had existed prior to the Beings who controlled and governed them. But to teach these ideas and to make them public to mankind, after so many ages of ignorance respecting them, had been reserved, according to his own arguments, for Brother Orson Pratt. We must do Brother Orson Pratt the justice, however, to say that he has never claimed to know these things by revelation; still he has published them to the world as facts and as doctrines of the Church of Jesus Christ of Latter-day Saints.

In remarks which Bro. Pratt made in Great Salt Lake City, Jan. 29, 1860—remarks which were prompted upon learning our views respecting the doctrines that he had published, and which he delivered without giving intimation of any such intention—while speaking in relation to the things which were deemed objectionable and erroneous by the First Presidency and Twelve—he confessed that he had erred and done wrong in publishing them; he said that "So far as revelation from the heavens is concerned, I have had none in relation to those points of doctrine;" and he further said, on this same subject: "There is one thing I will assure you of, God will never reveal anything to me, or to any other man, which will come in contact with the views and revelations which he gives to the man who holds the keys. We never need expect such a thing." These remarks were published in the DESERET NEWS, July 25th, 1860, and the First Presidency appended to them the following comments ...

At this point, the 1860 declaration appears, along with four quotations from the *Seer* and one from Pratt's pamphlet on the *Great First Cause,* over the signatures of Brigham Young, Heber C. Kimball, and Daniel H. Wells. The 1865 declaration then continues:

In an article, entitled "The Holy Spirit," published by br. Pratt in the *Millennial Star,* of October 15th, and November 1st, 1850, pages 305-309, and pages 325-328, it is stated, among other things, in relation to the Holy Spirit, that,

"Each part of this substance is all-wise and all-powerful, possessing the same knowledge and the same truth. The essence can be divided into parts like all other matter, but the truth which each part possesses is one truth, and is indivisible; and because of the oneness of the quality, all these parts are called but ONE God. There is a *plurality* of substance, but a *unity* of quality; and it is this unity which constitutes the one God which we worship. When we worship the Father, we do not worship merely His substance, but we worship the attributes of that substance; so, likewise, when we worship the Son, we do not merely worship the essence or substance of the Son, but we worship because of his qualities or attributes; in like manner when we worship the Spirit, we do not merely worship a personal substance or a widely diffused substance, but we worship the attributes and qualities of this substance; it is not then the essence alone which is the object of worship, but it is the qualities of the essence. These attributes and qualities, unlike the essence, are undivided; they are whole and entire in every part. A truth is not truths because it dwells in two or more beings, but we worship it as one truth wherever we find it. Hence if the qualities and attributes are the principal cause of our worship, we worship them as one and the same, wherever they are found, whether in a million of substances or only in one. If these qualities and attributes dwell in all their fulness in every substance of the universe, then one and the same God would dwell in every substance, so far as the qualities are concerned. That the qualities are the real object of worship, and not the essence, is evident from the fact that all essences without their qualities, must be alike in nature, if not in form and magnitude. Therefore one essence without qualities has not more claim to our worship than another."

And again he says:

"We can form some conception of the extreme minuteness of these all-powerful and all-wise atoms of substance when we reflect that they are capable of being in and through all things. Now there are many solids, so dense that many millions of millions of particles are collected in a space not larger than a grain of mustard seed; now the pores between these particles must be still more minute than the particles themselves; therefore, the particles of that all-wise substance, which is in and through all things, must be sufficiently minute to enter these extremely small pores, surrounding every atom, and pervading the whole mass, governing and controlling it according to fixed and definite laws."

In a tract, bearing the same title as the article just quoted from, one of a series of eight tracts which br. Pratt published in England in the year 1856,[15] in reasoning upon the difference between the Holy Spirit and the being known as the Holy Ghost, it is stated on page 51, par. 11, that,

"On this occasion (the day of Pentecost), portions of this Holy Fluid assumed the form of 'Cloven Tongues like as of Fire.' It is very doubtful whether a permanent personal spirit would dissolve its personality, and transform its parts into one hundred and twenty tongues, having the appearance of fire. But a living, self-moving fluid substance might transform itself into any shape it pleased, and render itself visible in the form of tongues, or in the form of a dove, or in a personal form, resembling the image of man."

And further on page 53, par. 18, he says,

"This boundless ocean of spirit possesses in every part, however minute, a will, a self-moving power, knowledge, wisdom, love, goodness, holiness, justice, mercy, and every intellectual and moral attribute possessed by the Father and the Son. Each particle of this Holy Spirit knows, every instance, how to act upon the other materials of nature with which it is immediately associated: it knows how to vary the gravitating tendency of a particle of matter, every moment, precisely in the inverse ratio of the square of its distance from every other particle of the universe. Where an infinite number of particles of matter are in motion, and every instance changing their relative distances from each other, it must require an overwhelming amount of discernment and knowledge, for each particle of the spirit to perceive every motion of every other particle, and every instant to know the relative positions and distances of every particle in the universe. And yet without such knowledge, the gravitating intensity could not be varied according to

---

15. This collection of pamphlets first appeared in 1852.

the strict law which is known to exist. For the Holy Spirit to move all the materials of nature, according to this one law, requires a wisdom and knowledge incomprehensible to mortal man."

Again, on page 53, par. 20, it is stated that,

"Man has been accustomed to associate wisdom, knowledge, love, joy and all the other faculties and passions, with an organized being or personality. Therefore, when he is informed that the Holy Spirit possesses all these attributes, he, from habit, supposes it to be a person; but there is no necessary connection between these attributes and a personality. Indeed, there is no reason why these attributes may not also belong to a fluid substance. We see life and voluntary motion exhibited by beings of every conceivable shape and magnitude, from man down through every grade of existence to the microscopic animalcules. Many of these inconceivably small beings appear to be merely minute globules or particles of living substance. Such being the case, why may not the still smaller particles of the Holy Spirit be alive also? and why may they not also possess all the elementary attributes of a spiritual personage or organization? Is there anything in the mere shape or magnitude of organized spirit-matter, that should cause it to differ in its elementary attributes from unorganized spirit-matter? Certainly not. Therefore, it is perfectly analogous with what we see in nature, to attribute life, voluntary motion, and numerous other attributes and qualities, to a fluid substance, or to each of its particles."

And on page 55, paragraph 25, it is said that,

"By the power of Their (the Father and the Son) word the Spirit would set those worlds into harmonious motion; by the power of Their word the Spirit would move the particles in nature according to the law of gravitation; by Their word the Spirit would move every substance according to the varied laws which now exist. By the power of Their word the Spirit could suspend its operations in one way, and operate in another, directly opposite, causing what the world generally calls a miracle. Through the agency of such a universal Spirit, a person could exercise almighty power throughout every department of nature. Particles, worlds and universes would obey, the Spirit being the great grand executor of all the sublime and majestic movements exhibited in boundless space."

On the same page, paragraph 27, it reads,

"But if the body of each Saint is full of the Holy Ghost, it is evident that this holy substance dwelling in each temple must assume the same shape and magnitude as the temple which it fills. If any one should, by vision, behold the tabernacle of man filled throughout with this substance, he would perceive it existing in a personal form of the same size and shape as the human spirit or tabernacle. And if he should behold a million of such bodily temples thus filled, he would see a million of personal beings called the Holy Ghost; but each one of these, though one with all the others in the attributes, would be distinct in substance from all the rest. They are distinct personal forms which the spiritual fluid assumes, upon entering human bodies, so as to accommodate itself to the size and form of the respective human temples which it inhabits."

"We have quoted some of the items," the Smith-Richards-Cannon committee explained, "which stand out most prominently in the publications referred to, and which strike us as being most objectionable.

They are self-confounding and conflict one with another, and, to our minds, some of the statements, if pursued to their legitimate conclusion, would convey the idea that the physical and spiritual organization of a human being conferred no additional powers or benefits on the creature thus organized, but that any single atom of the "spiritual fluid," however minute, possessed every attribute that an organized being could possess. Yet it will readily be perceived, upon reflection, that attributes never can be made manifest in any world except through organized beings.

There are great and important truths connected with the eternities of our God and with man's existence past, present and future, which the Almighty, in His wisdom, sees fit to conceal from the children of men. The latter are evidently unprepared to receive them, and there could be no possible benefit accrue to them, at present, from their revelation. It is in this light that we view the points of doctrine which we have quoted. If they were true, we would think it unwise to have them made public as these have been. But the expounder of these points of doctrine acknowledges that he has not had any revelation from the heavens in relation to them, and we know that we have had no revelation from God respecting them, except to know that many of them are false, and that the publication of all of them is unwise and objectionable. They are mere hypotheses, and should be perused and accepted as such; and not as doctrines of the Church. Whenever Br. Orson Pratt has written upon that which he knows, and has confined himself to doctrines which he understands, his arguments are convincing and unanswerable, but, when he has indulged in hypotheses and theories, he has launched forth on an endless sea of speculation to which there is no horizon.[16] The last half of the tract entitled "The Holy Spirit," contains excellent and conclusive arguments, and is all that could be wished; so also with many of his writings. But the *Seer*, the *Great First Cause*, the article in the *Millennial Star* of October 15th, and November 1, 1850, on the Holy Spirit, and the first half of the tract, also on the *Holy Spirit*, contain doctrines which we cannot sanction, and which we have felt impressed to disown, so that the Saints who now live, and who may live hereafter, may not be misled by our silence, or be left to misinterpret it. Where these objectionable works, or parts of works, are bound in volumes, or otherwise, they should be cut out and destroyed; with proper care this can be done without much, if any, injury to the volumes.

It ought to have been known, years ago, by every person in the Church—for ample teachings have been given on the point—that no member of the Church has the right to publish any doctrines, as the doctrines of the Church of Jesus Christ of Latter-day Saints, without first submitting them for examination and approval to the First Presidency and the Twelve. There is but one man upon the earth, at one time, who holds the keys to receive commandments and revelations for the Church, and who has the authority to write doctrines by way of commandment unto the Church. And any man who so far forgets the order instituted by the Lord as to write and publish, what may be termed, new doctrines, without consulting with the First Presidency of the Church respecting them, places himself in a false position and exposes himself to the power of darkness by violating his priesthood.

---

16. Readers will notice how closely this parallels Young's public criticism of 18 June 1865, quoted above.

"While upon this subject," they closed with reference to Pratt, "we wish to warn all the Elders of the Church, and to have it clearly understood by the members, that, in the future, whoever publishes any new doctrines without first taking this course will be liable to lose his priesthood."

A month later, addressing a public gathering on Temple Square, Young would wax more blunt: "He [Young] spoke his Feelings in great plainness Concerning O. Pratt & his publications. He said Orson Pratt would go to Hell. Joseph Smith said he would when Orson said that he would believe his wife Sarah before he would Joseph Smith. He will go to Hell as Joseph Said. He would Sell this people for gold. What would I give for Such an Apostle? No[t] much and yet we hold him in Fellowship in the Church."[17]

The church proclamation was not published abroad until 21 October when it appeared in the English *Millennial Star.* Four days later, Pratt, in London, handed *Star* editor Brigham Young Jr. a short notice addressed "TO THE SAINTS IN ALL THE WORLD." "Dear Brethren," Pratt's open letter began as published the following 4 November:

> Permit me to draw your attention to the proclamation of the First Presidency and Twelve, published in the *Deseret News,* and copied into the *Millennial Star* of the 21st., in which several publications that have issued from my pen are considered objectionable. I, therefore, embrace the present opportunity of publicly expressing my most sincere regret, that I have ever published the least thing which meets with the disapprobation of the highest authorities of the Church; and I do most cordially join with them in the request, that you should make such dispositions of the publications alluded to, as counselled in their proclamation.[18]

Less than two months later while recovering from a respiratory

---

17. Qtd. in Kenney, *Wilford Woodruff's Journal,* 6:249.

18. *Latter-day Saints' Millennial Star,* 4 Nov. 1865, 698; see also Clark, *Messages of the First Presidency,* 240.

illness, Pratt wrote President Young a two-and-a-half-page letter
in which he came as close to acknowledging the error of his reasoning as at any time in the past. The vicissitudes of the past twelve
years had clearly taken a heavy toll on the independent Pratt who
by now was too exhausted to protest what his biographer termed
"the sacred holocaust of his works."[19] "From the proclamation of
the First Presidency and Twelve, published in the Deseret News and
copied into the Millennial Star," Pratt meekly wrote,

> I learn that many of my writings are not approbated; and it is consid-
> ered wisdom for them to be suppressed. Any thing that I have written
> that is *erroneous*, the sooner it is destroyed the better, both for me and
> the people; for *truth* is our motto, and eternal truth alone will stand.
> Permit me to express my most sincere regrets, in having put you and
> the highest authorities of this church to so much trouble and expense. I
> most sincerely hope that the experience of the past may have a salutory
> influence on the future, and that I may live near enough to the Lord, to
> avoid all error, and cleave most steadfastly to the light. In the mean
> time, let me humbly crave your forgiveness, and the forgiveness of the
> council, and the forgiveness of all saints, as touching any thing which
> may have come from my pen, either erroneous or unwise. In relation
> to doctrine, or prophecy, or philosophy, or science, *truth, and truth alone*,
> is all that I desire. Let my name be recorded among the righteous; let
> me enjoy the society of my brethren; let me bear a humble part with
> them in bringing forth and establishing Zion, and my soul will be satis-
> fied—this only is the height of my ambition; this is the great joy of my
> life—my hope—my salvation—my all. (Emphasis in original.)

"Please present my kind love to the Council," he closed, "and m[a]y
God bless you and them for ever, is the humble sincere prayer of
your brother in Christ."[20]

---

19. England, *Life and Thought*, 229.
20. Orson Pratt to Brigham Young, 12 Dec. 1865, Brigham Young Papers.

TWELVE

Regret for Past Sins

Nine months following his apology to Brigham Young, Orson Pratt began publishing a series of articles on Adam, the first install-ment running in the 15 September 1866 issue of the *Millennial Star* in England. He knew that his biblically based writings contradicted the president's belief that Adam was the father, both spiritually and physically, of the human race, but since his criticisms of Young's teachings had never been explicitly repudiated, he must have con-cluded that they were not erroneous and that he was free to publish his own interpretations.[1] If Young read Pratt's tightly reasoned, strongly worded articles on Adam, he chose to ignore them and in-stead condemned the apostle's views on omniscience, which he found either more offensive or easier to discount.

---

1. With regard to Adam being formed "out of the ground" and "from the dust of the ground," the First Presidency wrote simply in 1860 and reiterated in 1865, "it is deemed wise to let that subject remain without further explanation at present, for it is written that we are to receive 'line upon line,' according to our faith and capacities, and the circumstances attending our progress" (qtd. in Clark, *Messages of the First Presidency*, 2:233-34).

Three months after the series began appearing in London, Young took to the pulpit in Salt Lake City:

> Some men seem as if they could learn so much and no more. They appear to be bounded in their capacity for acquiring knowledge, as Brother Orson Pratt, has in theory, bounded the capacity of God. According to his theory, God can progress no further in knowledge and power; but the God that I serve is progressing eternally, and so are his children: they will increase to all eternity, if they are faithful.

Young continued to poke fun at Orson Pratt's ability to progress in knowledge: "But there are some of our brethren," he said, "who know just so much, and they seem to be able to learn no more. You may plead with them, scold them, flatter them, coax them, and try in various ways to increase their knowledge; but it seems as if they would not learn."[2]

Home from England the next year, the much-besieged Pratt began to rethink his theology and determined to distance himself, at first privately and then publicly, from several of his disputed theories. In addition to the censures of 1860 and 1865 and his oldest son's excommunication, he was aware of the recent heresy of Amasa M. Lyman, a member of the Twelve whom thirty-five years earlier Pratt had baptized into the church. Lyman's troubles portended possible repercussions for other obdurate church authorities. According to his biographer, Lyman "asserted that man, coming from a perfect spirit father, was innately good and could redeem himself by correcting his own mortal errors. Thus there was simply no need for a personal savior. The historical figure, Jesus, whom most worshiped as the Christ, was in reality only a moral reformer, teacher, and exemplar of great love."[3] Before the end of the year, Lyman would be expelled from the Twelve for teaching that Christ's suffering and death were not necessary to God's plan of salvation. "When

---

2. *Journal of Discourses*, 11:286.
3. See Hefner, "From Apostle to Apostate," *Dialogue*, 90-104.

you wish to see the principle upon which God designed to save mankind," he had pronounced in early 1862,

> you will see there, when you look at it, a truthful reflection of the principles upon which he purposed to exalt poor sinful human-ity—of how man, who was so pure and holy before he became a den-izen of the earth, was to return to the scenes of hallowed felicity from whence he had come; not on the crimson tide of Emmanuel's blood poured forth on Calvary's mount, but by ceasing the perpetration of those wrongs which have brought misery, suffering, and death upon the family of man.[4]

"It is not with a view to get people to believe less in the blood of Jesus and all the advantages that accrue to humanity by his death that I speak," he added less than a month later;

> but would to God that I could awaken the world to a sense of the benefits mankind derived from his living! It does me more good to know that Jesus lived, a Teacher of righteousness; ... that he taught the principles of life and pointed the way to salvation, to happiness and bliss, [and] that through obedience to the requirements of the Gospel we could find rest and peace.[5]

Pratt could not have failed to appreciate that Lyman's sin, like his own, was intellectual and doctrinal in nature, compounded by Lyman's stubbornness—an inability to admit error or to submit wholly, if not willingly, to authority.

Meeting with other church officials on 10 September 1867, Pratt announced that "[h]e did not worship Atributes asside from the Personage of God." A striking change of position, it still in-cluded an ambiguous corollary: "But [Orson said he] Believed that God was an organized Being the same as Man & that Man possessed the Atributes of God & would become a God if he kept the Celes-

---

4. *Latter-day Saints' Millennial Star*, 16 Mar. 1862, 212.
5. Ibid., 13 Apr. 1862, 180.

tial Law."[6] Two days later, he met again with "[t]he President & Twelve" because of their "difference of opinion with O. Pratt."[7] The details of their meeting were not specified, but Pratt either volunteered or was instructed to repeat his "further light and understanding" to church faithful less than four weeks later at that fall's general conference. This was the same conference at which Apostle Lyman would be ejected with Pratt's consent from the Quorum of the Twelve. Intent on tempering the positions he had enunciated during the 1840s and 1850s, although not entirely repudiating them either, Pratt began cautiously:

> I do not know, but that in my teachings in years past, when teaching upon these two distinct subjects [God as a person and God's attributes], I may have left an impression upon the minds of the people that I never intended to convey[,] in reference to the qualities, perfections, glories and attributes of these personages, for attributes always do pertain to substances, you can not separate one from the other. Attributes can not exist without substance; everywhere it shows its bearing and relation to substance and person, and if in any of my preaching or teachings I have ever conveyed the impression that attributes could exist separate and apart from substances I never intended to do so.

"I do not know that I have ever declared any such in my writings," he continued.

---

6. Kenney, *Wilford Woodruff's Journal*, 6:364. Pratt's admission followed an exchange between Young and Hyde on the "baby resurrection." Hyde confessed that "Preside[n]t Young told me in 1850 that my views on the Baby resurection was not true, that I might Believe what I pleased if I would not Preach fals doctrin. But I am ready to follow in the beaten tract [sic]." Young said: "No man Could know much about the resurrection untill he passed through the resurrection & had the keys of it. For that reason I have been silent upon the subje[c]t ..." (363-64). Two days earlier, Young had told the Twelve "he herd Joseph Smith say that children would not Grow after death & at another time that they would grow[,] & he hardly knew how to reconcile it" (363).

7. Ibid., 364.

I have said that God is love, and that he is truth because the revelations say so. I have said that he oftentimes represents himself by his attributes. The same as when he says I am in you; but he does not mean that his person, his flesh and bones are in us. When Jesus says I am in the Father, he does not mean that his person is in the Father. What does he mean? He means that the same attributes that dwell in his own person also dwell in the person of the other.

"I think I have heard this doctrine taught from the commencement, by the authorities of the Church," he said, laying his teachings at the feet of Joseph Smith, "and I think it is taught, more or less, now, almost every Sabbath day. We are exhorted to develop and perfect those attributes of God that dwell within us in embryo, that we may more and more approximate to that high state of perfection that exists in the Father and the Son."

Effectively denying that he had ever previously written otherwise on the subject, he stressed that "[a]ttributes belong in all cases, in this and all other worlds, to personages and substances, and without personages and substances, they cannot exist.

"In the 'Kingdom of God,' published in October, 1848," he explained, avoiding mention of his other writings and especially those formally condemned two years earlier in mid-1865,

I have set forth the personality of the Father and the Son, and the glorious attributes that pertain to each. And again in many of my writings, to which I might refer, and could perhaps give the page, I have taught the same thing, and my views to-day concerning this matter are just the same as they were then, and then the same as they are now; only I think, by searching more fully, I have progressed and obtained some further light and information more than I had twenty or twenty-five years ago.

"I do not know, that, in my remarks this morning, concerning the atonement, and the personalities and glorious attributes of God," he concluded his nearly 90-minute sermon with the hope that his bow to Young would not go unnoticed, "I have varied in my views from those of the rest of the authorities of the Church. If I have I hope they will correct me and tell me wherein I am wrong, for it is my desire, and ever has been, to do in accordance with the revelations of heaven, to abide in the word of God, and to have that word abide in me."[8]

Young arose and briefly noted that he "was satisfied with O Pratts views upon the Godhead in the Main but[,] when He or any man published or preached his views[,] not to say they are the views of the church But his own."[9] At the close of the session, Young "talked vary Plain," directing his comments "to O Pratt about his saying that such & such were the doctrine of the Church & about his telling what would have been if Christ had not died & if Adam had not have fallen. If there had not been a savior prepared," Young insisted—the memory of Lyman's apostasy still fresh—"the world would not have been Created."[10]

"Brother Pratt keeps telling you what the Latter Day Saints believe," the president publicly vented about this same time,

> that they believe this and they believe that. Now he has no business to preach anything like this ... Brother Pratt philosophizes too much ... [T]he elders ... when they read what he writes or hear what he speaks ... find themselves in the swamp, in the fog ... Speculations are ruinous ... I warn him not to get up to talk more unless he knows what he talks about, ... and not enswamp us with speculations about what would have been if Christ had not died ... if Eve had not eaten ... if man had not fallen ... if Joseph Smith had not been killed, and what would have been if it hadn't have been, and what would have been if it had have been. If Brother Pratt will stick to the truth and come out of the swamp, I will be thoroughly satisfied with him.[11]

---

8. *Journal of Discourses,* 19:320-21.

9. Kenney, *Wilford Woodruff's Journal,* 6:368.

10. Ibid.

11. Qtd. in Daniel S. Tuttle, *Reminiscences of a Missionary Bishop* (New York: Whittaker, 1906), 345-46.

Throughout the ensuing years until the president's death in mid-1877, conflict between the two men dissipated as the infirmities of age and a variety of sacred and secular assignments assumed greater priority in their lives. At least in his formal writings, Pratt moved away from theological speculation in favor of astronomical and mathematical ruminations.[12] Only one more incident, public or private, is known to have struck a sour chord between the two leaders.

The Reorganized Church of Jesus Christ of Latter Day Saints (RLDS, renamed Community of Christ in 2001), a rival of the larger Utah church, released during the closing months of 1867 Joseph Smith's "Inspired Translation" of the *Holy Scriptures*. This was Smith's version of the King James Bible, never printed in toto during his lifetime. Leery of the new church headed by Smith's thirty-five-year-old son and namesake, Joesph Smith III, who condemned polygamy and denied that his father had ever practiced it, Young asked Pratt to evaluate the publication. Pratt either overstepped Young's mandate or reached the wrong conclusions when on at least two occasions he publicly expressed approval of Smith's Bible. Elder Woodruff wrote of the first instance, which occurred during a Sunday meeting on 31 May 1868 in the Salt Lake City 14th Ward chapel:

> O Pratt spoke upon the New Translation of the old & New Testament as Translated By the Prophet Joseph Smith before his death[,] & it had Been Published of Late by the followers of [y]oung Joseph & a Copy had been sent to Preside[n]t Young[,] & it was published in its purity & we felt much rejoiced that a copy had fallen into Preside[n]t Youngs hands. Brother Pratt showed the difference Between the old & New Translation on the second Coming of the Mesiah.[13]

Pratt's enthusiasm for the publication was genuine. "Sarah," he re-

12. See Hazen's discussion of Pratt in his *Village Enlightenment*, 15-64.
13. Kenney, *Wilford Woodruff's Journal*, 6:409-10.

portedly said to his wife after reviewing the new book, "these men have done their work honestly! This translation is just as it was left by the Prophet Joseph in 1833. I could quickly have detected it had they tampered with or altered what he wrote. I am delighted with it, and I thank God that I have received this copy."[14]

Pratt and Young knew that Smith's version of the Bible supported Pratt's belief in the creation of Adam from the dust of the earth—a position Young's Adam-God teaching rejected.[15] It was about this time that Provo's School of the Prophets (an auxiliary group composed of male priesthood holders) discussed, as recorded by one of its members,

[t]he doctrine preached by Pres[iden]t Young for a few years back wherein he says that Adam is our God—the God we worship[, and] that most of the people believe this—[S]ome believe it because the Pres[iden]t says so, others because they can find testimony in the B[ook] of Mormon & Book of Doc[trine] & Cov[enants.] Amasa Lyman stumbled on this[;] he did not believe it—[H]e did not believe in the atonement of Jesus—Orson Pratt has also told the Pres[iden]t that he does not believe it—[T]his is not the way to act—[W]e should not suffer ourselves to entertain one doubt—[W]e are not accountable on points of Doctrine if the President makes a statement [and] it is not our prerogative to dispute it.[16]

The next month, Pratt met with members of the Salt Lake School of the Prophets and found Brigham Young in attendance. Following the apostle's brief remarks, Young "bore testimony in strong terms that Joseph did not finish the New Translation of the old & new Testament which young Joseph Smith [Joseph III] had

---

14. Qtd. in Mary Audentia Smith Anderson, ed., "The Memoirs of President Joseph Smith (1832-1914)," *Saint's Herald*, 22 Jan. 1935, 109.

15. Seven years earlier, Young had commented favorably on Smith's revision of the Pentateuch, which included the Creation narrative: "The translation by Joseph Smith could be depended upon" (President's Office Journal, 26 Mar. 1861).

16. Minutes of the Provo School of the Prophets, 8 June 1868, LDS church archives (Abraham O. Smoot speaking).

lately published."[17] Others agreed, adding their own memories of what they believed Smith had intended.[18] Pratt could see that he had too eagerly embraced Smith's translation, much as he had earlier championed Lucy Smith's history, and by the end of the month, he appeared before the school to "ma[k]e a confession of his error in printing Mother Lucy Smith's book without first consulting Pres. Young." Members read and discussed excerpts from some of Pratt's writings.[19] One week later, on 4 July 1868, sensing the very real possibility of renewed conflict, Pratt sent Young a brief but compassionate letter acknowledging not only their disagreements over the Adam theology but all past differences of belief and doctrine.

> To Prest B. Young
>
> Dear brother, since the last two meetings at the school [of the Prophets], I have, at times, reflected much and very seriously, upon the feelings which I have suffered myself for years to occasionally entertain, respecting certain doctrines, or rather, items of ante-diluvian history, now believed by the Church, and have tried to justify myself in taking an opposite view, on the supposition that I was supported by the letter of the word of God; but as often as I have yielded to this influence, I have felt an indescribable wretchedness which fully convinces me that I am wrong. I wish to repent of these wrongs; for I fully realize that my sins, in this respect, have been very great, and of long continuance, and that it has been only through your great forbearance and long suffering, and the patience of my Quorum, that I have been continued in the high and responsible calling of the Apostleship to this day.
>
> I am deeply sensible that I have greatly sinned against you, and against my brethren of the school, and again[st] God, in foolishly trying to justify myself in advocating ideas, opposed to these which have

---

17. Qtd. in Kenney, *Wilford Woodruff's Journal*, 6:412. School members discussed the "new translation" the entire month. See Journal History of the Church, 6, 13 June 1868.

18. See Historian's Office Journal, 20 June 1868.

19. Journal History of the Church, 27 June 1868.

been introduced by the highest authorities of the Church, and accepted by the Saints. I humbly ask you and the school to forgive me. Hereafter, through the grace of God assisting me, I am determined to be one with you, and never found opposing anything that comes through the legitimate order of the Priesthood, knowing that it is perfectly right for me to humbly submit, in all matters of doctrine and principle, my judgement to those whose right it is by divine appointment, to receive revelation; and guide the Church.

There is no one thing in this world, or in that which is to come, which I do more earnestly desire, than to honor my calling, and be permitted to retain the same, and, with my brethren of the Twelve, enter the Celestial kingdom; with a full preparation to enjoy the glory thereof for ever.

With regard to all that portion of my printed writings which have come under the inspection of the highest authorities of the Church, and judged incorrect, I do most sincerely hope that the same may be rejected, and considered of no value, only to point out the imperfections of the author, and to be a warning to others to be more careful. This request I made formerly, but feel to renew it again in this letter.

With feelings of great sorrow, and deep regret for all my past sins, I subscribe myself your humble brother in Christ.

Orson Pratt, Sen.[20]

The tempering effect of time showed Pratt the futility of an extended conflict from which he had no hope of emerging victorious. Three days later, he again appeared before the Salt Lake School of the Prophets and "made a full confession," either reading from or summarizing his letter to Young, "in opposing doctrines revealed: said whenever he had done so & excused himself because of what

---

20. Pratt to Young, 1 July 1868, Brigham Young Papers. "It is reported on good authority," a leader of the RLDS church wrote thirteen years later, "that Elder Orson Pratt, on receiving a copy of the Inspired Translation, spoke in high terms of it in a discourse in one of the ward meeting houses in Salt Lake City some years ago, and afterwards took it all back as counseled by President B. Young" (W. W. Blair, "The Inspired Translation," *Saint's Advocate* 4 [July 1881]: 108).

was written[,] his mind [on such occasions had] become darkened
and he felt bad. He asked forgiveness of Pres[iden]t Young, of the
Twelve and the whole school." President Young "expressed his sat-
isfaction with Elder Pratt's confession & preached in relation to
Adam &c. &c," while Wilford Woodruff said he "felt happy at bro.
Pratt's position & present feelings."[21] Before the end of the month,
Young explained to Provo's School of the Prophets:

> If we become of one heart we will prosper—but if like a worm we
> divide[,] we are broken[. B]ut when [the president] speaks & says do
> this or that[,] all the faith of the people should be united in that word
> ... Orson Pratt has with stood me as he did Joseph [Smith]—I asked
> Orson to look over the "New Translation" [of the Bible] and found
> him speaking in [favor of it in] the school[. T]he Translation is incor-
> rect—and it says it shall not be published until completed.

The scribe noted that Young also referred to Pratt's letter and
quoted from it: "[W]hen I oppose[d] you I felt bitterness etc.; and
when I agreed with you I have felt well and rejoiced."[22]

Over the next few years, Pratt would do his best to conform to
Young's difficult theology, even referring to Adam as a god in an
address two years later: "Now, how are the angels of God after the
resurrection? According to the revelations which God has given,
there are different classes of angels. Some angels are Gods, and still
possess the lower office called angels. Adam is called an Archangel,

---

21. Qtd. in the Historian's Office Journal, 4 July 1868. "Some have though[t]
it strange what I have said Concerning Adam," Young told the Salt Lake School of
the Prophets late the next year. "But the period will Come when this people of
faithful will be willing to adopt Joseph Smith as their Prophet Seer Revelator &
God But not [as] the father of their spirits[,] for that was our Father Adam"
(Kenney, *Wilford Woodruff's Journal*, 6:508).

22. Minutes of the Provo School of the Prophets, 20 July 1868. It is unclear
what "it" refers to in "it says it shall not be published until completed." For more
on Young's opinion, see Robert D. Matthews, *"A Plainer Translation": Joseph Smith's
Translation of the Bible, a History and Commentary* (Provo, UT: Brigham Young University Press, 1975), 207-18.

yet he is a God."[23] That same month he urged local church leaders to try a pair of prominent Salt Lake City dissidents for apostasy. "[I]t always had been a principle in this Church for the members to receive the Councils & instructions of the authorities of the Church and to abide by their decisions in all things," he said.[24] In 1876 he abandoned—or at least significantly qualified—his belief in a "great first cause" in favor of Young's view of a universe without a beginning:

> There never was a time but what there was a Father and Son. In other words, when you entertain that which is endless, you exclude the ideas of a first being, a first world; the moment you admit of a first, you limit the idea of endless. The chain itself is endless, but each link had its beginning. ... There never will be a time when fathers, and sons, and worlds will not exist; neither was there ever a period through all the past ages of duration, but what there was a world and a Father and Son ...[25]

A year before his death, Pratt publicly revised his teachings on the self-existing attributes of godliness and contingency of the divine person to better reflect Young's doctrine:

> God has given laws to what might be termed intelligent nature; but let me say, that what is termed intelligent nature is ... an intelligent power that encircles itself through, or over, or round about every particle or every atom, that these atoms act in accordance with the law that is ordained, and do not deviate from it unless commanded by the same authority that gave the law. The same Being who gave the law to materials by which they act, can counteract the law. ... God is the great Author of all law, and is just as able to counteract a law, as he is to continue a law. Let him withdraw the command that materials shall attract all other materials; let him say to matter, "I no longer require

---

23. *Journal of Discourses,* 13:187.

24. Minutes of the Salt Lake Stake High Council, 25 Oct. 1869, LDS church archives (this was the trial of William S. Godbe and E. L. T. Harrison).

25. *Journal of Discourses,* 18:293.

you to act according to that law," and you would not find the earth in an orbit around the sun.[26]

Over time Pratt would occasionally and inevitably drift into old habits, again broaching such controversies as divine omniscience,[27] as well as quoting publicly and approvingly from Joseph Smith's "new translation."[28] Young's successor as church president, John Taylor, enlisted Pratt's expertise in 1877-78 in publishing several of Smith's revelations which had previously appeared in the small English pamphlet called *The Pearl of Great Price* (1851). In preparing these texts for publication, Pratt used the RLDS church's edition of Smith's *Holy Scriptures* as a basis of comparison and correction—though he did so silently, without alerting readers to the changes or their source. His edition of The Pearl of Great Price was canonized by the LDS church as scripture in 1880, three years after Brigham Young's death, and was later used in revising the text of the temple endowment ceremony.[29]

As for himself, Young never quoted from Smith's "new translation," and only rarely from the King James Version. "As I read the Bible," he confessed in 1871, "it contains the words of the Father and Son, angels, good and bad, Lucifer, the devil, of wicked men and of good men, and some are lying and some—the good—are telling the truth; and if you believe it all to be the word of God you can go beyond me. I cannot believe it all to be the word of God ..."[30] He continued to expound Adam-God at meetings of the Salt

---

26. Ibid., 21:238.

27. See ibid., 21:257: "They [the Father and Son] are possessed of all the fullness of glory. They have a fullness of happiness, a fullness of power, a fullness of intelligence, light and truth, and they bear rule over all other kingdoms of inferior glory, of inferior happiness, and of inferior power." See also Journal History of the Church, 21 Mar. 1872: "Elder Orson Prat lectured in the Old Tabernacle, upon the subject of 'Pre-existence.'"

28. See *Journal of Discourses*, 15:247-49; 20:71, 73; 21:200.

29. See L. John Nuttall, Journal, 15 June 1884, BYU Library.

30. *Journal of Discourses*, 14:208.

Lake City School of the Prophets and elsewhere and encouraged others to believe similarly,[31] though he sometimes wondered if he had been too indiscriminate in promulgating his controversial doctrine:

> Pres[iden]t Young queried w[he]ther the brethren thought he was too liberal in launching out on this doctrine [Adam-God] before the Gentiles [non-Mormons]. He was positive of the truth of the doctrine, but thought we should be cautious about preaching on doctrine[s] unless we fully understand them by the power of the Spirit, then they commend themselves to the hearts of our hearers. Spoke of the vain theories of men with regard to the Great first Cause. Said there were many revelations given to him that he did not receive from the Prophet Joseph [Smith]. He did not receive them ... as Joseph Smith did but when he did receive them he knew of their truth as much as it was possible for him to do of any truth.[32]

Six months before his death in late August 1877, Young began a revision of the temple ceremony to privilege his own account of the Creation over that found in Genesis. "We have heard a great deal about Adam and Eve[,] how they were formed &c," he dictated to one of his secretaries:

> [S]ome think he was made like an adobie and the Lord breathed into him the breath of life[,] for we read "from dust thou art and unto dust shalt thou return[.]" Well he was made of the dust of the earth but not of this earth. [H]e was made just the same way you and I are made but on another earth. Adam was an immortal being when he came. on this earth[. H]e had lived on an earth similar to ours [and] he had received the Priesthood and the Keys thereof. and had been faithful in all things and gained his resurrection and his exaltation and was crowned with glory[,] immortality[,] and eternal lives and was numbered with the Gods[,] for such he became through his faithfulness.

---

31. See Kenney, *Wilford Woodruff's Journal*, 6:508; Minutes of the Salt Lake City School of the Prophets, 9 June 1871, LDS church archives.

32. Minutes of the Salt Lake City School of the Prophets, 9 June 1871.

[A]nd [he] had begotten all the spirit[s] that was to come to this earth. [A]nd Eve our common Mother who is the mother of all living bore those spirits in the celestial world. [A]nd when this earth was organized by Elohim[,] Jehovah[,] & Michael[,] who is Adam our common Father[,] Adam & Eve had the privilege to continue the work of Progression. [C]onsequently[, they] came to this earth and commenced the great work of forming tabernacles for those spirits to dwell in. [A]nd when Adam and those that assisted him had completed this Kingdom[,] our earth[,] he came to it. and slept and forgot all and became like an Infant child. [I]t is said by Moses the historian that the Lord caused a deep sleep to come upon Adam and took from his side a rib and formed the woman that Adam called Eve—this should be interpreted that the Man Adam like all other Men had the seed within him to propagate his species. [B]ut not the Woman. [S]he conceives the seed but she does not produce it. [C]onsequently she was taken from the side or bowels of her father. [T]his explains the mystery of Moses' dark sayings in regard to Adam and Eve. Adam & Eve when they were placed on this earth were immortal beings with flesh[,] bones[,] and sinues[,] but upon partaking of the fruits of the earth while in the garden and cultivating the ground[,] their bodies became changed from immortal to mortal beings with the blood coursing through their veins as the action of life[.] Adam was not under transgression until after he partook of the forbidden fruit[. T]his was necessary that they might be together[,] that man might be. [T]he woman was found in transgression[,] not the Man ... Father Adam's oldest son (Jesus the Saviour) who is the heir of the family is Father Adams first begotten in the spirit World[,] who according to the flesh is the only begotten as it is written.[33] (In his divinity he [Adam,] having gone back into the spirit World[,] ...[34] c[a]me in the spirit to Mary and she conceived[,] for when Adam and Eve got

---

33. Young seems to distinguish between Adam's mortal children and a child conceived after Adam reclaimed his immortality, as he may be explaining in the next sentence.

34. The ellipses replace a conjunction. The full line reads: "In his divinity he having gone back into the spirit World. and come in the spirit to Mary and she conceived for when Adam and Eve got through with their Work in this earth."

through with their Work in this earth[,] they did not lay their bodies down in the dust, but returned to the spirit World from whence they came.[35]

John Taylor's subsequent decision to use Pratt's edition of the Pearl of Great Price in refining the temple ceremony, coupled with other scriptural reflections, effectively undermined Young's innovation as official doctrine, though it would continue to surface periodically as one of Mormonism's gnostic mysteries.

The closing bittersweet years of Orson Pratt's life were witness to further achievements and profound disappointments. In mid-August 1870, the Tabernacle walls rang with his now-famous debate on plural marriage against the Christian rhetoric of Dr. John P. Newman, chaplain of the United States Senate. From 1869 until 1880, he served as needed as the territorial Speaker of the House. In the summer of 1874, he was officially appointed LDS Church Recorder and Historian. The following year saw his demotion from a position of seniority in the Quorum of the Twelve, a blow that would crush any possibility that he would one day succeed to the presidency of the church.

---

35. Nuttall Journal, 7 Feb. 1877. For context, see David John Buerger, *The Mysteries of Godliness: A History of Mormon Temple Worship* (San Francisco: Smith Research Associates, 1994), 110-13.

THIRTEEN

Adjusting Matters

*B*y April 1856, when the *Deseret News* published Joseph Smith's history dealing with Orson Pratt's 1843 difficulties, Church Historian George A. Smith knew that Pratt had been fully restored to his position in the Twelve. How then to account most satisfactorily for Brigham Young's *ex post facto* realignment nineteen years later in 1875—his demotion of Apostles Hyde and Pratt?

Young complained in October 1856 that Orson Hyde was "no more fit to stand at the Head of the Quorum of the Twelve than a dog."[1] In May 1867, he predicted that Pratt would not be "enabled to do any good."[2] Previously, he had not expressed any concern with Hyde's or Pratt's position in the quorum. When Young succeeded

---

1. Qtd. in Kenney, *Wilford Woodruff's Journal,* 4:477.
2. Qtd. in ibid., 6:341. T. Edgar Lyon asserted that Pratt's seniority was debated during a closed meeting of the Twelve sometime between 1860 and 1868. According to Lyon, Young opposed Pratt's demotion because he did not believe Pratt had ever been "officially excommunicated" but finally capitulated to a majority who felt that Pratt was unsuited to be his successor (Lyon, "Orson Pratt—Early Mormon Leader," 160-62). Lyon's conclusion was based on Stenhouse's *Rocky Mountain Saints,* 494, which he reinterpreted, and on information

Joseph Smith, it was by virtue of his own status as senior apostle,[3] and he must have anticipated that Hyde might succeed him on the same principle. In April 1861, President Young mentioned during general conference that seniority within the Twelve depended on an apostle's age.[4] "The oldest man—the senior member of the first Quorum will preside, each in his turn," he explained, "until every one of them has passed away. ... Bro. Orson Hyde and br. Orson Pratt, sen., are the only two that are now left in the Quorum of the Twelve that br. Joseph Smith selected. Perhaps there are a great many here who never thought of these ideas, and never heard anything said about them."[5] Six months later he corrected himself. Now seniority now would depend on the date of one's ordination as an apostle rather than on one's birth date. Young "spoke of it now, because the time would come when a dispute might arise about it."[6] Consequently, John Taylor, who had been ordained

---

supplied by one of Pratt's daughters-in-law. Using available contemporary sources, I have not been able to confirm that such a meeting occurred.

3. "I am the pres of the 12—the head of the people," Young said shortly before the organization of his presidency in late 1847; "I am mouth—I will say as I please, do as I please." He viewed the Twelve the "same as I do my pet young ones, that I could put them in my pockets same as my Wives and Children ... so that when I want to talk with you, I put my hand in my pocket, take you out, and talk with you" ("Minutes of Councils, Meetings, & Journey," 16, 17 Nov. 1847).

4. See Reed C. Durham Jr. and Steven H. Heath, *Succession in the Church* (Salt Lake City: Bookcraft, 1970), 65-66. Less than three months after the Twelve were first organized in 1835, Joseph Smith commented: "It will be the duty of the twelve when in council to take their seats together according to their ages" (Remarks, 2 May 1835, in "A record of the transactions of the Twelve apostles"). Not quite three years later, the First Presidency instructed Brigham Young to "appoint the oldest of the Twelve who were firs[t] appointed, to be the President of your Quorum" (Sidney Rigdon, Joseph Smith, and Hyrum Smith to Heber C. Kimball and Brigham Young, 16 Jan. 1839, Joseph Smith Papers).

5. *Deseret News Weekly,* 6 Apr. 1861, 44.

6. Journal History of the Church, 7 Oct. 1861. See also John Taylor's discussion in *Succession in the Priesthood,* 2, 16-17. By this time, Young had ordained two of his sons to the apostleship and would later ordain two more, only one of whom

three months before Wilford Woodruff, was advanced to a position ahead of Woodruff even though he was twenty months younger. Pratt was unaffected by the change and remained second in line behind Hyde. Every six months to one year thereafter during sessions of general conference, each member of the quorum was sustained by church members in their new order of seniority.

Young had not forgotten Pratt's disaffection in Nauvoo and was no doubt reminded of it every time the two disagreed on doctrine. On more than one occasion since 1853, Pratt's dissent was compared to his earlier episode with Joseph Smith.[7] "Wild," "uncertain," "contradictory," and "at heart an infidel" were Young's descriptions of Pratt during such periods of conflict.[8]

The earliest known suggestion that Young might limit Pratt's future was an address he delivered in St. George, Utah, on 5 May 1867 when he condemned what he viewed as Pratt's and another apostle's false teachings. He said that "Orson Pratt ... would have been Cut off from the Church long ago had it not been for me. ... Neither of those brethren will be enabled to do any good."[9]

According to John Taylor's 1881 recollection, George A. Smith,

---

would be admitted to the Quorum of the Twelve. Basing seniority on either chronological age or date of ordination, Young may have hoped that one of his sons would one day succeed him. At the same time, it is unclear if he expected seniority to be the only factor. Another modification introduced in April 1900 based seniority on the date of one's admittance into the quorum rather than the date of one's ordination. This refinement resolved a dispute about Brigham Jr. who had been ordained four and a half years before he entered the quorum. See Durham and Heath, *Succession in the Church*, 111-16.

7. See, e.g., Kenney, *Wilford Woodruff's Journal*, 5:427, 6:249, and Minutes of the Provo School of the Prophets, 20 July 1868.

8. See *Journal of Discourses*, 11:121; Lorenzo Brown, Journal, 12 Sept. 1864, typescript, BYU Library.

9. Qtd. in Kenney, *Wilford Woodruff's Journal*, 6:341. The context of the speech suggests that Amasa Lyman was the second apostle since he had been dropped from the quorum the previous day and would be excommunicated the following October. It is also possible that Young meant Orson Hyde since Young went on to criticize his idea that the resurrection included a literal rebirthing.

Young's first counselor since 1868, drew Taylor's and presumably Young's attention to the succession question in the mid-1860s, a period when doctrinal disputes between Young and Pratt were at their height.[10] As Taylor recalled the exchange, Smith felt that the question might become serious since he believed Taylor would "st[an]d before them [Hyde and Pratt] in the quorum" if seniority depended—based on Young's reordering in late 1861—on date of ordination. Taylor answered that he was aware of the "correctness" of Smith's position "and had been for years" but had chosen not to bring up "a question of that kind." He added that he "personally cared nothing about the matter, and moreover, entertain[ed] a very high esteem for both the parties named." But in retrospect, at least, Taylor agreed that "complications might hereafter arise, unless the matters were adjusted." In other words, Taylor's memory was that he had not been sure about the proper method of succession at that time and had hoped that Young would outlive Pratt and Hyde.

According to Taylor, George A. Smith's role was pivotal. One of Smith's biographers agreed that "[i]t was principally due to George A.'s advice, it appears, that President Young rearranged the seniority of the Quorum of the Twelve."[11] Smith was present at Pratt's 1842 suspension and his 1843 reinstatement. He was appointed Church Historian and General Church Recorder in 1854, a position he

---

10. Taylor, *Succession in the Priesthood,* 16-17. Perhaps this Smith-Taylor conversation was what T. Edgar Lyon's informant had in mind. See n2.

11. C. Kent Dunford, "The Contributions of George A. Smith to the Establishment of the Mormon Society in the Territory of Utah," Ph.D. diss., Brigham Young University, 1970, 284-85. George A. Smith's son, John Henry, reported in 1893 that he was present when "the question of moving Bro. Hyde and Orson Pratt back in the quorum came up." He remembered his father telling Brigham Young: "I have always counselled against making this change, hoping that Brother Hyde might die and thus be spared that humiliation, but seeing how sick you have been for some time I feared the consequences if you should have died. I shall no longer oppose the move" (qtd. in Anthon H. Lund, Journal, 16 Apr. 1893). Taylor's 1881 account (*Succession in the Priesthood,* 16) places the responsibility for the realignment squarely with George A. Smith.

held for sixteen years, and he helped draft the 1865 official censure of Pratt. He was also "a devoted friend and brother" to Young, who reportedly depended on Smith "perhaps more than any other, 'to bear off the burden of the Kingdom.'"[12] As a historian, Smith wore his biases proudly. "The characteristics of the Latter-day Saints, for Smith," wrote Davis Bitton and Leonard J. Arrington, "were faith, dedication, courage—in a word, heroism."[13] Clearly, he could not accept that a man of Pratt's disloyalties could be fully qualified to lead the church. While Smith did not effect the 1875 realignment single-handedly, by virtually all accounts he pursued it with more determination than anyone else.

Given the intensity of George A.'s feelings on the topic, it should be noted that he chose not to edit Joseph Smith's history differently in the 1850s when he had official charge of the records. If he believed the prophet had erred in returning Pratt to his previous seniority, he could have clarified the situation by making Pratt's 1842 suspension a legal excommunication and his 1843 reordination less than a full return to his former standing. He was either unwilling to rewrite the prophet's record to such an extent or was cautioned not to do so. It is possible that in 1856 he was not yet convinced that Joseph had erred in overturning Orson's "excommunication."

Young could have more easily adjusted Hyde's and Pratt's standing in 1861 when Taylor and Woodruff traded places. The fact that no change was made suggests that he either did not share Smith's interpretation or was not as anxious to move so quickly. Possibly George A. Smith and others felt that they could not push the subject too far with their strong-willed president, or maybe Young believed

---

12. Preston Nibley, *Brigham Young—The Man and His Work* (Salt Lake City: Deseret News Press, 1936), 516. See also Dunford, "The Contributions of George A. Smith."

13. Davis Bitton and Leonard J. Arrington, *Mormons and Their Historians* (Salt Lake City: University of Utah Press, 1988), 25.

that Hyde and Pratt would die before him. Ironically, the topic was next broached, not by church leaders but by the weekly *Salt Lake Tribune,* which was well known for its anti-Brigham sentiment. In mid-September 1871, the *Tribune* explicitly asserted in an article entitled "The Two Orsons and the Succession" that "[t]he President of the Twelve Apostles, whoever he might be at Brigham's death, cannot be set aside by an ordinary rule, much less by a usurped ... and a stolen ordination." The anonymous writer was surprisingly prescient: "Nothing but an extraordinary act of legislation of his quorum, sustained by the voice of the entire church, could displace Orson Hyde, and that would amount to a grand impeachment ..."

Of Pratt's future prospects, the reporter ventured an equally irreverent assessment:

> When brother Orson [Pratt] while on a mission was informed of the rumors that the President had ordained his son Brigham to succeed him, the veteran Apostle smiled, and with quiet significance replied, "I guess the Twelve will choose their own President. ..."
>
> [T]he best part of Mormon theology has been derived, after Joseph [Smith], from Parley and Orson [Pratt]. Orson was also the mast of nearly all the Utah Protestants, and of all the thinkers and rebels of Mormonism; but to-day, they have outgrown their teacher, being younger and consequently more progressive. But Orson's disciples still venerate their old master, whose example they are following in measuring intellects with Brigham Young, and refusing to be subdued by the absolute will and mind of any mortal man.[14]

Hyde's reaction to the article was one of stunned embarrassment, and worried that Young would think he had been weighing his chances of becoming church president. "I suppose some have imagined I would seek for that station if I outlived President Young," he wrote to George A. Smith, now Young's first counselor, "but such thoughts are vain and groundless. They may exist in the minds of

---

14. "The Two Orsons and the Succession," *Salt Lake Tribune* (weekly), 16 Sept. 1871, 4.

some, but they never existed in my mind at any period of my life."[15] Whether or not Pratt responded to the inflammatory article is not known.

Whatever the intentions or consequences of the *Tribune* article, the matter of succession went unaddressed for the next several years until September 1874 when the president became "gravely ill" for the first time since the mid-1850s due to an enlarged prostate gland.[16] With no guarantee that such an affliction would not be fatal, George A. Smith and others likely urged a final resolution to the seniority question.[17] By this time, Young had changed his mind about the need for clarification, no doubt fearing the consequences if the church were led by either of the two senior apostles.

The mechanics of the decision, its announcement to the quorum, and the reactions of Hyde and Pratt remain unclear. On 10 April 1875, both apostles were demoted behind Elders Taylor and Woodruff. There was no public comment on the action until shortly after Young's death in late August 1877. Six weeks later, on 8 October, George Q. Cannon announced in general conference that Young had been "moved upon to place [Taylor] ahead of two others, until by the unanimous voice of the Apostles he [Taylor] was acknowledged the Senior Apostle, holding the oldest ordination without interruption of any man among the Apostles." Cannon mistakenly reported that the change had taken place not in Salt Lake City in April 1875 but two months later in southern Utah.[18]

His misstatement was perpetuated in John Taylor's official ren-

---

15. Orson Hyde to George A. Smith, 23 Sept. 1871, qtd. in Hyde, *Orson Hyde*, 457.

16. See Lester E. Bush Jr., "Brigham Young in Life and Death: A Medical Overview," *Journal of Mormon History* 5 (1978): 90.

17. William G. Hartley, "The Priesthood Reorganization of 1877: Brigham Young's Last Achievement," *BYU Studies* 20 (Fall 1979): 5, agrees that Young's failing health may have prompted the realignment. But Hartley sees it as a coincidental first step in a general reorganization of priesthood offices, quorums, and jurisdictions which occurred two years later.

18. *Journal of Discourses*, 19:234-35. Cannon did not name the "two others"

dering of the realignment, which influenced the accounts of subsequent writers.[19] According to Taylor, "Brigham Young brought up the subject of seniority, and stated that John Taylor was the man that stood next to him; and that where he was not, John Taylor presides. He also made the statement, that Brother Hyde and Brother Pratt were not in their right positions in the Quorum."[20] It is true that Young's entourage toured southern Utah settlements

---

because Pratt and Hyde were both alive. See also *Journal of Discourses,* 23:365, where Cannon repeats this mistake in chronology. He tended to be more certain in public than in private. Cf. Moses Thatcher, Journal, entry titled "The October Conference 1880," photocopy, BYU Library.

19. Writers who used the Taylor account include Arrington, *Brigham Young,* 376; Talbot, *Acts of the Modern Apostles,* 146; and England, *Life and Thought,* 271. Only Smith, *Essentials in Church History,* 575, and D. Michael Quinn, *The Mormon Hierarchy: Extensions of Power* (Salt Lake City: Signature Books in association with Smith Research Associates, 1997), 770-71, provided the correct date. Apostle John Henry Smith later asserted that he had privately asked Young in the spring of 1874, "In the case of your death to whom should I look to lead the Church[?]" Young reportedly told the twenty-five-year-old, "To any one of the Council of the Apostles in the order of ordination, bar[r]ing Orson Hyde and Orson Pratt, who had forfeited their right" (qtd. in Jean Bickmore White, ed., *Church, State, and Politics: The Diaries of John Henry Smith* [Salt Lake City: Signature Books in association with Smith Research Associates, 1991], 241). The official minutes of the meeting in which John Henry recounted his conversation with Young read: "John Henry Smith asked President Brigham Young once in St. George [Utah] as to the positions of Orson Hyde and Orson Pratt. In case of President Young's death who should preside. He answered, 'The Twelve, and their President was the President of the Church, unless he had forfeited his right to do so.' That Orson Hyde and Orson Pratt had forfeited their right to preside, therefore it went to John Taylor" (Minutes of the Quorum of the Twelve Apostles, 3 Aug. 1887). Heber J. Grant recorded: "John Henry Smith[:] Pres[iden]t Brigham Young had told him that he had never done any thing of importance without first getting it endorsed by seven of the Apostles, and that in case of his (Brigham's) death that John Taylor, then the President of the quorum of the Apostles was the man to lead the Church" (Heber J. Grant, Diary, 3 Aug. 1887, LDS church archives). John Henry probably misremembered when his conversation with Young occurred. (In another quorum meeting three years later, George A. Smith perpetuated the idea that the change in seniority was first announced in St. George [Abraham H. Cannon, Journal, 1 Oct. 1890, BYU Library].)

20. Taylor, *Succession in the Priesthood,* 17.

for ten days in June 1875, but no contemporary account substanti-
ates Cannon's and Taylor's reminiscences.[21] Cannon and Taylor
accompanied the party, and Young may have mentioned that Taylor
should be his successor according to seniority, but this would have
been commentary on an action that had already taken place more
than two months earlier.

On the strength of this realignment, John Taylor, acting as senior member of the Quorum of the Twelve Apostles, assumed leadership of the church upon Young's death on 29 August 1877.[22] He
was sustained as president of the Quorum of the Twelve Apostles—a position that had gone unfilled since the realignment—the
following 6 October,[23] but a First Presidency would not be organized for another three years. Instead, Taylor and the Twelve would
jointly preside over the church. Some of the apostles felt the previous First Presidency had been autocratic and that it had ignored the
role of the Twelve as a governing body of equivalent, if not identical, rank and were reluctant to see this pattern repeated. ("*The
Twelve have no right* to ask the Presidency why they do this or that,"
Young had insisted, saying that their duty was "ownly [to] go & do
as they are told."[24]) Cannon recorded his astonishment at discover-
ing, four months after Young's death, that

---

21. Journal History of the Church, 19, 29 June 1875. Neither Pratt nor
George A. Smith accompanied the group south (ibid., 25, 27 June 1875). Brigham
Young Jr., who did, summarized his father's public talks during this period without reference to such an announcement. He does mention his father's public criticism of Hyde on 22 June 1875 in Mt. Pleasant, Utah: that Hyde "was not fit to be
an apostle ... Bro Hyde had not the spirit ... [but] would lead the people to hell."
Afterwards, Brigham Jr. recorded, "Father had a long talk with bro Hyde and
warned him to be careful" (Brigham Young Jr., Diary, 22 June 1875).

22. See Franklin D. Richards, Journal, 4 Sept. 1877, LDS church archives; Historian's Office Journal, 6, 8 Sept. 1877. Less than two years later, Wilford Woodruff
would explain publicly: "Elder Taylor is the oldest in *Ordination* and that is why he
presides today" (in Moses Thatcher, Journal, 5 Jan. 1879; emphasis Thatcher's).

23. Journal History of the Church, 6 Oct. 1877.

24. Qtd. in Kenney, *Wilford Woodruff's Journal*, 4:382; emphasis Woodruff's.
Once the First Presidency was reorganized in late 1847, Young believed, the pri-

some of my brethren ... did have feelings concerning his [President Young's] course. They did not approve of it, and felt oppressed, and yet they dared not exhibit their feelings to him, he ruled with so strong and stiff a hand, and they felt that it would be of no use. In a few words, the feeling seems to be that he transcended the bounds of the authority which he legitimately held. I have been greatly surprised to find so much dissatisfaction in such quarters.[25]

Apostle Franklin D. Richards added several years later: "Brigham used to love to display his powers, his absolute and arbitrary influence."[26] "To use the language of business," twentieth-century

---

mary mission of the Twelve would be to preach Mormonism to the world, not to direct the affairs of the church at home.

25. George Q. Cannon, Journal, 17 Jan. 1878, qtd. in Joseph J. Cannon, "George Q. Cannon—Relations with Brigham Young," *The Instructor* 80 (June 1945): 259. Cannon's most recent biographer summarizes this entry, then quotes Cannon directly: "The thought that ever was with me was: If I criticize or find fault with, or judge Brother Brigham, how far shall I go; if I commence[,] where shall I stop? I dared not to trust myself in such a course. I knew that apostasy frequently resulted from the indulgence of the spirit of criticizing and fault-finding. Others, of greater strength, wisdom and experience than myself, might do many things and escape evil consequences, which I dare not do" (in Davis Bitton, *George Q. Cannon: A Biography* [Salt Lake City: Deseret Book Co., 1999], 212).

26. Franklin D. Richards, "Reminiscences," 1884, Bancroft Library, University of California, Berkeley. See also Heber J. Grant, Letterbook, 8 Sept. 1887, LDS church archives: Brigham Young "had not counseled as much with the Council of the Apostles as with those persons with whom he was surrounded."

Consider the case of Jacob Weiler and John Wayman, both members of the Salt Lake School of the Prophets. At one of its meetings in mid-1874, Young asked if members would be willing to live the United Order, a communal plan, to which everyone except Weiler raised his hand. Weiler thought "he should require a little more time to reflect before deciding on the matter." Young moved that Weiler "be excused from acting hereafter as Bishop." When Wayman objected that his colleague should be allowed some time to think, Young expelled both of them from the school (Minutes of the Salt Lake City School of the Prophets, 25 May 1874). "Certainly," wrote one historian of this episode, "if one wished to remain in the good graces of church leaders, it paid to support the[ir] policies ... whether approving of them or not" (John R. Patrick, "The School of the Prophets: Its Development and Influence in Utah Territory," M.A. thesis, Brigham Young University, June 1970, 115).

church historians Leonard Arrington and Ronald Esplin subsequently explained, "President Young considered himself to be both
the chairman of the policy-making board and the company president chosen to administer the policies." While he "did involve the
apostles in several important ways," they continued, "[t]his is not to
say that the President trod softly on the Twelve[, and] ... Young's
capacity for sarcasm assured that his administration was not devoid
of some tension."[27]

Seniority was not the sole factor in their approach to reconstituting a new First Presidency. In October 1877, Young's former
counselor Daniel H. Wells proposed that Joseph F. Smith, one of the
youngest members of the quorum and son of Hyrum Smith, be
named church president. The Twelve voted down the proposal,
though whether inspired by a general reluctance to form a First
Presidency or out of committment to seniority is not clear.[28] Wells,
a "counselor to the Twelve" at the time and hence not a formal
member of the quorum, had spent his entire tenure in the First
Presidency, and either ignored or was oblivious to the Twelve's concern for cooperation and balance. Taylor repeatedly reassured his
associates during this "apostolic presidency" that his would be a different kind of administration. As he told a group of church authorities meeting in his office in February 1878:

> While Pres[iden]t Brigham Young was alive, there were some

---

27. Leonard J. Arrington and Ronald K. Esplin, "The Role of the Council of
the Twelve during Brigham Young's Presidency of the Church of Jesus Christ of
Latter-day Saints," *Task Papers in LDS History*, No. 31 (Salt Lake City: Historical
Department of the Church of Jesus Christ of Latter-day Saints, Dec. 1979), 55-56,
57, 58.

28. Franklin D. Richards, Journal, 3-4 Oct. 1877. Wells told the apostles that
he was prompted by a vision (see *Journal of Discourses*, 19:235). Twenty years later,
Heber J. Grant recorded Richards's reflection: "When Bro Young died Counselor
Daniel H. Wells said that Joseph F. Smith should be chosen to be the President of
the Church, but the apostles did not accept of this and it was some time before
there was a perfect union so that the Presidency could be organized" (Grant, Journal, 4 Oct. 1898).

things in which my views differed from his, but did I ever permit them to stand in the way of my doing the will of God? No; I submitted my will to the will of God. When I was in St. George last winter [1877], President Young spoke to me, and I believe, some others of the Twelve, with regard to the Deseret Alphabet.[29] He said he knew that through our traditions and education we were opposed to it, but if we would help him he would carry it through. I acknowledged that in my feelings I was not favorably disposed towards it; but I said Pres[iden]t Young, if you will tell me that it is the mind and will of the Lord that it should be adopted, I will back you up to the utmost of my influence and ability; and I wish to say to my brethren that I don't want them to be scared of one another, but let us present our ideas to each other and adopt the best ones. Let us have free intercourse one with another, and converse on doctrine and principle, and upon all things in which the Kingdom of God is interested as pointed out in the revelation ...[30] I am always willing to swap bad ideas for good ones.[31]

---

29. A phonetically based alphabet that Young hoped would replace standard English among the multi-ethnic Saints.

30. Taylor quotes here from Doctrine and Covenants 88:77-81.

31. "Minutes of a Meeting in the President's Office, 23 Feb. 1878," L. John Nuttall Collection, BYU Library. See also Samuel W. Taylor, *The Kingdom or Nothing: The Life of John Taylor, Militant Mormon* (New York: Macmillan Publishing Co., 1976), 159-74. Apparently, at around the same time and in the same place, another disagreement—possibly more serious—arose between Taylor and Young. As Lorenzo Snow later recalled:

John Taylor also was similarly tested by the then Pres. B. Young at the time the St. George temple was dedicated [April 1877]. The United Order was then a favorite theme of Pres. Young, but in his views[,] John Taylor did not fully coincide. Because of this the latter was most terribly scourged by the tongue of Pres. Young in the temple before all the people. Bro. Taylor was then President of the Twelve. It looked for a time as though these two great men would separate in anger, for Pres. Y had forbidden John to travel through Kanab and Panguitch Stakes and organize them with Bro. L. Snow as had been intended and said he had better return home and make wagons until he knew what was right. Bro. Snow saw the danger and knew the disposition of the two men. He therefore visited Pres. Taylor and after considerable argument induced him to go and visit Pres. Young. They were coolly received at the latter's house, but as soon as Pres. Taylor said, "Bro. Brigham, if I have

Despite Taylor's assurances, when he called for the quorum to organize a First Presidency late the next year, the Twelve vetoed it "as altogether uncalled for & unbefitting of the Church. The 12 ought first [to] attain a full unity with each other & [the] people first."[32]

Taylor continued to push for a new presidency, convinced that a division of authority was not only decreed by revelation but was in the church's long-term best interests. Early the following October 1880, he shocked the quorum by insisting that a First Presidency "be organized during the present [general] Conference." While the consensus was that the most senior member of the Twelve was quorum president and *de facto* church president, not all of the apostles believed that the senior apostle became *de jure* church president on the death of the incumbent.[33] For example,

---

done or said anything wrong I desire to make it right," every feeling of anger vanished and these two men were reconciled. Thus the Lord will try us wherever we seem to be strong ... (Abraham H. Cannon, Journal, 9 Apr. 1890.)

Young left Salt Lake City for St. George in November 1876, dedicated the temple there in early April 1877, and returned to Salt Lake City on 27 April. Thus, it is possible that Snow remembered the event Taylor described but was confused as to the topic of disagreement, or perhaps Taylor and Young sparred over several topics. (Young did publicly criticize Orson Hyde's cautious support of the United Order in June 1875 while on a tour of Sanpete County [(Hyde, *Orson Hyde,* 471-75].)

D. Michael Quinn has speculated that Young's decision not to appoint Taylor as president of the quorum was evidence of the "depth of his disapproval of Taylor" (Quinn, *Mormon Hierarchy: Extensions,* 60). "It is beyond question," Quinn wrote, "that Young did not want Taylor to become president through automatic succession as senior-ranked apostle" (Quinn, *Mormon Hierarchy: Origins,* 254). It is also likely that Young simply did not want to draw attention to Hyde's and Pratt's demotions.

32. Franklin D. Richards, Journal, 6 Sept. 1879. The Twelve may have felt little urgency due to the Saints' millennialist beliefs at this time.

33. Less than seven years later, Apostle Grant would muse, "I do not think it is absolutely necessary that in case of the death of the President of the Church and the subsequent reorganization of the First Presidency that the President of the Twelve Apostles should be made the President of the Church" (Heber J. Grant, Journal, 5 Apr. 1887). Elder Cannon reportedly remarked that while both Young and Taylor were president of the Twelve before becoming church president, "it

did not follow that that principle would be carried out hereafter" (in Wilford Woodruff to Heber J. Grant, 28 Mar. 1887, Wilford Woodruff Papers, LDS church archives). Lorenzo Snow told the apostles in 1896 when he was president of the Twelve that they "had the right and power to select a First Presidency either in or outside of the Council of the Twelve" (Minutes of the Quorum of Twelve Apostles, 29 Sept. 1896).

On the other hand, Woodruff responded forcefully to Grant's question about, "in case of the death of the president of the Church[,] why the Twelve Apostles should not choose some other person to be the president of the Church instead of the president of the Twelve Apostles":

> First, when the president of the Church dies, who *then* is the presiding authority of the Church? It is the *quorum of the Twelve Apostles* (ORDAINED AND ORGANIZED BY THE REVELATION OF GOD & NONE ELSE). Then, while these Twelve Apostles preside over the Church[,] who is the president of the Church? It is the president of the Twelve Apostles. And He is virtually as much the President of the Church ... as He is when organized into the presidency ... If the president of the Twelve Apostles is not fit to be the president of the Church[,] He is not fit to be the president of the Twelve Apostles. ... And I certainly do not believe[,] should president Taylor Die to day[,] that Brother George Q. Cannon nor any other Man could use influence or argument Enough to convert a Majority of the Twelve Apostles to depart from the Beaten track laid out and followed by the Almighty God for the last 57 years ... As far as I am concerned[,] it would require not ownly a much stronger argument than I ever heard but a Revelation from the Same God who had organized the Church and guided it by inspiration in the Channel in which it has tar[ried] for 57 years ... Now Brother Grant[,] With this declaration and Charge ringing in my Ears, should I outlive presid[en]t Taylor (AN EVENT I NEVER EXPECT TO SEE) I should strongly urge my brethren of the Twelve Apostles to follow the beaten track ... And I have full confidence to believe that the Twelve Apostles have had experience and light enough to shun any path pointed out to gratify the private interest of any Man or set of men against the interest of the Church and Kingdom of God on the Earth (Wilford Woodruff to Heber J. Grant, 28 Mar. 1887, emphasis in original).

Following a year and a half of infighting in the Quorum of the Twelve, Woodruff was sustained as church president on 7 April 1889. According to the most recent "official" explanation of succession: "Since a fundamental doctrine of the Church is the reality of continuing REVELATION, and since the Twelve Apostles are sustained as PROPHETS, SEERS, AND REVELATORS, there is no apparent reason that the Quorum of the Twelve could not depart from this precedent and select someone other than the senior apostle to lead the Church, if so directed by revelation" (Martin B. Hickman, "Succession to the Presidency," in Ludlow, *Encyclopedia of Mormonism,* 3:1421).

Orson Pratt surveyed his colleagues following Taylor's announcement and found that, whereas he personally favored a younger, more physically able man for the vacancy, others were unprepared to venture a preference at all and remained silent.[34]

At a second meeting of the Twelve the next day, 8 October, Wilford Woodruff concluded that Taylor "might, if he choose to claim it, be president of the Church, by virtue of his calling and position as the Chief and oldest Apostle." Several others agreed. However, the issue of timing was important. According to Apostle Moses Thatcher, "Many of the brethren seemed unsettled" and asked Taylor if he "had the mind of the Lord on the matter." Taylor "declined" to answer, pointing out that "it should be left with the Quorum of the Twelve to decide—it rested upon them." Orson admonished his quorum that they already had the "will of the Lord" as found in the Doctrine and Covenants and that "it only remains for us to do it." Wilford Woodruff, Charles C. Rich, George Q. Cannon, Albert Carrington, and, to a lesser extent, Lorenzo Snow and Franklin D. Richards concurred with Pratt.

Those who were reluctant included Moses Thatcher, who had replaced Hyde upon his death in 1879, and Joseph F. Smith, another junior member of the quorum. Smith felt there was not "any necessity for such a move at this time" and said "the Spirit had not impressed on [me] that the organization at this time was either very important or required." He asked if his associates recalled Young having said, "You think I have been hard in many things but I want to say to you that the little finger of my successor will rest more heavily upon this people than my whole body has ever done." No one remembered it. Cannon commented that he "thought he had heard [Young] say that 'John Taylor would be his successor,'" but

---

34. See Moses Thatcher, Journal, "October Conference 1880." In the early 1870s, one knowledgeable writer reported that possible successors to Young included George A. Smith, Brigham Young Jr., and George Q. Cannon (see Stenhouse, *Rocky Mountain Saints,* 661-64).

Young's former counselor, Daniel Wells, "said that he did not believe that any man ever heard President Young say that—for he knew, that he never thought so." Thatcher hoped that Erastus Snow and Brigham Young Jr., both absent, would be allowed to express their views. As for himself, he believed that "in the multitude of counselors there is safety," and was "sorry that I could not feel like some of the brethren who had spoken; but I could not, and the idea of a change—an organization of the most important quorum in the Church at this time—brought with it, to me, feelings of apprehension." As they had the previous day, the Twelve adjourned without reaching a decision.[35]

Not surprisingly, given Taylor's "anxious" desire to resolve the issue, the subject was again raised the following afternoon. Upon motion by Woodruff, "Elder John Taylor was nominated and sustained as president by the vote of all present."[36] He was formally set apart and immediately called George Q. Cannon and Joseph F. Smith to be his first and second counselors.[37] Wilford Woodruff was sustained as president of the Quorum of the Twelve. Despite

---

35. Moses Thatcher, Journal, "October Conference 1880"; see also Kenney, *Wilford Woodruff's Journal,* 7:594.

36. Moses Thatcher, Journal, "October Conference 1880"; Kenney, *Wilford Woodruff's Journal,* 7:595. Thatcher writes that Charles C. Rich nominated Taylor to be president. However, both Woodruff (ibid.) and George Q. Cannon (Cannon, *Instructor,* 410-11) say that Woodruff made the motion. George Q. adds that it occurred on 8 October; Thatcher and Woodruff say 9 October. Bitton, *George Q. Cannon,* 239, quoting George Q. on his new appointment, suggests that it occurred on the 9th. The changes were announced publicly on the 10th; see Journal History of the Church, 10 Oct. 1880.

37. Ironically, within two years, members of the Twelve would complain that Taylor, much like Young, was autocratic, oblivious to the Twelve, and a usurper of power. John Henry Smith, one of the newest members of the quorum, commented in his journal: "I am satisfied that before another President over our Church is sustained[, t]he Twelve apostles will be compeled to have an understanding in relation to the duties of their respective quorums. The first [new] President [will be the one who] takes the whole business in his hands" (qtd. in White, *Church, State, and Politics,* 85). "I may have differed from him [Taylor] upon some

his earlier call for a younger president, Orson Pratt defended the quorum's decision in general conference the next day. "Every time we [the Twelve] thought upon the subject [of organizing the church]," he explained, "we saw that one Council, the most important of all, was still vacant. Could we ignore it? No. We therefore considered the propriety of organizing it at the present Conference; and Brother John Taylor, by the voice of his brethren, the Twelve, being the person holding the legal right to that office, ... was selected to occupy the position of the President of the whole Church."[38]

Taylor added that afternoon:

> Now let me refer with pride to my brethren of the Twelve here, which ... as a quorum held the right by the vote of the people to act in the capacity of the First Presidency, yet when they found ... that they had performed their work, they were willing to withdraw from that Presidency, and put it in the position that God had directed, and fall back into the place that they have always held, as the Twelve Apostles ... I say it is with pride that I refer to this action and the feeling that prompted it. I very much question whether you could find the same personal exhibition of disinterested motives and self-abnegation, and the like readiness to renounce place and position in deference to principle, among the same number of men in any other place.[39]

Throughout the closing months of 1880 and much of 1881, Pratt's health declined markedly as he battled the ravages of late-onset diabetes. On 18 September 1881, he struggled to the Taber-

points," George Q. Cannon recorded at Taylor's death in 1887; "but I have always submitted to his judgment" (qtd. in Bitton, *George Q. Cannon*, 288). Concerns about the misuse of power, particularly Cannon's potential in this regard, delayed the reorganization of the First Presidency for nearly two years following Taylor's death in 1887.

38. *Journal of Discourses*, 22:37; also Journal History of the Church, 10 Oct. 1880.

39. *Journal of Discourses*, 22:40; Journal History of the Church, 10 Oct. 1880.

nacle podium to deliver his last public sermon. The next day he turned seventy—also the fifty-first anniversary of his baptism into the Church of Christ. "[A]fter having been brought so low, so near the gates of death," he confessed to the Saints,

> how happy I feel that I am permitted once more to lift up my voice before you. I do not know that I can make you all hear, but I trust that my voice will be strengthened, I trust that my body will be strengthened, I trust that my mind—if it has been weakened at all by sickness—may also be strengthened, and that I yet may have the humble privilege of lifting up my voice and testifying, before thousands of people in these mountains, if not abroad among the inhabitants of the earth, of God's power. ... [A]lthough feeble in body, I do not know but what the Lord may yet strengthen me to again publish glad tiding of great joy abroad among the nations of the earth, or perform whatever duties may be assigned unto me by the general authorities [of] His Church.[40]

Fifteen days later, on 3 October, Pratt died at the home of one of his plural wives in Salt Lake City. His epitaph, which he reportedly dictated shortly before his death, read simply: "My body sleeps but a moment; but my testimony lives and shall endure forever."[41]

---

40. *Journal of Discourses,* 22:225-26.

41. Recorded by Joseph F. Smith in "Life and Labors of Orson Pratt," *Contributor* 12 (Oct. 1891): 462.

Because He Faltered

If Orson Pratt's demotion in the Twelve was based—publicly, at least—on a faulty assumption that he had been excommunicated in 1842, how can one best account for his acquiescence? To be sure, the episode was devastating, no doubt the most painful of his life and one that forced him to choose between his wife and his equally beloved prophet. That he decided to remain with the church demonstrates his resolution, but the decision exacted a terrible price. At the very least, he had to conclude that his wife had misinterpreted the prophet's intentions, and at worst, that she had lied about a liaison with John C. Bennett. In many ways, Pratt chose not only between two people whom he loved but between his family and his faith, between exaltation and damnation. His silence regarding the circumstances surrounding his wrenching decision is not surprising, nor that he spent the remainder of his life defending the controversial teaching that had nearly destroyed him. In fact, his apologetics seemed to have been directed as much to himself as to potential converts.

Having sided with Joseph Smith, Pratt eventually accepted the interpretation of others about what had happened during that summer of 1842. His inability—or unwillingness—to entertain alternative explanations must have been based on his realization of the ramifications. By 1856 when Brigham Young's retrospective history was compiled, Pratt was able to announce that he had "been in the Church almost twenty-six years, lacking about four months."[1] Despite Joseph Smith's assurances that he had not been "legally cut off" or dropped from the quorum, Pratt had reinterpreted the past in a way that allowed him to maintain his faith and fellowship as well as his own mental and emotional stability.

Why was Pratt demoted in 1875? Put simply, ranking church leaders—Brigham Young, George A. Smith—did not want him to become president. This was because of Pratt's reluctance to side with Joseph Smith in Nauvoo as well as his protracted doctrinal disagreements with Young. In both instances, Young judged Pratt to be disloyal—a condition that rendered him unworthy of the presidency. By reconstructing Pratt's Nauvoo difficulties, Young and others reduced the likelihood that he would ever assume quorum or ultimately church leadership. As President Joseph F. Smith explained to the Twelve in 1901, "No man in the quorum of Apostles who falters or rebels can ever attain to the presidency of the Church. And because they faltered, Orson Pratt and Orson Hyde lost their place of seniority in the quorum, and were consequently thrown out of the line to the presidency."[2] It is interesting that, given his age and debility, if Pratt had become president, his counselors certainly would have exercised as much practical influence as Pratt himself.

Still, time has been unusually kind to Orson Pratt. In the words

---

1. *Journal of Discourses*, 3:306.

2. Qtd. in Rudger Clawson, Diary, 24 Oct. 1901, Special Collections, Marriott Library, University of Utah, Salt Lake City. Apostle Moses Thatcher's explanation was blunt: Brigham Young "was prejudiced against Orson Pratt" (qtd. in Abraham H. Cannon, Journal, 3 Apr. 1895). Eleven years earlier, Apostle Abraham H. Cannon, quoting John Henry Smith, had used the term "faithlessness" in reference to Pratt and Hyde (ibid., 1 Oct. 1890).

of one biographer: "As one pauses at a vantage point and looks back over the first century of Mormonism, it becomes increasingly evident that Orson Pratt did more to formulate the Mormons' idea of God, the religious basis of polygamy, the pre-existence of spirits, the doctrine of the gathering of Israel, the resurrection, and eternal salvation than any other person in the Church, with the exception of Joseph Smith."[3] He was "the most prolific and perhaps most influential early apologist for the Church of Jesus Christ of Latter-day Saints," added contemporary LDS scholar David J. Whittaker. "Influential during his lifetime, from his conversion in 1830 to his death in 1881, he wielded even more influence after his death. ... He was at his best in developing the ideas of others and expanding them into fully elaborated statements. Without question, all religious movements in their infancy need such disciples."[4]

Even after Brigham Young's death, speculations about Adam-God continued as no small controversy among church members. The president's belief that Adam was both the spiritual and physical father of all men and women born into this world, including Jesus Christ, proved difficult for many to accept despite continuing reference to it by various church officials. Even within the presiding quorums, Pratt was not alone in his discomfort. Apostle George Q. Cannon, Young's former counselor, alluded to Adam-God in his journal when he wrote that "[s]ome of my brethren ... even feel that in the promulgation of doctrine he [Young] took liberties beyond those to which he was legitimately entitled."[5] While plural marriage enraged the American populace, Young's ill-fated Adam-God doctrine exerted a similar, albeit somewhat less divisive, effect within Mormonism. Official support declined during the succeeding administrations of John Taylor,[6] Wilford Woodruff, and Lorenzo

---

3. Lyon, "Orson Pratt—Early Mormon Leader," 125.

4. David J. Whittaker, foreword, *Essential Orson Pratt,* xv, xxv.

5. George Q. Cannon, Journal, 17 Jan. 1878, qtd. in Cannon, "George Q. Cannon," *Instructor,* 259.

6. Taylor was understanding of Pratt's intellectual activities. "With regard to

Snow. Mormons who promulgate the doctrine today risk formal expulsion from the church.

Several of Pratt's problematic theories found acceptance among influential, conservative, twentieth-century Mormon leaders including Apostles Joseph Fielding Smith and Bruce R. McConkie. Pratt would have echoed Smith's authoritative-sounding assertion: "I believe that *God knows all things* and that *his understanding is perfect, not 'relative.'* I have never seen or heard of any revealed fact to the contrary. I believe that our Heavenly Father and his Son Jesus Christ are *perfect.* I offer no excuse for the simplicity of my faith" (emphasis in original).[7] McConkie, Smith's son-in-law and theological torchbearer, was equally adamant: "God is omnipotent, omniscient, and omnipresent. He knows all things, he has all power, and he is everywhere present by the power of his Spirit. And unless we know and believe this doctrine we cannot gain faith unto life and salvation."[8] Elder McConkie's encyclopedic *Mormon Doctrine* shows a similar debt to Pratt in his sections on "God," the "Godhead," and "Eternal Progression."[9] Reliance on Pratt has continued to be pervasive and unmistakable in Mormonism to the present.[10]

---

your proposed work on that wonderful structure of the Great Pyramid," he wrote to Pratt in 1879, "we are quite agreeable that you should publish whatever you deem desirable therein; but we suggest that you do it as you are doing with your work on the Mechanism of the Universe [*A Key to the Universe*]: let it be based on scientific principles rather than on revelation, and be published as your own production as an Elder, as are other of your scientific publications" (Taylor to Pratt, 25 Apr. 1879, in Samuel W. Taylor and Raymond W. Taylor, eds., *The John Taylor Papers, Volume II, 1877-1887; The President* [Redwood City, CA: Taylor Trust Publisher, 1985], 88).

7. Qtd. in Joseph Fielding Smith, *Doctrines of Salvation,* comp. Bruce R. McConkie (Salt Lake City: Bookcraft, 1954), 1:8. Smith's views on Adam-God parallel those of Pratt. See ibid., 97-106.

8. Qtd. in Mark L. McConkie, ed., *Sermons and Writings of Bruce R. McConkie* (Salt Lake City: Bookcraft, 1998), 25.

9. Bruce R. McConkie, *Mormon Doctrine,* 2nd ed. (Salt Lake City: Bookcraft, 1966), 317-21, 238-39.

10. Several of Pratt's views on the attributes of God and the omnipresence of

"Although most moderns would probably smile at Orson's system," observed his biographer, "rooted as it is in old assumptions about the atom, it continues to this day to influence Mormon thinking about these fundamental scientific questions."[11]

Recent attention to Joseph Smith's "inspired translation" of the Bible has endowed it with respect equal to what Pratt wanted to see it granted.[12] The 1979 LDS edition of the King James Bible was augmented by the inclusion of Smith's emendations, which effectively lay to rest any reservations about Smith's work. Similarly, later research has largely vindicated Lucy Mack Smith's book.[13]

Orson Pratt and Brigham Young were inextricably united in a common goal: the expansion of Mormonism. Each pursued this end from a different point of view which as a consequence produced two seemingly separate paths. As the overseer of official church doctrine, Young saw his fundamental responsibility as the maintenance of unity within the church, and he tolerated freedom of thought insofar as it remained subservient to the authority of the First Presidency, the dissemination of sound doctrine, and the cultivation of church unity. Pratt sensed the potential danger in individualism, but he did not believe his own views ran contrary to the doctrines Joseph Smith had established alongside biblical authority.

---

the Holy Spirit were adapted by later church writers. See, e.g., Charles W. Penrose, discourse, 16 Nov. 1884, in *Journal of Discourses*, 26:18-29; B. H. Roberts, *The Seventy's Course in Theology, Third Year: The Doctrine of Deity* (Salt Lake City: Church of Jesus Christ of Latter-day Saints, 1910), 198; and Hyrum L. Andrus, *God, Man and the Universe* (Salt Lake City: Bookcraft, 1968), 109-43.

11. England, *Life and Thought*, 102.

12. See especially Robert J. Matthews, *"A Plainer Translation": Joseph Smith's Translation of the Bible—A History and Commentary* (Provo, UT: Brigham Young University Press, 1975); and Stephen R. Knecht, *The Story of Joseph Smith's Bible Translation—A Documentary History* (Salt Lake City: Associated Research Consultants, 1977).

13. "Lucy Smith's memories of the early years of the rise of Mormonism have a demonstrable degree of accuracy" (Richard L. Anderson, "Circumstantial Confirmation of the First Vision through Reminiscences," *BYU Studies* 9 [Spring 1969]: 391).

Indeed, Pratt consistently affirmed the unifying aspect of his theology. Young's controversial teachings, on the other hand, were scripturally unsound and divisive, according to Pratt's view.

In retrospect, the primary issues were not the attributes of God or the identity of Adam or the publication of Lucy Mack Smith's history and Joseph Smith's Bible. Rather, they were conflicts over authority—Young's notion of dynamic revelation and the primacy of contemporary statements by living prophets on the one hand and Pratt's fundamentalist adherence to a literal interpretation of divine canon on the other. As each man came to perceive his own biases, reconciliation became increasingly impossible. Further exacerbating the tensions were jurisdictional ambiguities in the hierarchy, communication problems as Pratt continued to serve foreign missions away from church headquarters, the backdrop of unresolved past conflicts, restrictions on Pratt's writing and preaching, and the need for unanimity among the leading brethren.

Young's efforts, beginning in 1855 with his public letter to the editor of the *Latter-day Saints' Millennial Star,* were calculated to reduce the influence of Pratt's theories, not to diminish the status of the apostle himself. Whether out of unusual naivete or passive aggression, Pratt held that since he had not been told explicitly what points were under official condemnation, he could therefore continue to promulgate his ideas. He was careful not to disagree directly with Young until Young addressed the issues publicly. Then Pratt demanded to know exactly which of his teachings were in error and why. Where Young was reluctant to engage in such a debate, Pratt continued to press the issue privately and publicly. Finally, the president issued his final response: the official denunciations of 1860 and 1865. In their appeal to authority rather than to reason, the statements proved effective in the short run, and support for Pratt's theories began to wane. But the rhetorical, logical, and scriptural power of Pratt's arguments would not die out completely and eventually experienced a renaissance.[14] As sometimes occurs over

---

14. In mid-1892, President Wilford Woodruff addressed local leaders in St.

time, the boundaries separating both men's positions have since become blurred, and ultimate victory—so often pyrrhic—a matter of perspective.

George, Utah. Several of the brethren had been "advancing [the] false doctrine" that "it was right to worship the intelligence that was in God the Eternal Father and not God." Woodruff refuted this, as recorded by Charles Lowell Walker, saying that this was

> [a]lso [one] of the false teachings of the late Orsen Pratt, one of the Twelve, arguing that every particle of matter which imposed the elements had all the attributes of the Deity in it, and that they, i.e., the particles of Matter, [were] by some unaccountable way united together and became god. Pres Woodroof told of Orson's unyielding stubbornes, and of upbraiding the Twelve for not being manly, for not declaring their views the way he looked at it, and branding them as cowards &c &c. Spoke of the firmnes of Pres Young in correcting Orson Pratt and setting him aright: Of Orson wishing to resign his position in the Quorum: of Pres. Young saying "No you wont Orson, I'll rub your ears until I get you right;" and had it not been for [the] firmnes of Pres Young in maintaining the right, and assiduously laboring and showing him his gross errors, Orson would have been out of the Church.

At the same meeting, George Q. Cannon, Woodruff's counselor in the First Presidency, advised that "it was not necessary that we should or [will] endorse the doctrine that some men taught that Adam was the Father of Jesus Christ. Counsel was given for the Elders to teach that which they knew, not that which they did not" (qtd. in Larson and Larson, *Diary of Charles Lowell Walker*, 2:741).

BOOKS

Allen, James B., Ronald K. Esplin, David J. Whittaker. *Men with a Mission, 1837-1841: The Quorum of the Twelve Apostles in the British Isles.* Salt Lake City: Deseret Book Co., 1992.

Anderson, Lavina Fielding. *Lucy's Book: A Critical Edition of Lucy Mack Smith's Family Memoir.* Salt Lake City: Signature Books, 2001.

Andrus, Hyrum L. *God, Man and the Universe.* Salt Lake City: Bookcraft, 1968.

Arrington, Leonard J. *Brigham Young: American Moses.* New York: Alfred A. Knopf, 1985.

————. *Great Basin Kingdom: An Economic History of the Latter-day Saints, 1830-1900.* Lincoln: University of Nebraska Press, 1958.

Bagley, Will. *Blood of the Prophets: Brigham Young and the Massacre at Mountain Meadows.* Norman: University of Oklahoma Press, 2002.

Barlow, Philip L. *Mormons and the Bible: The Place of the Latter-day Saints in American Religion.* New York: Oxford University Press, 1991.

Barron, Howard H. *Orson Hyde: Missionary, Apostle, Colonizer.* Bountiful, UT: Horizon Publishers, 1977.

Bennett, John C. *History of the Saints; Or an Exposé of Joe Smith and Mormonism.* Boston: Leland and Whiting, 1842. rpt. 2000 by University of Illinois Press.

Bennett, Richard E. *Mormons at the Missouri, 1846-1852: "And Should We Die ..."* Norman: University of Oklahoma Press, 1987.

————. *We'll Find the Place: The Mormon Exodus, 1846-1848.* Salt Lake City: Deseret Book Co., 1997.

Bergera, Gary James, ed. *Line Upon Line: Essays on Mormon Doctrine.* Salt Lake City: Signature Books, 1989.

Bitton, Davis. *George Q. Cannon: A Biography.* Salt Lake City: Deseret Book Co., 1999.

——————, and Leonard J. Arrington. *Mormons and Their Historians.* Salt Lake City: University of Utah Press, 1988.

Bloxham, V. Ben, James R. Moss, and Larry C. Porter, eds. *Truth Will Prevail: The Rise of the Church of Jesus Christ of Latter-day Saints in the British Isles, 1837-1987.* Solihull, Eng.: Church of Jesus Christ of Latter-day Saints, 1987.

Brooks, Juanita, ed. *On the Mormon Frontier: The Diary of Hosea Stout.* 2 vols. Salt Lake City: University of Utah Press/Utah State Historical Society, 1964.

Buerger, David John. *The Mysteries of Godliness: A History of Mormon Temple Worship.* San Francisco: Smith Research Associates, 1994.

Burton, Richard. *The City of the Saints and across the Rocky Mountains to California.* New York: Harper & Brothers Publishers, 1862.

Cannon, Donald Q., and Lyndon W. Cook, eds. *Far West Record: Minutes of The Church of Jesus Christ of Latter-day Saints, 1830-1844.* Salt Lake City: Deseret Book Co., 1983.

Clark, James R., ed. *Messages of the First Presidency of the Church of Jesus Christ of Latter-day Saints, 1833-1964.* 6 vols. Salt Lake City: Bookcraft, Inc., 1965.

Collier, Fred C., comp. *The Teachings of President Brigham Young, Vol. 3: 1852-1854.* Salt Lake City: Collier's Publishing Co., 1987.

Compton, Todd. *In Sacred Loneliness: The Plural Wives of Joseph Smith.* Salt Lake City: Signature Books, 1997.

Cook, Lyndon W., comp. *Nauvoo Deaths and Marriages, 1839-1845.* Orem, UT: Grandin Book Co., 1994.

——————. *William Law.* Orem, UT: Grandin Book Co., 1996.

Cooley, Everett L., ed. *Diary of Brigham Young.* Salt Lake City: University of Utah Library/Tanner Trust Fund, 1980.

Cooper, Rex Eugene. *Promises Made to the Fathers: Mormon Covenant Organization.* Salt Lake City: University of Utah Press, 1990.

Daynes, Kathryn M. *More Wives than One: Transformation of the Mormon Marriage System, 1840-1910.* Urbana: University of Illinois Press, 2001.

The Doctrine and Covenants of the Church of Jesus Christ of Latter-day Saints.

Durham, Reed C., Jr., and Steven H. Heath. *Succession in the Church*. Salt Lake City: Bookcraft, 1970.

Ehat, Andrew F., and Lyndon Cook, eds. *The Words of Joseph Smith: The Contemporary Accounts of the Nauvoo Discourses of the Prophet Joseph*. Provo, UT: Brigham Young University Religious Studies Research Center, 1980.

England, Breck. *The Life and Thought of Orson Pratt*. Salt Lake City: University of Utah Press, 1985.

The Essential Brigham Young. Salt Lake City: Signature Books, 1992.

The Essential Joseph Smith. Salt Lake City: Signature Books, 1995.

The Essential Orson Pratt. Salt Lake City: Signature Books, 1991.

The Essential Parley P. Pratt. Salt Lake City: Signature Books, 1990.

Evans, Richard L. *A Century of "Mormonism" in Great Britain*. Salt Lake City: Publishers Press, 1984; 1st ed. 1937.

Faulring, Scott H., ed. *An American Prophet's Record: The Diaries and Journals of Joseph Smith*. Salt Lake City: Signature Books in association with Smith Research Associates, 1987.

Firmage, Edwin Brown, and Richard Collin Mangrum. *Zion in the Courts: A Legal History of the Church of Jesus Christ of Latter-day Saints, 1830-1900*. Urbana: University of Illinois Press, 1988.

The First Annual Church Educational System Religious Educators Symposium. Provo, UT: Brigham Young University, 1977.

Foster, Lawrence. *Religion and Sexuality: Three American Communal Experiments of the Nineteenth Century*. New York: Oxford University Press, 1981.

Froiseth, Jennie Anderson. *The Women of Mormonism*. Detroit: C. G. G. Paine, 1884.

Hansen, Klaus J. *Quest for Empire: The Political Kingdom of God and the Council of Fifty in Mormon History*. East Lansing: Michigan State University Press, 1967.

Hardy, Carmon B. *Solemn Covenant: The Mormon Polygamous Passage*. Urbana: University of Illinois Press, 1992.

Hazen, Craig James. *The Village Enlightenment in America: Popular Religion and Science in the Nineteenth Century*. Urbana: University of Illinois Press, 2000.

Hill, Donna. *Joseph Smith: The First Mormon*. Garden City, NY: Doubleday, 1977.

Hyde, Myrtle Stevens. *Orson Hyde: The Olive Branch of Israel*. Salt Lake City: Agreka Books, 2000.

Jensen, Richard L., and Malcolm R. Thorp, eds. *Mormonism in Early Victorian Britain*. Salt Lake City: University of Utah Press, 1989.

Jessee, Dean C., ed. *The Papers of Joseph Smith*. 2 vols. Salt Lake City: Deseret Book Co., 1992.

Kane, Elizabeth Wood. *Twelve Mormon Homes Visited in Succession on a Journey through Utah to Arizona*. Everett L. Cooley, ed. Salt Lake City: University of Utah Library, 1974.

Kenney, Scott G., ed. *Wilford Woodruff's Journal*. 9 vols. Midvale, UT: Signature Books, 1983-85.

Kimball, Stanley B. *Heber C. Kimball: Mormon Patriarch and Pioneer*. Urbana: University of Illinois Press, 1981.

Knecht, Stephen R. *The Story of Joseph Smith's Bible Translation—A Documentary History*. Salt Lake City: Associated Research Consultants, 1977.

Larson, Andrew Karl. *Erastus Snow: The Life of a Missionary and Pioneer for the Early Mormon Church*. Salt Lake City: University of Utah Press, 1971.

——————, and Katharine Miles Larson, eds. *Diary of Charles Lowell Walker*. 2 vols. Logan: Utah State University Press, 1980.

LeSueur, Stephen C. *The 1838 Mormon War in Missouri*. Columbia: University of Missouri Press, 1987.

Ludlow, Daniel H., ed. *Encyclopedia of Mormonism*. 4 vols. New York: Macmillan Publishing Co., 1992.

Madsen, Truman G., and Charles D. Tate, Jr., eds. *To the Glory of God: Mormon Essays on Great Issues*. Salt Lake City: Deseret Book, 1972.

Matthews, Robert J. *"A Plainer Translation": Joseph Smith's Translation of the Bible—A History and Commentary*. Provo, UT: Brigham Young University Press, 1975.

McConkie, Bruce R. *Mormon Doctrine*. 2nd ed. Salt Lake City: Bookcraft, 1966.

McConkie, Mark L., ed. *Sermons and Writings of Bruce R. McConkie*. Salt Lake City: Bookcraft, 1998.

Newell, Linda King, and Valeen Tippets Avery. *Mormon Enigma: Emma Hale Smith*. 2nd ed. Urbana: University of Illinois Press, 1994.

Nibley, Preston. *Brigham Young—The Man and His Work*. Salt Lake City: Deseret News Press, 1936.

Pratt, Orson. *The Key to the Universe; Or, a New Theory of Its Mechanism ...* Liverpool: William Budge, 1879.

Pratt, Parley P. *Key to the Science of Theology*. Liverpool: F. D. Richards, 1855.

Pratt, Parley P. [Jr.], ed. *Autobiography of Parley P. Pratt*. Salt Lake City: Deseret Book Co., 1938. first ed. 1873.

Quinn, D. Michael. *The Mormon Hierarchy: Extensions of Power*. Salt Lake City: Signature Books in association with Smith Research Associates, 1997.

————. *The Mormon Hierarchy: Origins of Power*. Salt Lake City: Signature Books in association with Smith Research Associates, 1994.

Roberts, B. H. *A Comprehensive History of the Church of Jesus Christ of Latter-day Saints*. Century I. 6 vols. Provo, UT: Brigham Young University Press, for the Church, 1965.

————. *The Seventy's Course in Theology, Third Year, the Doctrine of Deity*. Salt Lake City: Church of Jesus Christ of Latter-day Saints, 1910.

————. *Succession in the Presidency*. Salt Lake City: Deseret News Publishing Co., 1894. Expanded 1900.

Sessions, Gene, ed. *Mormon Democrat: The Religious and Political Memoirs of James Henry Moyle*. Salt Lake City: Historical Department of the Church of Jesus Christ of Latter-day Saints, 1975; rpt. 1998, Signature Books in association with Smith Research Associates.

Smith, Andrew F. *The Saintly Scoundrel: The Life and Times of Dr. John Cook Bennett*. Urbana: University of Illinois Press, 1997.

Smith, George D., ed. *An Intimate Chronicle: The Journals of William Clayton*. Salt Lake City: Signature Books in association with Smith Research Associates, 1995.

Smith, Joseph. *History of the Church of Jesus Christ of Latter-day Saints, Period I*. B. H. Roberts, ed. 7 vols. Salt Lake City: Deseret Book Co. for the church, 1974.

Smith, Joseph Fielding. *Doctrines of Salvation*. Bruce R. McConkie, comp. 3 vols. Salt Lake City: Bookcraft, 1954.

————. *Essentials in Church History*. Salt Lake City: Deseret Book, 1969; first ed. 1922.

Stenhouse, T. B. H. *Rocky Mountain Saints.* New York: D. Appleton and Co., 1873.

Stenhouse, Mrs. T. B. H. [Fanny]. *Tell It All: The Tyranny of Mormonism, or an Englishwoman in Utah.* Hartford: A. D. Worthington, 1874.

Talbot, Wilburn D. *The Acts of the Modern Apostles.* Salt Lake City: Randall Book, 1985.

Taylor, Samuel W. *The Kingdom or Nothing: The Life of John Taylor, Militant Mormon.* New York: Macmillan Publishing Co., 1976.

——————, and Raymond W. Taylor, eds. *The John Taylor Papers, Volume II, 1877-1887, The President.* Redwood City, CA: Taylor Trust Publisher, 1985.

Tullidge, Edward W. *The Women of Mormondom.* New York: Tullidge and Crandall, 1877.

Tuttle, Daniel S. *Reminiscences of a Missionary Bishop.* New York: Whittaker, 1906.

Van Wagoner, Richard S. *Mormon Polygamy: A History.* Salt Lake City: Signature Books, 1986; 2nd ed., 1989.

——————. *Sidney Rigdon: A Portrait of Religious Excess.* Salt Lake City: Signature Books, 1994.

Waterman, Bryan, ed. *The Prophet Puzzle: Interpretive Essays on Joseph Smith.* Salt Lake City: Signature Books, 1999.

Watson, Elden J., comp. *The Orson Pratt Journals.* Salt Lake City: by the editor, 1975.

Webster's Third New International Dictionary.

White, Jean Bickmore, ed. *Church, State, and Politics: The Diaries of John Henry Smith.* Salt Lake City: Signature Books in association with Smith Research Associates, 1991.

Wyl, W., pseud. [Wilhelm Ritter von Wymetal]. *Mormon Portraits.* Salt Lake City: Tribune Printing and Publishing Co., 1886.

PAMPHLETS

Affidavits and Certificates, Disproving the Statements and Affidavits Contained in John C. Bennett's Letters. Broadside. Nauvoo, 31 Aug. 1842.

Pratt, Orson. *The Absurdities of Immaterialism.* Liverpool: R. James for the author, 1849.

——————. *Great First Cause, Or the Self-Moving Forces of the Universe.* Liverpool: R. James for the author, 1851.

——————. *A Series of Pamphlets.* Liverpool: Franklin D. Richards, 1852.

Pratt, Parley P. *Immortality and Eternal Life of the Material Body*. Milwaukee: W. T. Courier, 1841.

————. *Intelligence and Affection*. Milwaukee: W. T. Courier, 1841.

————. *The World Turned Upside Down, Or Heaven on Earth*. Liverpool: Millennial Star Office, [1842].

Taylor, John. *Succession in the Priesthood*. Salt Lake City: n.p., 1881.

Young, Brigham. *The Resurrection*. Salt Lake City: Deseret News Co., 1884.

PERIODICALS

Anti-Polygamy Standard

Interview with Arthur Pratt, Feb. 1882.

BYU Studies

Allen, James B., and Malcolm R. Thorp, "The Mission of the Twelve to England, 1840-41: Mormon Apostles and the Working Class," summer 1975.

Anderson, Richard L. "Circumstantial Confirmation of the First Vision through Reminiscences," spring 1969.

Buerger, David John. "'The Fulness of the Priesthood': The Second Anointing in Latter-day Saint Theology and Practice," spring 1983.

Cannon, Donald Q. "The King Follett Discourse: Joseph Smith's Greatest Sermon in Historical Perspective," winter 1978.

Cracroft, Richard. "Liverpool, 1856: Nathaniel Hawthorne Meets Orson Pratt," spring 1968.

Ehat, Andrew F., ed. "'They Might Have Known That He Was Not a Fallen Prophet'—The Nauvoo Journal of Joseph Fielding," winter 1979.

Hale, Van. "The Doctrinal Impact of the King Follett Discourse," winter 1978.

Hartley, William G. "The Priesthood Reorganization of 1877: Brigham Young's Last Achievement," fall 1979.

Jessee, Dean C. "The Writing of Joseph Smith's History," spring 1971.

Kimball, Stanley B. "Brigham and Heber," spring 1978.

Larson, Stan, ed. "The King Follett Discourse: A Newly Amalgamated Text," winter 1978.

Quinn, D. Michael. "The Practice of Rebaptism at Nauvoo," winter 1978.

Searle, Howard C. "Authorship of the History of Brigham Young: A Review Essay," summer 1982.

—————. "Willard Richards as Historian," spring 1991.

Contributor

"Life and Labors of Orson Pratt," Oct. 1891.

Deseret News

"Annual General Conference," 13 Apr. 1875.

Brigham Young sermons: 27 June 1860, 6 Apr. 1861, 8 June 1873, 6 June 1877.

First Presidency statement, 23 Aug. 1865.

"History of Brigham Young," 17 Mar. 1858.

"History of Joseph Smith," 24 July 1852, 9 Apr. 1856; 3 July 1858.

Jedediah M. Grant sermon, 27 July 1854.

Orson Pratt sermon, 1, 22 Feb., 25 July 1860.

Dialogue: A Journal of Mormon Thought

Arrington, Leonard J. "The Intellectual Tradition of the Latter-day Saints," spring 1969.

Bates, Irene M. "William Smith, 1811-93: Problematic Patriarch," summer 1983.

Buerger, David John. "The Adam-God Doctrine," spring 1982.

Hefner, Loretta L. "From Apostle to Apostate: The Personal Struggle of Amasa Lyman," spring 1983.

Larson, Stan. "Intellectuals in Mormon History: An Update," fall 1993.

Smith, George D. "Nauvoo Roots of Mormon Polygamy, 1841-46: A Preliminary Demographic Report," spring 1994.

Walker, Ronald W. "Rachel R. Grant: The Continuing Legacy of the Feminine Ideal," autumn 1982.

Van Wagoner, Richard S. "Sarah M. Pratt: The Shaping of an Apostate," summer 1986.

Ensign

Whittaker, David J. "Orson Pratt: Early Advocate of the Book of Mormon," Apr. 1984.

The Historian

Bishop, M. Guy. "Eternal Marriage in Early Mormon Marital Belief," autumn 1990.

Historical Record

"Orson Pratt's Testimony," May 1887.

Instructor
Cannon, Joseph J. "George Q. Cannon—Relations with Brigham Young," June 1945.

Journal of Discourses
Cannon, George Q.: 19:234-35; 23:364, 365; 24:275-76.
Hyde, Orson: 8:234.
Penrose, Charles W.: 26:18-29.
Pratt, Orson: 1:53-66, 282-91, 328-34; 2:336-47; 3:306, 344-54; 7:224, 371-76; 8:111-13, 311; 13:187; 15:247-49; 16:335; 18:293; 19:320-21; 20:71, 73; 21:173, 200, 238, 257; 22:37, 225-26.
Snow, Erastus: 5:288-90.
Taylor, John: 22:40.
Wells, Daniel H.: 19:235.
Young, Brigham: 1:50, 93, 352-53; 2:32, 314; 3:80-96, 116, 203, 316-27; 4:266-67; 6:275; 7:228-29; 8:17-18, 32, 34, 138; 9:311; 10:192; 11:121, 286; 14:198, 208.

Journal of Mormon History
Bush, Lester E., Jr., "Brigham Young in Life and Death: A Medical Overview," May 1978.

Latter Day Saints' Messenger and Advocate
Reprint of *Brookville Enquirer* article, Feb. 1835.

Latter-day Saints' Millennial Star
Amasa Lyman sermons, 16 Mar., 13 Apr. 1862.
First Presidency statement, 21 Oct. 1865.
Letter from Brigham Young to Franklin D. Richards, 12 May 1855.
Open letter from Orson Pratt, 4 Nov. 1865.
Orson Pratt. Excerpts from the *Great First Cause,* 1 Feb. 1851.
————. "The Holy Spirit," 15 Oct., 1 Nov. 1850.
————. Sermon and First Presidency statement, 22 Sept. 1860.
"Report of Elders Orson Pratt and Joseph F. Smith," 16 Dec. 1878.
Smith, Joseph. "History," 27 Aug. 1853.
"Testimonial Presented to Elder Orson Pratt," 1 Feb. 1851.
Text of temple marriage ceremony, 2 Apr. 1853.
Young, Brigham. "History," 5, 12 Mar. 1864.

Messenger and Advocate of the Church of Christ
Rigdon, Sidney, "Tour East," Dec. 1845.

New York Herald
"Orson Pratt's Harem," 18 May 1877.

"The Utah Theocracy," 18 May 1877.

The Return
"Items of Personal History of the Editor," Nov. 1890.

The Saint's Advocate
Blair, W. W. "The Inspired Translation," July 1881.

The Saint's Herald
Anderson, Mary Audentia Smith, ed. "The Memoirs of President Joseph Smith (1832-1914)," 22 Jan. 1935.

Salt Lake Tribune
"City Jottings," 13 Apr. 1875.
"The Two Orsons and the Succession," 16 Sept. 1871.

The Seer
"Prospectus," Dec. 1852.
Various topics cited: Jan., Feb., Mar., May, Aug. 1853.

Task Papers in LDS History
Arrington, Leonard J., and Ronald K. Esplin. "The Role of the Council of the Twelve during Brigham Young's Presidency of the Church of Jesus Christ of Latter-day Saints," Dec. 1979.

Times and Seasons
"Letter from Tennessee," 15 June 1842.
Notices, Nov. 1839, 15 June 1842, 16 Jan. 1843.
Report of a public meeting, 1 Aug. 1842.
"To the Church of Jesus Christ of Latter Day Saints, and to All the Honorable Part of Community," 1 July 1842.

Utah Historical Quarterly
Irving, Gordon. "Encouraging the Saints: Brigham Young's Annual Tours of the Mormon Settlements," summer 1977.
Van Wagoner, Richard S. and Mary Van Wagoner. "Arthur Pratt, Utah Lawman," winter 1987.

The Wasp
Letter to the editor, 2 Sept. 1842.

Western Historical Quarterly
Whittaker, David J. "The Bone in the Throat: Orson Pratt and the Public Announcement of Plural Marriage," July 1987.

MANUSCRIPTS

Bancroft Library, University of California, Berkeley
Richards, Franklin D. "Reminiscences," 1884.

Chicago Historical Society
  Mormon Collection
    Demming, Arthur B. Letter to C. F. Gunther.
Harold B. Lee Library, Brigham Young University
  Bleak, James G. "Annals of the Southern Utah Mission" (typescript).
  Brown, Lorenzo. Diary (transcript).
  Cannon, Abraham H. Journal.
  Little, James Amasa. Journal (microfilm).
  Lundwall, Nels B. Papers
    Letter to T. Edgar Lyon, 9 Apr. 1947 (microfilm).
  Nuttall, L. John. Collection.
    "Minutes of a Meeting in the President's Office, 23 Feb. 1878."
    ——————. Journal.
  Pratt, Parley P. Collection.
    Letter from Orson Hyde, 2 Nov. 1846
    Letter to Orson Hyde, 9 Nov. 1846
    Letters from Orson Pratt, 10 Mar., 12 Sept., 2 Nov. 1853; 12 Feb.,
      4 Apr. 1854.
  Richards, Samuel W. Journal.
  Robinson, Joseph Lee. Journal.
  Thatcher, Moses. Journal.
LDS church archives
  Book of Anointings.
  Clayton, William. Diary.
  Fielding, Mary. Letter to Mercy Fielding Thompson, 8 July 1837.
  Grant, Heber J. Diary.
    ——————. Letterbook.
    ——————. Papers.
    Letter from Wilford Woodruff, 28 Mar. 1887.
  Historian's Office Journal.
  Hobbs, Henry. Journal.
  Jeremy, Thomas Evans. Journal.
  Journal History of the Church of Jesus Christ of Latter-day Saints.
  Kimball, Heber C. Letter to Parley P. Pratt, 17 June 1842.
  Lund, Anthon H. Diary.
  Manuscript History of the Church.
  "Minutes of Councils, Meetings, & Journey on a mission to the Saints
    on the Pottawatomie Sands."

Miscellaneous Minutes Collection.

Nauvoo City Council Meeting. Minutes.

Nauvoo Female Relief Society. Minutes.

Nauvoo High Council Minute Book.

Neibuhr, Alexander. Journal.

Patriarchal Blessings Book, vol. 1.

"A record of the transactions of the Twelve apostles of the Church of the Latter-Day Saints from the time of their call to the apostleship which was on the 14th Day of Feby. A. 1835."

Pratt, Orson. Collection.

Farewell note, 14 July 1842.

Letter from Parley P. Pratt, 25 May 1853.

Letter to Parley P. Pratt, 12 Sept. 1853.

Letter to Sarah M. Pratt, 18 Sept. 1878.

Pratt, Orson Jr. Letter to Brigham Young, 13 June 1863.

Pratt, Parley P. Papers.

Letter to John Van Cott, 7 May 1843.

President's Office Journal.

Provo School of the Prophets. Minutes.

Quorum of the Twelve Apostles, Minutes, 27 May 1843, 12 Feb. 1849, 3 Aug. 1887, 29 Sept. 1896.

"Remarks by Sister Mary E. Lightner, Who Was Sealed to Joseph Smith in 1842. [An Address Delivered at] B.Y.U., Apr. 14, 1905."

Revelations Collection.

Revelation to Joseph Smith, Sidney Rigdon, Vinson Knight, and George W. Robinson, 12 Jan. 1838, Kirtland, Ohio.

Richards, Franklin D. Journal.

————. Letter to John Taylor, 26 Dec. 1883.

Richards, Willard. Diary.

Salt Lake City School of the Prophets. Minutes.

Salt Lake Stake High Council. Minutes.

Smith, Joseph. Papers.

Marsh, Thomas B., and Orson Hyde. Letter to Brother [Lewis] and Sister [Ann] Abbot, ca. 25 Oct. 1838.

Minutes, 5 Oct. 1839.

Rigdon, Sidney, Joseph Smith, and Hyrum Smith. Letter to Heber C. Kimball and Brigham Young, 16 Jan. 1839.

Smith, Joseph F. Affidavit Books.

Woodruff, Wilford. Papers
  Letter to Heber J. Grant, 28 Mar. 1887.
"Workings of Mormonism Related by Mrs. Orson Pratt, Salt Lake
  City, 1884."
Young, Brigham. Diary.
————. Letter to Parley P. Pratt, 17 July 1842.
————. Manuscript History and Autobiography.
————. Papers.
  "'A few words of Doctrine' Given by President Brigham Young
    in the Tabernacle in Great Salt Lake City[,] Oct 8th 1861.
    A.M. Reported by G. D. Watt."
  Galley sheets, Orson Pratt sermon, 22 Feb. 1860.
  "Great Salt Lake City, Council of the Twelve in Historian's upper
    room, April 5, 1860, 10 a.m."
  Letter from William Clayton, 4 Oct. 1852.
  Letters from Orson Pratt, 12 Jan. 1846; 31 Dec. 1852; 4 Mar., 4
    Nov. 1853; 12 Dec. 1865; 1 July 1868.
  Letter from Sarah M. Pratt, 19 Sept. 1869.
  Letter to Orson Pratt, 1 June 1853.
  "Minutes in office, of Pres. Young, April 5[, 18]60."
  "Minutes of Meeting at Historian's Office, Apr. 4, 1860, 7 p.m."
  Patriarchal Blessing, delivered by John Young, 25 Dec. 1857.
  Quorum of the Twelve Apostles, Minutes, 20 Jan. 1843.
  "Remarks," 6 May 1865, recorded by E. O. Sloan.
  Unpublished speech, 19 Nov. 1854.
Young, Brigham, Jr. Journal.
Marriott Library, University of Utah
  Clawson, Rudger. Diary.
Utah State Archives
  Tax Assessment Rolls, Salt Lake County, 1861 (microfilm).
Utah State Historical Society
  Gottfredson Family History (typescript).

THESES AND DISSERTATIONS

Bachman, Danel W. "A Study of the Mormon Practice of Plural Marriage before the Death of Joseph Smith." M.A. thesis, Purdue University, 1975.
Dunford, C. Kent. "The Contributions of George A. Smith to the

Establishment of the Mormon Society in the Territory of Utah."
Ph.D. diss., Brigham Young University, 1970, 284-85.

Ehat, Andrew F. "Joseph Smith's Introduction of Temple Ordinances and
the 1844 Mormon Succession Question." M.A. thesis, Brigham
Young University, 1982.

Lyon, T. Edgar. "Orson Pratt—Early Mormon Leader." M.A. thesis, University of Chicago Divinity School, 1932.

Patrick, John R. "The School of the Prophets: Its Development and Influence in Utah Territory." M.A. thesis, Brigham Young University,
June 1970.

Searle, Howard. "Early Mormon Historiography: Writing the History of
the Mormons, 1830-1858." Ph.D. diss., University of California, Los
Angeles, 1979.

Whittaker, David J. "Early Mormon Pamphleteering." Ph.D. diss.,
Brigham Young University, 1982.

OTHER

Anon. "Orson Pratt and Brigham Young," n.d., privately circulated.

"Early Coal Mining History," www.pitwork.net/history1.htm.

"Glossary of Welsh Coal Mine Sayings," www.welshcoalmines.co.uk/
Glossary.htm.

Taylor, Mark J. "Orson Pratt: Conflict and Restoration," 1973, privately
circulated.

58, 59, 60; performed unauthorized plural marriage, 57n12; materialistic philosophy of, 90n18, 92n22; letters to brother Orson, 102–103; murder of, 135n43

Pratt, Parley, Jr., 135n43

Pratt, Sarah Marinda (Bates), 44, 48, 49, 51, 221–22, 243, 251; rebuffed Smith's advances, 17–20, 18n36, 21–22; Smith's threat to ruin character of, 17; told husband of Smith's advances, 16, 18, 19, 23, 24; confided in a friend, 18; learned of Smith's plural wives, 18; publicly attacked by Smith, 22; no action taken against by church authorities, 27, 41; alleged affair with John C. Bennett, 30–31, 31n78, 41–42; responded to accusations, 30n74; rebaptism, 36; confirmed Bennett's version of events, 43; gave permission for husband to marry plural wife, 47–48; sealed to Orson, 47–48; voted into Anointed Quorum, 48; confronted by Parley Pratt regarding break-up of marriage, 50–51; unhappy about husband's marrying young girls, 222–23; excommunication, 223, 224; raised children to disbelieve Mormonism, 223–24; left Orson, 222, 224; on polygamy, 226; death, 226

"Pre-Existence of Man," 99, 105

"Questions on the Origins of Man," 89

"Questions on the Present State of Man," 89

Quinn, D. Michael, 12–13n16, 23n52, 36n10, 53, 115n6, 273

Quorum of the Anointed, 21

Quorum of Fifty, 73, 73–74n44

Quorum of Seventies, 61, 73; meeting concerning Orson Pratt's theology, 137–51

Quorum of Twelve Apostles, 41n26, 53, 81, 126, 133, 146, 160, 167, 172n8, 175n9, 178n14, 193n3, 235, 237, 242, 248, 260, 269, 270n26, 271; assumed harmony of, vii; reorganization, 2–3, 2n4, 261–78; Orson Pratt's reinstatement in, 4n11, 33–38; Smith teaches plural marriage to, 15; majority needed to transact business, 34, 34n4, 43–44, 56, 60, 61, 62, 64; Smith's teachings concerning discipline of members, 39–40, 40n25; meetings featuring conflicting opinions of Orson Pratt and Brigham Young regarding authority, 53–83; mission to England, 55, 57n12; meetings concerning Orson Pratt's theology, 137–51, 173–75n9, 175–87, 189–202; statement concerning Pratt's publications, 232–44; seniority based on order of ordination rather than age, 262–63, 262n3, 262n4, 262–63n6; expressed dissatisfaction with Brigham Young following his death, 269–70; resisted John Taylor's effort to organize First Presidency, 271–87. *See* conflict; First Presidency

Ramus (IL), 182n21

Relief Society, 16, 29

Reorganized Church of Jesus Christ of Latter Day Saints (Community of Christ), 251, 254n20

Rich, Charles C., 83n56, 148, 173, 189, 190n1, 199, 275; advised Pratt concerning conflict with Young, 193–94

Richards, Franklin D., 6n13, 83n56,